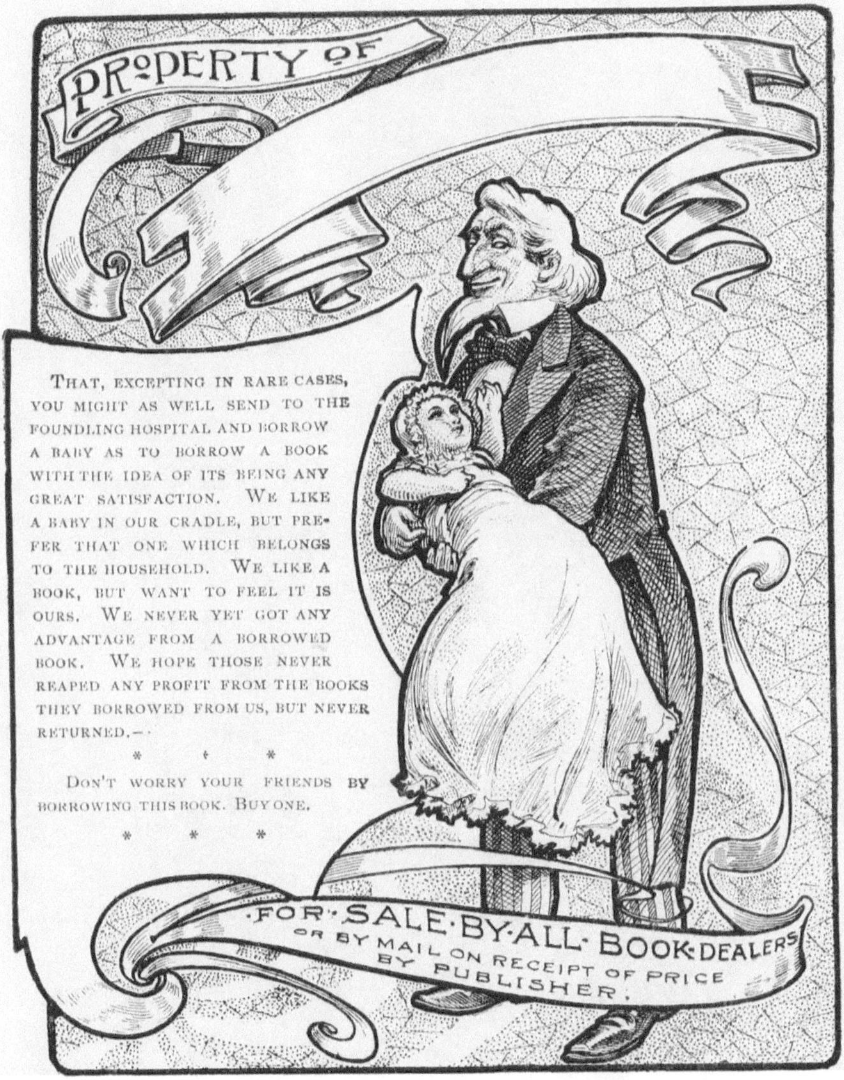

Property of

That, excepting in rare cases, you might as well send to the foundling hospital and borrow a baby as to borrow a book with the idea of its being any great satisfaction. We like a baby in our cradle, but prefer that one which belongs to the household. We like a book, but want to feel it is ours. We never yet got any advantage from a borrowed book. We hope those never reaped any profit from the books they borrowed from us, but never returned.—·

* · *

Don't worry your friends by borrowing this book. Buy one.

* * *

For sale by all book dealers or by mail on receipt of price by publisher.

Peschel Press ~ P.O. Box 132 ~ Hershey, PA 17033 ~ Email: Bpeschel@Gmail.com ~ www.PeschelPress.com

The Best Sherlock Holmes Parodies & Pastiches: 1888-1930

ALSO FROM THE PESCHEL PRESS

THE 223B CASEBOOK SERIES
The Early Punch Parodies of Sherlock Holmes
Sherlock Holmes Victorian Parodies & Pastiches: 1888-1899
Sherlock Holmes Edwardian Parodies & Pastiches I: 1900-1904
Sherlock Holmes Edwardian Parodies & Pastiches II: 1905-1909
Sherlock Holmes Great War Parodies & Pastiches I: 1910-1914
Sherlock Holmes Great War Parodies & Pastiches II: 1915-1919
Sherlock Holmes Jazz Age Parodies & Pastiches I: 1920-1924
Sherlock Holmes Jazz Age Parodies & Pastiches II: 1925-1930
The Best Sherlock Holmes Parodies & Pastiches: 1888-1930

THE RUGELEY POISONER SERIES
The Illustrated Life and Career of William Palmer
The Times Report of the Trial of William Palmer
The Life and Career of Dr. William Palmer of Rugeley

ANNOTATED EDITIONS
The Complete, Annotated Murder on the Links
By Agatha Christie
The Complete, Annotated Secret Adversary
By Agatha Christie
The Complete, Annotated Mysterious Affair at Styles
By Agatha Christie
The Complete, Annotated Whose Body?
By Dorothy L. Sayers

OTHER BOOKS
Sew Your Own Cloth Grocery Bags
The Dictionary of Flowers and Gems
Suburban Stockade
The Bride from Dairapaska

ALSO BY BILL PESCHEL
Hell's Casino
Writers Gone Wild (Penguin)

The Best Sherlock Holmes Parodies & Pastiches: 1888-1930

Edited by Bill Peschel

PESCHEL PRESS ~ HERSHEY, PA.

THE BEST SHERLOCK HOLMES PARODIES AND PASTICHES: 1888-1930. Notes and essays copyright 2019 Bill Peschel. All rights reserved. Printed in the United States of America. No part of the notes or essays may be used or reproduced in any manner without written permission except in cases of brief quotations embodied in critical articles or reviews. For information, email peschel@peschelpress.com or write to Peschel Press, P.O. Box 132, Hershey, PA 17033.

Cover design by Bill Peschel.

"The Adventure of the Whyos," copyright © 2011 by Bill Peschel, reprinted by permission of the publisher.

www.peschelpress.com

ISBN-13: 978-1-950347-04-9
ISBN-10: 1-950347-04-4

Edition: May 2019, version 1.0

Table of Contents

Introduction by Charles Press i

An Interrupted Honeymoon 3
    "A. Cone and Oil" (Charles C. Rothwell)
The Mystery of the Spot Ball 20
    "C"
The Man Who "Bested" Sherlock Holmes 30
    Joseph Baron
The Adventures of Chubblock Homes 39
    Jack Butler Yeats
Sherlock Holmes and the Missing Box 45
    Anonymous
The Identity of Miss Angela Vespers 48
    "Ka"
Picklock's Disappearance 57
    R.C. Lehmann
Mrs. Dr. Sherlock Holmes 63
    Anonymous
The Reappearance of Sherlock Holmes 65
    Roy L. McCardell
The Adventure of the Child's Perambulator 68
    "Another Conan Doyle" (Charles Loomis)
The Adventure of the Pink Pearl 75
    Anonymous
Notes of a Bookman 81
    James MacArthur
Mr. Homes Solves a Question of Authorship 89
    John Kendrick Bangs
The Adventure of the Missing Bee 103
    P.G. Wodehouse
The Last of Sherlock Holmes 107
    A.B. "Banjo" Paterson
Sherlock Holmes' Daughter 115
    H.H. Ballard

The Great Suit Case Mystery 135
    Jacques Futrelle
By a Hair 170
    Jean Giraudoux
Herlock's One Mistake 175
    Henry A. Hering
The Adventure of the Lost Manuscripts 189
    Edmund L. Pearson
The Adventure of Shamrock Jolnes 206
    O. Henry
Maddened by Mystery 214
    Stephen Leacock
The Adventure of the Lost Baby 224
    Carolyn Wells
Water, Water Everywhere and Not a Drop For Tea 233
    Anonymous
The Mystery of the Leaping Fish 238
    Tod Browning and Anita Loos
Narpoo Rum 246
    Anonymous
The Looking-Glass 257
    Anonymous
When the Spirits Rapped 260
    Anonymous
Baffled 264
    Anonymous
The Case of the Sinn Feiners 267
    "Peter Todd" (Charles Hamilton)
The Master Mind 275
    Dashiell Hammett
The Mystery of the Murdered Major 277
    James Thurber
The Teapot Dome Case 282
    "A. Conan Oyle" (N.H.)
Intelligence Service 309
    "Z. 4.999"

The Rollo Boys with Sherlock in Mayfair 315
  Corey Ford
The Adventure of the Missing Hatrack 326
  Frederic Dorr Steele
Expert Assistance 336
  James J. Montague
The Mystery Than Which 338
  Rupert Hughes

Appendix
The Adventure of the Whyos (1894) 342
  Bill Peschel
About the Editor 374

Conan Doyle amid his characters, newspaper illustration, 1905.

Introduction: Forever Sherlock

Back in 1944, the mystery writers known as Ellery Queen published a book of twenty-seven Sherlockian parodies they called *The Misadventures of Sherlock Holmes*. The Conan Doyle heirs moved quickly to suppress the book. They considered it an outrageous insult to the memory of The Great Detective.

But the genie was out of the bottle, the yellow fog swirled around offbeat Sherlockian adventures, and Sherlock Holmes was revealed to have been a subject of irreverent comment, almost from the day Conan Doyle wrote the stories about him.

Members of the group known as the Baker Street Irregulars began unearthing more of these early Sherlockian parodies. They traded their finds with each other and some appeared as "incunabulum" in *The Baker Street Journal* or in now out-of-print publications. And inevitably these turned up later in library holdings or became available through diligent internet searches.

These first researchers concentrated on parodies published in the days before World War I, the period of Sherlock's many triumphs. These writers also had first crack at devising the twists that are the glory of humorous parody and have been repeated many times since.

Both Bill Peschel and I extended our collections of early parodies to 1930, the year in which the creator of Sherlock Holmes, Sir Arthur Conan Doyle, died. It seemed a reasonable cutoff, and one that also raises the question of what Conan Doyle might have thought of the outpouring of Sherlockian lampoons. He never said.

During Conan Doyle's lifetime, more than 450 parodies have so far been discovered, published almost exclusively in England and the United States. And many, many more Sherlockian parodies have appeared since 1930, now over 10,000 by one count, and the number continues to climb.

This makes Sherlock Holmes the subject of more parody than any other fictional character or living person.

Why? Many theories exist. My guess is it's because Sherlock's logical deductions do not always lead to correct solutions, as readily as Watson makes it seem. And it's also that in democracies, and especially so in America, we like to point out the flaws and defects in the high and mighty. Australians call it lopping off the tall poppies.

At about the same time, unknown to each other, Bill Peschel and I each began reviewing our bulging parody collections with an eye to publishing the most amusing. My book appeared first, and Bill, stifling his chagrin, introduced himself to me via e-mail, and congratulated me handsomely; a true gentleman.

But as I noted in the opening remarks in my collection, choosing among the Sherlockian parodies available was extremely difficult because it left so many first-rate items still unpublished. Add to this the number of others Bill, via the internet, has independently unearthed for the first time since their original publication.

He has selected these parodies he considers as among the very best.

And this is the feast of Sherlockian parody he now lays before you.

So read on and enjoy! enjoy! and enjoy!

Charles Press
New Era, Michigan

Sherlockian Charles Press is the author of *Parodies and Pastiches Buzzing 'Round Sir Arthur Conan Doyle*, (The Battered Silicon Dispatch Box, 2006), which was consulted for this series, and *A Bedside Book of Early Sherlockian Parodies and Pastiches* (MX Publishing, 2014).

Editor's Introduction

This book represents the cream of the parody crop, culled from the eight volumes I published in the 223B Casebook series. But there are two caveats.

First, this book does not duplicate the stories in Otto Penzler's excellent *The Big Book of Sherlock Holmes Stories*. Not because they don't deserve publication, but there are so many more equally deserving of preservation that we can set that aside. That way, buyers of both books are assured they'll get the most fun and enlightenment for their money.

The other caveat: Some stories are more interesting as historical pieces than as entertainment. Conan Doyle's lifetime saw enormous changes in Western civilization. Britain witnessed the zenith of its empire, and the start of its dismantling. The United States closed its western frontier, stabled the horse in favor of the automobile, and rode into the age of cheap energy with all the societal upheavals that we're still learning to live with today.

Over the course of this book, Sherlock and Watson, too, changed. Like Doctor Who, they traveled through space and time. They swapped roles, personas, and even genders. They trailed communists, gave beauty tips to women, and mocked each other. They met ghosts, investigated government malfeasance, and even solved a few mysteries. These stories also spoke to the concerns of readers, some are still worth hearing now.

My goal with the 223B project was to bring into print as much vintage fanfiction as I could find. It was a fool's errand. Bill Mason's recent *A Holmes By Any Other Name* (Wildside Press) uncovered more period parodies. Matthias Boström and Matt Laffey's ongoing *Sherlock Holmes and Conan Doyle in the Newspapers* series promises even more along with other treasures.

The search is not over, oh, no. In fact, it's barely begun.

Or, as the tall gent in the deerstalker might put it:

The game's still *afoot!*

Bill Peschel
Hershey, Pa.

Acknowledgments

A great effort was made to determine the copyright status of these pieces and obtain permission to publish from the rightful copyright holders. If I have made a mistake, please contact me so that I may rectify the error.

As each volume went to press, I'm reminded again of how many people helped make this series larger and better than I could have done alone. Research assistant Scott Harkless provided rare and crucial stories. Denise Phillips at Hershey Public Library worked hard to acquire the books and articles I asked for. Peter Blau generously shared the fruits of his researches. Charles Press provided me with a shopping list from his *Parodies and Pastiches Buzzing 'Round Sir Arthur Conan Doyle*, and happily filled in the gaps with extremely rare items from his researches.

Then there are the writers whose books led the way: Otto Penzler for *The Big Book of Sherlock Holmes Stories*; Bill Blackbeard for *Sherlock Holmes in America*; Frederic Dannay and Manfred Lee ("Ellery Queen") for their ill-fated *The Misadventures of Sherlock Holmes*; Philip K. Jones for his massive (10,000 entries!) database of Sherlockian pastiches, parodies, and related fiction; John Gibson and Richard Lancelyn Green for *My Evening With Sherlock Holmes* and *The Uncollected Sherlock Holmes*; Paul D. Herbert for *The Sincerest Form of Flattery*; Peter Ridgway Watt and Joseph Green for *The Alternative Sherlock Holmes: Pastiches, Parodies and Copies*; The Sciolist Press, Donald K. Pollock, and the other editors behind *The Baker Street Miscellanea*.

By digitizing the nation's newspapers and making them searchable, The National Library of Australia enabled me to find previously unknown parodies and research their local references so we can appreciate what was going on in New South Wales, Mudgee, and Perth.

Andrew Malec has my thanks as well for contributing his articles on the career of Frederic Dorr Steele and his involvement with the Players Club.

Finally, my love to Teresa, wielder of the red pen and owner of my heart.

👉 **Get the newsletter:** If you want to learn more about my books, my researches and the media I eat, sign up for the Peschel Press newsletter. You'll get an intermittent chatty letter about what we're publishing plus a glimpse behind the scenes at a growing publishing house. Visit either www.planetpeschel.com or www.peschelpress.com and look for the sign-up box.

👉 **Got a review?** If you like this book — or even if you don't — could you leave a word or two at the online book retailer of your choice? I would really appreciate it.

The 223B Casebook Collection

An Interrupted Honeymoon

"A. Cone and Oil" (Charles C. Rothwell)

Although Conan Doyle began Sherlock Holmes' career with two novels, it wasn't until the first short stories appeared that he captured the public's imagination. The first known parody — "My Evening with Sherlock Holmes" by Peter Pan's creator J.M. Barrie — appeared just four months after The Strand *published "A Scandal in Bohemia."*

While The Strand *was publishing the first 12 stories between July 1891 and June 1892, other writers were picking up their pens, such as the one below. Writing as "A. Cone and Oil," Charles C. Rothwell wrote two stories that appeared in the penny magazine* The Ludgate Weekly. *"An Interrupted Honeymoon" was published in the April 9, 1892, edition. Of Charles C. Rothwell, we know only that he published more two short stories — "The Umbrella-Man" and "The Chinaman's Spider" — and the novel* The Stolen Bishop (1895).

My first introduction to Mr. Sherwood Hoakes, that eminent specialist in crime, took place under circumstances of the following singular nature. I was walking home inoffensively enough one evening in a late autumn, when, about half-way down Butcher-avenue, in the City, an open house door attracted my attention. It was a very ordinary door, in a very ordinary row of flat-faced houses, but on the panel below the knocker there was the following inscription in chalk:

"PUT IT DOWN WITHOUT KNOCKING."

I smiled, and wondered, and would have passed on, but at that instant, as my eye travelled down the short lobby and into a room beyond, I perceived to my astonishment and alarm that the fringe of the carpet adjoining the grate was on fire, and that the flame was eating its way towards the window curtains. Without a moment's hesitation I entered the house, hurried into the room, and crushed out the fire under my boot. Contrary to my expectation, the room was occupied by a gentleman, who slowly rose from a basket chair, showing neither annoyance nor surprise at my intrusion. I was about to offer explanations, but he intercepted me by speaking first.

"Good evening, sir. No apologies, I beg. You are welcome. I perceive that you are a cheesemonger[1] by trade. And a widower. Also I regret to observe that you lost your eldest son two years ago — from the measles, I think. Your daughter is married to a jeweller, who, I am afraid, is not quite so steady as he might be. Won't you take a seat? Ah I perceive you were at Margate last month with your grandchildren."

I stood looking in amazement at this man, whom I had never seen before in my life, who, as his eyes travelled over me, read out the biographical details I have given above.

"Now, how on *earth*—?"

"Do I know all these things?"

He smiled a pleasant, if rather superior, smile.

"There's no magic in it. A trained eye and a logical brain. For instance, how do I discover that you are a cheesefactor? My nose tells me so, and my eyes corroborate it by observing the peculiar glossy yellowness of your right hand, which, of course, must handle many thousand cheeses a year. That you are lately a widower, that locket containing brownish-grey hair at your watchchain leads me to presume."

"And about my son — my poor dead son? How can you tell?"

"By your collar, sir. It was one of his. That is evident by the fact that not only is it half a size too small for you, and therefore not your own purchasing, but the collar is one which came into fashion two years ago, and was much in vogue among young men, which leads one to conclude that he bought it then, and probably died soon after of the measles, which you will remember caused great mortality that year."

"Well, well! And the jeweller, my drunken son-in-law — and Margate—" I gasped.

"Nothing could be simpler. A glance at the bridge of your

---

[1] A seller of cheese and other dairy products.

nose assures me that you rarely use those gold eye-glasses dangling before you, and the fact that you wear plain bone studs in your shirt affords a strong presumption that you wouldn't be the man to buy a pair of useless gold pince-nez; they have therefore been presented to you, but presumably by someone not thoroughly acquainted with your habits, and yet sufficiently intimate to make you a handsome personal gift; this being so, the additional fact that the eyeglasses are an old pattern, evidently furbished up and refitted with new cork nose-clips, points strongly to their having been presented by someone in the trade, no doubt a son-in-law anxious to make a handsome gift and to get rid of an unsaleable article. The burin-scratches on one of the glasses seem to indicate the unsteady hand of a drinker." [1]

"Oh, you wizard!" I said, in gay reproach. "You scandalous old sorcerer!"

"As regards your trip to Margate, those three long stiff donkey's hairs—"

"Never mind about Margate and the donkey's hairs. What's under that hat on the table?"

He lifted the silk hat in some confusion and betrayed the flat bottle underneath.

"Won't you sit down and take some?"

I sat down, and while my host moved about the room, I took note of his appearance and surroundings. He looked a man of about forty, whom time and fortune had conspired to ill-use. His face was long and blanched, his eye large and boiled, his red hair was cropped so short that it might have been under a lawnmower, his general expression was badgered and harassed, and that of a man constantly striving to accomplish something against adverse conditions. He wore a frock coat with inked seams;[2] and his vest, which was but-

---

[1] As a burin is a tool used in engraving, the connection with excessive drinking is not apparent.

[2] Inking the seams disguised the fact that thread of a different color was used to repair his frock coat (which is a coat characterized by its knee-

toned askew, showed that he was one of those few remaining individuals who take snuff.

Having equipped me with a cigar and a glass, he resumed his chair. "By the way," I said, "I can tell you something interesting about these Manila cheroots.[1] I was asked to analyse one the other day, in the ordinary course of my business —"

"Analyse? But, my good sir, you — a cheesefactor—"

"Not for the world! I am a chemist and druggist, sir, from my youth up."

Mr. Hoakes fixed a puzzled jaded eye upon me.

"Dear me! That's odd now. But how comes it — your yellow hand — the odour of cheese — I can smell it this moment, distinctly!"

"No wonder, sir," said I, "with half a pound of Gorgonzola on your own sideboard there. And as for my hand, it was mixing iodoform ointment all morning, which may well account for its colour."

The badgered look on the poor man's face deepened perceptibly.

"At any rate you are a widower," he urged.

"Quite the contrary. Nor am I wearing up my poor dead son's linen. The collar is all my own buying and the hair in this locket is said to be Queen Charlotte's; I bought it at a sale."

"But at least your daughter is married to a jeweler—"

"Never had either son or daughter. Bought the eyeglasses myself. Haven't been to the seaside for years; these 'donkey's hairs' must have come out of the clothes-brush this morning."

Mr. Hoakes sighed, and gazed dejectedly into the fire.

"I don't know how it is, but try as I will I never seem to get the knack of it. It's most disheartening; yet I do my best. I strain every nerve. Induction, deduction, ratiocination — I

---

length skirt). Clearly Hoakes had fallen on hard times.
[1] A cigar made from tobacco harvested in the Philippines. It was notable for being made from inferior grades of the leaf and sold to foreign sailors who didn't know or couldn't afford better.

apply 'em all; but I'm almost always wrong. By every rule of evidence, you ought to have been a cheesemonger, and your daughter married to a tipsy jeweller."

"Well," I said, "I'm sorry to disoblige you. Have you been at this business long?"

"About three years."

"I suppose you would call yourself a private detective?"

"'Criminal pathologist' would be more suitable, sir. I have always had a strong leaning towards crime — I mean, of course, the detection of crime — and having been unfortunate in business, I took up my present profession some three years ago."

"Indeed I am myself a student of humanity, but without any special leanings towards crime, and your case interests me greatly. Have you had many successes?"

"Well — yes — perhaps one or two — partial successes. There was the notorious backgammon case, which I am confident I should have unravelled if the police had only left me alone. There was that remarkable case known as the 'Four and Twenty Jailbirds,' and the other, the great Hoxton Blue Pearl Robbery."

"Ah, yes, I remember that well."

"So do I," said Mr. Hoakes, gloomily, "for I served a light sentence at Millbank[1] in connection with it. How was I to know that those plausible ruffians were only using me as a cat's paw?"[2]

He groaned bitterly.

"And yet it eventually redounded to my advantage, for while in jail I was able to establish acquaintanceship with the elite of the criminal classes, much to my subsequent benefit in my profession."

"And do you work in connection with the regular police?"

---

[1] A prison built on marshland near the Thames in London's Pimlico area. It operated from 1816 to 1890, when it was demolished in stages until 1903 and the land redeveloped.
[2] Getting someone else to unwittingly do your dirty work. The phrase was inspired by a fable by French poet Jean de La Fontaine (1621-1695), in which a monkey convinces a cat to pull chestnuts for him from a hot fire, burning his paw in the process.

"Not now, sir. I went down to Scotland-yard[1] to offer them my co-operation but they declined; they even warned me off, and so far forgot themselves as actually to look me out in their Photograph Albums, and make references the reverse of considerate to — in short — to Millbank. Of course, I left the premises at once. My self-respect demanded it. And now, though I shall always try to work in harmony with the Force, they must understand that there can be no true intimacy between us for the future."

In this wise began my memorable friendship with Sherwood Hoakes. When I left him he pressed his card upon me, which I reproduce here in the hopes that publicity may be of service to him:—

> SHERWOOD HOAKES.
> Specialist in Crime and Mystery.
> Felonies a Speciality.
> 404, Butcher Avenue.

In the course of many subsequent interviews I gleaned the details of his craft and the methods he pursued in its practice. His early education had been obviously neglected, but he had made a creditable attempt to repair the deficiency by means of some back numbers of a *Popular Educator*,[2] and the conscientious study of three volumes of an Encyclopedia, ranging from "Lit" to "Sag," which he had picked up at an auction of cottage pianos and household furniture. "Induction, deduction, ratiocination" were his constant watchwords, and seemed to afford him as much occult satisfaction as "that blessed word Mesopo-

---

[1] London's Metropolitan Police. Although its original location was at 4 Whitehall Place, its rear entrance opened onto Great Scotland Yard, hence the name.
[2] A weekly magazine founded in 1852 by printer John Cassell (1817-1865) aimed at encouraging working-class readers to improve their education and employment prospects. Future Prime Minister Lloyd George said that reading it as a child in Wales helped shape his future.

tamia" did to the devout old lady in the story.¹

Mr. Hoakes had, on the whole, a taking personality. Simplicity of mind and warmth of heart were his most prominent traits. As I followed his calamitous career, at a judiciously safe distance, I was only too frequently pained to observe the endless troubles into which he was hurried by the unselfish zeal with which he espoused the causes of dubious and deceitful clients. His trustful, unshaken confidence in the face of failures innumerable, in the infallibility of his method of "lightning deductions," should have aroused the pity of the most callous of his dissembling clients. This I will say to my own credit that I was always the first to welcome him out of jail after he had served one or other of those many light sentences to which his benevolent indiscretions, on behalf of other people, subjected him.

On looking over my copious notes of his cases, I am tempted to extract the following and most recent adventure for publication:—

I was supping with him one evening, to celebrate a recent release, and was in the midst of an appeal to him to control for the future those "lightning deductions" which so often ended in Millbank, when a client was announced. Mr. Hoakes put on his skull cap (he had only been out four days)² and we repaired to the consulting room.

Here a lady in a heavy crape veil awaited us; but, oddly enough, her other attire was not mourning. As she raised the veil Mr. Hoakes took his usual plunge.

"You are recently from New York, I see."

"No, sir; I'm from Camberwell."³

---

¹ *Brewer's Dictionary of Phrase and Fable* tells of the old woman "who told her pastor that she found great support in 'that comfortable word Mesopotamia.'" This might be a variation of a story about Anglican preacher George Whitefield (1714-1770), whose voice was so powerful that actor David Garrick said that "he could make men laugh or cry by pronouncing Mesopotamia."
² As a prisoner, his hair had been cropped short as an anti-lice measure.
³ A district in the borough of Southwark in London, south of the Thames.

"But your glove-buttons are stamped with an American maker's name, and they don't ship such articles over here."

"My sister gave me them when she was over last year from Canada."

Mr. Hoakes looked annoyed, and sat down.

"You wish to consult me, madam?"

"Yes, sir, I do. I've read about you in the police reports, and I thought perhaps you might be able, though everyone else has failed, to help me in my terrible perplexity." The lady turned a pathetic white face upon each of us, and sobbed in a very hopeless way, very touching. She was about thirty, rather good-looking, with dreamy eyes, and an accent that plainly came from Camberwell as well as herself.

"My name is Bagworthy, Marian Bagworthy. I was married three weeks ago, from my parent's house in Camberwell, to a gentleman who travelled in tea and varnish, Mr. Arthur Bagworthy."

"You say 'travelled' in the past tense, Mrs. Bagworthy. Is your husband dead, then?"

"Alas, sir, I don't knows. All I know is, that he disappeared on the very day of our marriage, and hasn't been seen or heard of since."

"Not altogether an uncommon occurrence," said Hoakes, drily.[1] "Do you suspect foul play, or have you any grounds (pardon the supposition) for presuming his disappearance prearranged and intentional?"

"Oh, not the slightest! He bore an excellent character, and his accounts were found in perfect order. The circumstances of his disappearance were so unaccountably strange, Mr. Hoakes, that I don't know what to think, or where to turn for help! Why, he vanished *before my very eyes!*"

The unhappy woman looked from one to the other in haggard despair.

---

[1] A nod to a similar situation in "The Adventure of the Noble Bachelor," published in *The Strand* that month, when Lord St. Simon asked Holmes to discover why his bride disappeared immediately after her wedding.

"This seems strange," said Hoakes. "Let me have the story in detail."

"It was a quarter to eight on the evening of the twelfth of February when he vanished. But let me begin at the beginning. We were married at two o'clock — it was a very quiet wedding — and we went home to mother's after it, while I finished packing and changed my dress. Then we drove quietly into town and put up at Lakey's Hotel, intending to start early next morning for Folkestone."

"One moment. Be good enough to describe your husband's personal appearance."

"He was rather short and slim — a very elegant figure — dark, with black eyes, and a — a slight squint in the left one; but not a very noticeable squint."

"Inwards or outwards?"

"Outwards, sir, and it gave him a sort of — sort of poetic, far-away look, very taking. Well, as I was saying, we reached Lakey's at half-past six and had dinner, and then, as it was a nice calm night, Arthur suggested a little walk. So we went upstairs to put my things on, and then — then he — he vanished."

Mrs. Bagworthy wept into an already damp handkerchief.

"Control yourself, dear madam," said Hoakes, soothingly. "In what way did he vanish? through the door? — the window? — the chimney?"

"No," wailed the unhappy girl, "he was sitting on my tin trunk and he disappeared."

"Into the trunk?"

"No, into nothingness."

"What were you doing at the moment?"

"I was looking at him and putting on my ulster."[1]

Hoakes leaned back and took a heavy pinch of snuff.

"This is going to be a stickler, Chasemore"

---

[1] A long overcoat worn during the daytime. Until the 1890s, it was worn with a cape attached. Named for the Irish town where it was originally sold.

"Had you much ready money with you at the time, madam?" I asked.

"We had a matter of twenty pounds for the honeymoon, but it was all in my box. Arthur had only a few shillings on him when he disappeared."

"This occurred at a quarter to eight, you say," resumed Hoakes, in his most impressive style. "You would be an hour over dinner?"

"About, sir. But we had to order the dumplings beforehand, and that delayed it."

"Dumplings?"

"Yes, sir. Apple dumplings. My husband was always partial to them, and so we ordered three, and had one each."

"And left the third on the dish?"

"No."

"You divided it, then?"

"No. We had only one each."

"Then it must have been removed by the waiter."

"Oh no, it wasn't."

"Well, then, what became of it?"

"That's what I don't know," said Mrs. Bagworthy, tearfully.

"But why? If it wasn't on the dish, and you didn't eat it, and it didn't go out, what do you suppose happened to it?" The poor woman put up her handkerchief and sobbed.

"It vanished too."

Hoakes stared and whistled.

"Vanished? Before your eyes?"

"I was looking at it, and it turned into nothing on the dish."

"And you never saw it again?"

"Yes, sir, I did. That's how I know Arthur's alive. It came back to me by post three days afterwards, directed in his own writing."

Mrs. Bagworthy opened a small parcel done up in tissue paper, and displayed a rather large and unclean envelope, which bore the post-office stamps, and contained the withered yellow mummy of an apple dumpling.

We both started up to examine this interesting relic. Hoakes posed over it with his inevitable magnifying glass, and we sniffed it and nibbled at it. "I don't like the looks of this," said Hoakes, gravely. "I don't like it at all. You observed the envelope, Chasemore. He was not only in safety when he addressed that to his poor deserted wife, but he was actually enjoying comfort and leisure, and smoking a pipe at the time."

"O come now! How do you make—"

"Look at the handwritings! A man whose mind is distressed doesn't write such a natty hand as that, all flourishes and whipthongs.[1] He spread his elbows and took his time over it, and if you look narrowly you can see half a dozen brown spots in the middle of the '—worthy' where the ashes puffed out of his pipe and slightly burnt the paper. Depend upon it, we have to deal with some cowardly scamp who, for private ends of his own, has married the girl and then bolted."

On the following day we met Mrs. Bagworthy at Lakey's Hotel by appointment. This establishment is a third-rate house at the bottom of Bloater-street. We were not exactly welcomed by the proprietor.

"I'm gettin' sick of this here business," he shouted, angrily, into our faces.

"Police for breakfast, police for dinner; we've 'ad the 'ole blamed Force down at one time and another."

Hoakes explained blandly that we didn't belong to the Force.

"I dessay you don't, neither! But you look as if you'd come out of their 'ands only last week; you've got the proper Newgate cut, you 'ave! Here, Tom, show these tramps upstairs to number 17, and keep an eye on the towels."

It was a small, square, plainly-furnished apartment. There

---

[1] A whip attached to a short stick used in fox hunting. The thong refers to the flexible leather braided section of the whip. It is located in between the handle at one end and the popper and the fall at the other.

was no wardrobe, no cupboard, nor any valance to the iron bedstead. Tom Thumb could not have hidden himself in the room. Mrs. Bagworthy rehearsed the details of the mysterious disappearance, showing us where, at the foot of the bed, "Arthur" sat on the tin box, smoking a cigar, whilst she, standing before the closed door, put on her cloak. "He was wearing a chemical diamond pin[1] in his tie — he was always fond of jewellery, was Arthur — and it sparkled so prettily in the gaslight that I spoke about it to him, and the next minute — he had vanished."

"And what did you do then?"

"It gave me a proper turn, Mr. Hoakes, but I didn't go off. I called 'Arthur,' and told him not to be silly, but to come out again — though goodness knows there was nothing for him to hide behind in the room."

"They do say," observed the crumpled waiter Tom, hoarsely, "as the gent had been a amateur Moore and Burgess, and was a good 'and at playin' the 'anky-panky.'"[2]

"How dare they say such things of my husband!" cried Mrs. Bagworthy, indignantly. "I've never known him do anything but a little thought-reading, in fun; and as for playing the 'hanky-panky' on our wedding-day — it's wicked of you to suggest such things!"

I have never seen a man so almost inspired as Hoakes was during his examination of that room. The walls, the floors, the chimney, the bed, the washstand, were auscultated[3] with the loving care of a physician sounding a phthisical[4] patient. We stood reverently apart while the scrutiny lasted. As well as the

---

[1] The cubic zirconium of its day, this was a diamond created through a manufacturing process instead of by mining.
[2] *Moore and Burgess:* George "Pony" Moore (1820-1909) and Frederic Burgess (1827-1893) were American music hall performers, notable for appearing as part of the New Christy Minstrel before forming the Moore and Burgess Minstrels in 1871. *Hanky-panky:* Trickery, double-dealing or cheating. Later, it would be associated with sexual intercourse.
[3] In medicine, the act of listening to a patient's chest with a stethoscope.
[4] Tuberculosis or a similar wasting disease.

magnifying-glass, he had a small compass, which he deposited at different places and watched with rapt attention. He seemed to be gathering clues as he proceeded, for his eagerness increased, and once or twice he spoke half-aloud — "Yes, yes, as I thought, as I feared! Ah, when an unscrupulous tea-traveller takes to crime, 'tis indeed a corker. He has no match!" Finally he reached the window and searched the woodwork inch by inch with his glass. At length an exclamation burst from him, and he turned with a burning glance on the trembling woman.

"Did your husband wear a signet ring?"

"Yes."

"Shield-shaped — on his third finger?"

"Yes, yes."

Hoakes drew in a deep breath of triumph.

"One more question, madam, and I have done. Was your husband partial to a large umbrella?"

"He frequently carried a large one, as most travellers do."

"Did he bring it upstairs with him on the evening of his disappearance?"

Mrs. Bagworthy reflected a moment. "I believe he did, sir, but I wouldn't be quite positive."

"Thank you," said Hoakes, quietly, "but I am. And now, I think I can promise you, madam, to produce your lost husband within three days."

We next chartered a cab for Camberwell, where Hoakes desired to be introduced to the tin trunk and such personal effects of Mr. Bagworthy's as his wife was in possession of. On the journey a very curious thing happened. Mrs. Bagworthy and I occupied the back seat, and facing us sat Hoakes. His lens peeped over the edge of his vest-pocket and sparkled vividly in a ray of the March sunlight. Both my companion's and my own eyes were attracted by its brightness. Suddenly Mrs. Bagworthy remarked:—"

I wonder why Mr. Hoakes didn't come with us? I thought he said he wanted particularly to see my husband's clothing."

She turned a pair of dreamy eyes on me as I sat stupidly grinning at my astonishment.

"I think if you look closer, madam, you'll see Mr. Hoakes sitting there in front of us."

She looked, but obviously without seeing his very palpable presence.

"There's no one there," she said, smiling at what she appeared to think was my little joke. Then it flashed upon me that she was hypnotised, no doubt by the sparkle of the lens. Hoakes and I exchanged nods. In a few moments she came out of her partial trance and chatted to us as if nothing had happened.

In Bagworthy's clothes Hoakes read a world of subtle meaning in his most approved style. He construed characteristics of deceit in every fold and wrinkle. "This is no ordinary scoundrel's waistcoat, Chasemore; see here what I've found." It was a small brass dinner-check with the Queen's head neatly cut in it. "That's as good as a half-sovereign on a dark night to a tipsy cabman. And look at this overcoat; look at the long slit and the secret pocket it forms in the lining, right under the armpits. And those slippers — they reek of trickery! You see that bend in the sole, showing his habit of walking about, secretly, on tiptoe! The man's a monster of hypocrisy and crime!"

In discussing the case that night Hoakes was becomingly mysterious and reticent, as all good novelists and detectives should be. We agreed that the theory of the instantaneous disappearance was now satisfactorily explained on the assumption that Mrs. Bagworthy had been for the moment hypnotised, probably by the sparkle of the chemical diamond in her husband's tie, and that during her trance he had slipped away unobserved. But how? — for the employees at the hotel were unanimously confident that he had never come downstairs in the ordinary way.

Hoakes tapped me significantly on the knee.

"*What was he doing with that umbrella upstairs?*"

"But that explains nothing," I objected.

"It explains everything. *He used it as a parachute!* I saw

the marks of his boots and his signet-ring outlined in the soft ashwood of the window-sill. He climbed out that way and floated down into the stable-yard, unnoticed in the dark."

Next evening I called at Butcher-avenue, and found a seedy-looking cab-driver asleep in his hat by the fire. It was Hoakes.

"I've had a heavy day," he explained. "This is my third disguise since morning."

"Have you been successful?"

"Very. I've got my man well in hand, and I shall be up with him to-morrow. He thinks he's going to Antwerp on the noon boat, but I *don't!*"

"You've seen him, then?"

"Not yet. But I've seen his *other* wife and the children. Oh, yes — very much married man — nice little house and shop in the Commercial-road — sells German yeast — under an *alias*, of course. Ran him to earth by means of his trouser-buttons. You remember I cut one off yesterday and measured the trousers.

"Well, I found his tailor, to whom, of course, he figures under his German yeast *alias* — 'Augustus Bundelman.' Same initials, you observe. Had a chat with his little wife, and surprised the confession from her that *her* husband's favourite dish is — apple dumplings! That's corroboration I should hope? Oh, we've got him fairly!"

"And how will you proceed to-morrow? For heaven's sake, be careful, Hoakes, do nothing rash!"

"It's plain sailing now. I shall go down to St. Katherine's Wharf disguised as a dock-hand; Mrs. Bagworthy will be there to identify him, and we nail my little man as he steps on board."

"Well, good luck, and let me hear from you to-morrow night."

I did hear from him. At seven a policeman brought a note to my shop, as urgent as a four-line "whip." [1]

---

[1] In Parliament, a whip is a note sent by a political party official — usually the Chief Whip — to its members asking them to attend a particular ses-

"Come at once — identify me — bail me — save me!"

I found my friend extremely dishevelled and depressed. He looked so life-like a dock-hand that I did not wonder at the police discrediting his assertions to the contrary. Had we been Frenchmen we should have wept on each other's shoulders.

"My poor Hoakes, how did it all happen?"

"My cursed luck again," he moaned. "She didn't come in time — Mrs. Bagworthy — the boat was about to start — he came on board — something had to be done — I charged him — he denied it, denied everything — I dragged him ashore — there was an awful row — the boat went off — we fought and then gave each other in charge — they've let him go on his own recognizances, but they won't believe I'm not a dock-hand. It's too late to bail me to-night, so go down and bring up Mrs. Bagworthy, and let us have an explanation."

Away I posted to Camberwell. Imagine my surprise when I was precipitated, by a flurried servant-girl, into the presence of the re-united bride and bridegroom, sitting hand in hand by the fire.

"Oh, for shame of yourself, sirs," I cried, "dallying in the lap of pleasure while the man who dragged you from the Antwerp boat and the paths of crime is groaning on a bed of straw!"

My rhetoric was florid, but well-meant. Up started Mrs. Bagworthy.

"Sir, how dare you! And poor Arthur only just come out of hospital!"

"Well," I said, "it was his own fault. He shouldn't have struck Hoakes. He should have come off the boat quietly."

Then it all came out. We were talking at sixes and sevens. Mr. Bagworthy rose and explained, while I sat and humbly listened, for self and Hoakes.

---

sion. A "four-line whip" is a particularly important summons. It gets its name from the four lines underscoring the opening word "Important" and the concluding sentence "Your punctual attendance is most particularly requested."

He was not Mr. Bundelman, and never had been. On the evening of his disappearance, not noticing his wife's temporary trance, he had quietly walked downstairs to await her in the street. There he had been knocked down by a hansom and hurried off insensible to hospital, but for three weeks he had suffered from "aphasia"[1] or aberration of speech, and was quite unable to put his thoughts and wishes into intelligible words or writing. He couldn't even give his own name and address.

As for the incident of the apple-dumpling, he confessed, with some confusion, that he had removed it from the dish and popped it into a large envelope he had in his pocket, being extremely fond of cold dumpling, with the intention of eating it later on. He further supposed that the packet was jerked out of his pocket by the collision, and picked up eventually by some honest soul, who, finding it already addressed and stamped, consigned it to the post.

"This will be a sad blow for my poor friend," I said. "His chain of evidence was so complete, beginning with the parachute-descent and the trouser-buttons, and ending triumphantly at the German yeast shop. I will bid you goodnight and break the news to him in his lonely cell."

The action of *Bundelman v. Hoakes* resulted disastrously for my friend. I expect him out at the end of next week.

---

[1] An inability to speak or understand words after suffering brain damage.

The Mystery of the Spot Ball

"C"

Conan Doyle's ties to Edinburgh University began with his attendance there in 1876. His study of medicine was rewarded with an M.B. degree in '81 and an M.D. in '85. He maintained his connection to the school and the city throughout his life, paying frequent visits, lecturing at the school and running for Parliament for Central Edinburgh.

This parody came from an 1893 issue of the Student, Edinburgh University's official weekly magazine that had already published parodies of Lewis Carroll, the Brontës, and Jerome K. Jerome. Its author has not been identified. Conan Doyle apparently did not mind Holmes being an object of fun; three years later, he contributed "The Field Bazaar," an apocryphal Holmes story, as part of a fundraiser run by the magazine. "The Mystery of the Spot Ball" was republished in a limited-edition pamphlet in 1997 by Richard Lancelyn Green.

We were in our old rooms in Baker Street, the rain was falling fast, and the monotony of three consecutive days unenlivened by murder or mystery had begun seriously to affect the spirits of my friend Sherlock Holmes. All that dreary afternoon he had lain stretched upon a sofa sipping a concentrated solution of cocaine through a straw, an amusement which he varied at times by softly playing a few bars of "God Save the Queen" on a fine 'cello conveniently suspended above his head by a stout string.

Suddenly he exclaimed, "You were out last night, Watson."

I started in astonishment.

Holmes chuckled softly to himself. "Ah, my dear Watson, it is a very simple matter after all," he said, with his peculiarly penetrating smile.

"On your trousers I have noticed for some time two or three crumbs of a peculiar shape and colour. These I recognised at once as belonging to the common water biscuit. I may mention that I have written a monograph on the subject of biscuit crumbs. From the tenacity with which they retained their position I saw at once that they had been fixed by some fluid. What fluid could it be? The garments in question are so light that coffee would be at once seen, water you never drink; I know the resources of our cellar, therefore soda water it must have been.

"And why should you, a man of five foot six, in the best of health, breakfast off soda water and a biscuit if you had not been out last night?"

"But my dear Holmes," I exclaimed, "I went to bed last night at ten, and these are your trousers which I took the liberty of borrowing while my own were — well, while they were being repaired, if you must know."

Holmes smiled somewhat bitterly. "I never get any credit when I explain the steps by which I have arrived at my results," he said; "I always give myself away, I am afraid," and tossing off the remains of the cocaine, he closed his eyes wearily.

Suddenly we were startled by a loud peal on the bell. I rushed to the window, and was rewarded by a glimpse of a female figure entering the door. I could hardly control my excitement.

"Our visitor," said Holmes casually, "is a tall bulky gentleman, dressed in a long blue coat, and I think wears a red beard, though I am not certain as to this last point."

I perceived that he had a mirror let to the back of his 'cello, and arranged at such an angle that he could obtain an excellent view of the street.

"You have accurately described the policeman on the other side of the street," I said, "but our visitor will, I think, prove a somewhat more interesting person."

As I spoke the door opened, and a lady was shown in. She was a person of some forty winters, dressed neatly but plainly in black, and had an air of unusual agitation.

Holmes sprang to his feet, and greeted her with that ready courtesy which he knew so well how to assume. "I perceive," he said, "that you have just come from Glasgow, and that you received a severe cut over the right eye about four years ago; you have three teeth stopped with gold, you wear your boots down at the heel, have a taste for drink and a weakness for peppermints, are in comparatively poor circumstances, have had a love affair many years ago, and have something on your mind at present."

"Indeed, sir," replied the lady, in evident alarm. "I have something terrible on my mind, but I have never been to Glasgow, and my teeth—"

Holmes interrupted her with a wave of his hand. "To the point, my dear madam, to the point," he said; "tell me in your own words what is the matter with you." As he spoke he threw himself back in an easy-chair, and prepared to listen to her tale in a characteristic attitude.

She was, it seemed, a lady in reduced circumstances, who had for a number of years past let lodgings to a single gentleman, a certain Mr. Tollocks by name. She described him as a pleasant affable gentleman, of somewhat irregular hours, and, at times, habits, well off, and apparently in a good position. She had neither seen nor heard anything remarkable about him, and nothing at all eventful or suspicious had happened till that day.

The night before he had declared his intention of dining out, a by no means unusual course for Mr. Tollocks, and one that caused his landlady, Mrs. Boddle, no anxiety.

She retired to bed at ten o'clock, leaving her door locked, but not bolted, as her lodger was in the habit of carrying a latch key.[1]

About one o'clock, as nearly as she could say, she was awakened by strange sounds outside the house. She was quite certain that they came from the outside, and not from within, and for some minutes she lay awake with a beating heart. All was silent again, however, and Mrs. Boddle once more went to sleep.

Again, some hours later, she thinks she woke with a start for the second time, and then she clearly and distinctly heard

---

[1] A key consisting of a rod with a notched paddle at the end used to open a door's lock. This is a forerunner of the tumbler lock used today.

a deep grunting sound coming apparently from beneath the window. There was a moment's silence, then a long deep-drawn sigh sounded through the silent room, and all was still again.

Mrs. Boddle was too agitated for further slumber. Nothing more was heard save the ticking of the clock and the occasional moan of the wind, but for hour after hour the poor woman tossed restlessly from side to side, and as soon as it was daylight she got up.

With commendable prudence she at once summoned the police, and then, accompanied by an inspector and two constables, she knocked at Mr. Tollock's bedroom door. There was no reply, and as Mrs. Boddle said it would have seemed strange if there had been after a night so broken with incidents and presentiments. Entering, they found that the bed had not been slept in, and that Mr. Tollocks had evidently not been in his apartment since he left on the previous evening. Mrs. Boddle then left the house in charge of six detectives, and came straight to Baker Street.

At the end of this interesting narrative, told in a simple unaffected manner, and in a voice at times choked with emotion, Holmes sprang to his feet, his lassitude gone, his eyes gleaming with the excitement of the chase. "There is no time to be lost," he said, "call a cab, Watson — my colleague Dr. Watson — Mrs. Boddle. We will go at once to the house."

During the drive Holmes sat in a corner of the cab, his hat over his brows, buried in deep thought. All at once he started up, smiled mysteriously, and then launched forth into a conversation of the most various and desultory kind. No one would have thought that he had just been grappling with one of those intricate and vital problems which take inferior minds days of constant thought, and before which they have so often to retire baffled and dismayed.

We reached Tooral Terrace, E.W., after about an hour's drive. A quiet suburban road it seemed, a double line of semi-detached villas standing in small gardens, a grocer's van in front of one, and at No. 16, Mrs. Boddle's residence, two well-dressed men lounging at the front gate. These touched their hats to Holmes as he entered, Mrs. Boddle and I following. We were met at the door by Mugson, the Chief of the Metropolitan Detective Force.

"A strange business, Mr. Holmes," he remarked, shaking his bullet head sententiously, and looking wisely out of a pair of unintelligent green eyes, "— a strange business, but we have a clue, and I think we shall be at the bottom of this affair before very long."

Holmes smiled sarcastically. "Indeed, my dear Mugson, and may I ask what evidence you have acquired?"

Mugson gave a self-satisfied smirk, and putting his hand into his coat-tail pocket, produced a round white spherical object, much stained with mud, but most unmistakably recognisable as a billiard ball.

Holmes took it in his hand, and gazed at it intently. Suddenly he gave an exclamation of astonishment. "The spot ball!" he cried.[1]

Mugson looked the picture of envious surprise; he had evidently overlooked this fact. Recovering his composure, however, he remarked, in a tone of great importance, "We have something else," and with that he produced a narrow slip of paper.

Holmes seized it eagerly, and taking from his waistcoat pocket a lens of great power, examined it minutely for some time.

"My dear Mugson," he said at length, "you are really excelling yourself; this is most satisfactory."

Then pocketing the two pieces of evidence, he requested us to stand aside, and proceeded to make an exhaustive examination of the garden. Throwing himself flat on his face, he wriggled his way over the grass plots at the side, up and down the path in front — in short, through the entire garden. His

---

[1] A white ball marked with a red dot. In English billiards, each player has their own cue ball; one player gets the plain white ball, and the other the spot ball.

nose seemed actually in the mud at times, and his lens left not a blade of grass or the smallest pebble unnoticed.

"Well, Mugson," he said, as he rose at last to his feet, "of course you observed that two red pebbles near the gate had been turned over since last night, and that the word 'Betsy' had been cut on the stone work about three years ago, and, of course, you have formed your own conclusions."

Mugson looked baffled and mortified.

"Let us enter the house, Watson," he added. Having carefully examined every room in turn, taken down all the pictures, and turned up all the carpets, he at length paused and said, "Well, what do you make of this case?"

"I confess that I am completely at sea," I replied.

Holmes handed me the slip of paper, and said, "Perhaps this throws some light upon it."

I looked at the paper carefully. "It is rather more than half an inch wide, the edges are evenly cut and not torn, the writing has been printed in capitals, and it reads: 'Crowded house; several minor bills read.'[1] But what it means I haven't a notion," I said.

"Ah! my dear Watson," replied Sherlock Holmes, "it is just in the study of these seemingly mysterious but really very simple things that I have gained such renown as your very flattering notices of some of my cases have given me. I own at first that the case presented some difficulties. These apparently straightforward and simple problems generally are the hardest in reality.

"But a little reflection soon convinced me of two things. Mr. Tollocks had evidently come back to his house, and Mr. Tollocks had not gone inside. Mrs. Boddle's tale, though apparently so truthful, I at once rejected as improbable and inconsistent; and it is an elementary axiom that having eliminated the evidently doubtful, what remains must either be false or true. Therefore, I was driven to the conclusion that

---

[1] Readers of the time would recognize that this was a ticker-tape message referring to action in the British House of Parliament.

Mrs. Boddle has been murdered by Mr. Tollocks."

I started. "Impossible," I exclaimed; "Mrs. Boddle is in the garden at this moment."

"Mr. Tollocks, disguised as Mrs. Boddle, is in the garden, and I have told Mugson and his satellites not to let him out of their sight," replied Holmes.

"But how in the world did you find that out, Holmes?" I asked with an admiration which evidently gratified him, for it was with a pleased smile that he continued.

"Ah! my dear Watson, it was a very simple affair after all. I saw at once that a terrible tragedy had been committed. The sounds outside the house, the deep sigh, the external arguments drawn from my varied experience, convinced me of the truth of a suspicion which crossed my mind before Mrs. Boddle had entered my rooms."

"But," I suggested, "perhaps Mrs. Boddle, or rather, I should say, Mr. Tollocks may have invented these particulars."

"I thought of that," said Holmes, "but I dismissed the supposition at once as being untenable and inconvenient. The spot ball and the paper confirmed my suspicions, and my search through the house and garden placed the last links in this mysterious chain of events securely in my hands."

He paused for a moment in triumph, and then continued, "Listen, Watson, and you shall judge for yourself. This ball, you will observe, is spot, not plain; that is the first important point. How did it come here, and why? It must have been thrown over the wall by some one who was well acquainted with the house and the ways of its inmates, and it was obviously thrown with a meaning. It is for us to discover that meaning. What does the word itself suggest? 'Spot,' evidently this is the spot, the spot for the murder; the spot where the deed should be done. And the paper, what does that tell us? It is the record of some deadly secret society, and by putting the words backwards we shall see a new and a more insidious meaning; look at it now." And with that he rapidly wrote on the back of an envelope, "Red. bills. Minor several house crowded."

"What do you say to that, Watson?" he chuckled, rubbing his long lean hands together.

"I am simply overwhelmed," I replied.

"And you have rightly observed that it is printed in capitals; that proves that the man who wrote this was not in the habit of writing in English. What races print in capitals and commit murders on spots?"

Holmes drew from his pocket an *Encyclopaedia Britannica*, and read, "'The Hyti-Tytis inhabit the island of Blob, in the South Pacific. They average about four feet three in height, are plainly but tastefully dressed in corals, wear their hair in papers composed of the bark of the gum tree, &c. &c. Thanks to the efforts of our missionaries, they have learned to *print in capital* style. . . . They choose lonely spots for the celebration of these horrid rites.'

"There you are, Watson; Mrs. Boddle and Mr. Tollocks were both Hyti-Tytis. They were fellow-members of a secret society."

"But, my dear Holmes," I interrupted, "this person Boddle or Tollocks, or whoever he or she is, is considerably above four feet three."

"He is a giant Hyti-Tyti," replied Holmes, with unanswerable logic, and then he continued—

"Last night this ball and this paper were thrown into the garden. They were the signal for the 'red bill' to be put into execution; and now, Watson, it only remains to find the body."

He had just finished speaking, when a sharp knock on the door was followed by the entrance of Mugson in a state of extreme excitement. In his hand he carried a mud-stained blue Melton coat. "Well, Mr. Holmes, while you been thinking, we have been working, and this is what we have found. We discovered it beneath the two red pebbles," he said, complacently.

Holmes started, but immediately recovered himself. "I suppose you have searched the pockets," he said, carelessly.

It was Mugson's turn to start; he had evidently omitted to take the precaution.

Muttering "idiot" under his breath, Sherlock Holmes seized the coat, and proceeded to turn out the pockets. We stood round watching with breathless interest. A cigar case, a theatre bill, and a few loose fusees,[1] in turn emerged; and then, with a low exclamation, Holmes drew forth first a plain and then a red billiard ball.

Putting his hand hastily into the other pocket, an extraordinary mass of stuff was brought to light. Yard after yard of the same mysterious paper strips appeared, covered, like our previous find, with printed matter.

"It is an archive!" cried Holmes, in his excitement; "the whole records of the society are here! This is indeed a find, Mugson."

As we crowded round him, eager to read the multitudinous messages, we were arrested by a low cry from the garden.

"He cannot have escaped," muttered Holmes, as we all rushed out.

"We have found him, sir," said a detective, coming forward to meet us in the garden.

"Found him? Found whom?" demanded Holmes.

"Mr. Tollocks, sir."

"Mr. Tollocks — nonsense," said Holmes, quickly.

"Come here then, sir."

We followed the man, and found the five other detectives and Mrs. Boddle grouped round the water-butt at the back of the house.

Gazing into the butt, an extraordinary spectacle met our view. At the bottom, in about eighteen inches of water, sat a middle-aged gentleman in evening clothes. His button boots had been carefully taken off, but otherwise he was in full dress. He had evidently been drinking pretty heavily over night, and apparently his brain was not yet very clear; for, in answer to Mrs. Boddle's almost tearful entreaties that he should get up and come in, he replied in bibulous accents,

---

[1] A conical-shaped gear used to help spring-powered watches keep time.

"Go 'way, go 'way, dear. Call me 'gain — half-pasht nine, thatsch a dear."

With some difficulty, and in spite of his expostulations that he was "perfidy comferrable" where he was, we got him into the house, and sobered him sufficiently to answer our questions.

It seemed that he had been dining not wisely but too well at his club, and on his return home, after an abortive attempt to enter by the front door, he had taken off his coat, and quietly gone to sleep in the water-butt.

"And the balls — how do you account for these?" asked Sherlock Holmes.

"The ballsh?" said Mr. Tollocks, with a puzzled expression.

"Yes, the billiard balls we found in your pockets?"

Mr. Tollocks laughed gaily. "Alwaysh shtick the chalk in my pocket; shupposh I shtuck ballsh by mistaksh," he explained, brimming over with mirth at the recollection.

"And all this stuff — how did you come by this?" asked Mugson, holding up the mass of paper.

"Thatsh the tape. Put penniesh in the shlot of the tape machine[1] and got all that — all that blooming paper. Shplendid fun," said Mr. Tollocks, still laughing merrily.

"I think we had better leave him to Mrs. Boddle," said Mugson. "We worked well, sir," he added to Holmes, "and I am much obliged, I am sure, for any little assistance you were able to give us."

"That's always the way, Watson," said Sherlock, bitterly; "I do all the work, they get the credit. All the evening papers will be full of Mr. Mugson's intelligence and energy, I suppose."

As we drove away together, Holmes remarked to me: "I tell you what, Watson, next time you can do the detecting, and I shall do the writing."

---

[1] Some gambling halls accepted bets on horse races and used telegraph-driven tape machines to print the race results. As we saw earlier, the message had nothing to do with horse racing.

The Man Who "Bested" Sherlock Holmes

Joseph Baron

This story debuted as "entertaining Christmas reading" in a special 1892 holiday edition of the Burnley Express *newspaper. An editorial note in the previous week's edition told readers that Conan Doyle himself "has gone through the MS. of this story, and emphatically pronounced it 'good'," placing Baron alongside James M. Barrie as the only authors whose parodies Doyle publicly praised. Two years later, the story also won the annual Christmas fiction contest in* The Strand's *sister magazine* Tit-Bit.

Baron (1859-1924) was a Blackburn journalist who also wrote stories in the Lancashire dialect under the penname "Tom o'Dick o'Bobs."

"I don't care what you say," I claimed, enthusiastically; "my opinion is that Sherlock Holmes will be as great a favorite with posterity as Pickwick or Count Fosco,[1] or anybody else you can name in fiction."

"Bosh! Rot!" replied my friend. "Don't libel posterity in that reckless manner; it never did you any harm, and the poor body cannot speak for itself. And why should you imagine it will be so easily imposed upon?"

"But look at his unique individuality — his wonderful reasoning powers," I retorted.

"Unique and wonderful fiddle-de-dee! I could tell you a story which might somewhat alter your opinions."

My friend Anderson was a particularly smart private detective, specially retained by a burglary insurance company, and I gave him credit for speaking with a touch of professional jealousy. Still, he had brought off some clever captures and

---

[1] Two fictional characters whose personalities inhabit opposite ends of the moral spectrum. Pickwick is the comic character from Charles Dickens' *The Pickwick Papers* (1836), while Count Fosco is the villain in Wilkie Collins' *The Woman in White* (1859).

exposed a few people who had attempted to defraud his company, so I was compelled to regard him as an authority. I invited him to proceed with this wonderful yarn of his.

Well — he began — I was just putting the finishing touches to my breakfast one lovely morning — it was the beginning of July — when I heard the sound of wheels in the street, and looking through the window, I saw a neat little dog-cart pull up at my own door. The driver got down and rang the bell, and a minute later my servant brought in a letter, which I opened. It was brief, and ran as follows:—

"Luton Square, E———,
"5th July, 1892.

"Dear Sir,
"I shall be glad to see you as early as possible. A burglary was committed at my house late last night or early this morning, and very valuable property stolen. If you can make it convenient to accompany the bearer, so much the better.

"Yours faithfully,

"J.H. McDonald."

"The driver is to wait for an answer, sir," my servant reminded me as I stared at the letter.

"Say I will be with him in less than five minutes," I replied. So I finished my breakfast, and after referring to the directory for information respecting McDonald, who was, it appeared, a retired army captain, I went downstairs and entered the dog-cart.

On arriving at Luton Square I was shown into the drawing-room, and the captain joined me almost before I was seated. I noticed that his agitation was very great.

"Good morning, Mr. Anderson," he said, giving me his hand; "I am exceedingly obliged by your prompt compliance with my wishes, and I trust — but before going any further, may I ask if you have any objection to working, if necessary, with a fellow-expert in matters of this kind?"

"None whatever," I answered; "who is he?"

"A Mr. Sherlock Holmes," he said; "I understand he is a specialist?"

"He is a remarkably clever man," I replied.

"Then perhaps you will kindly follow me," he said; and he led the way to the dining-room and unlocked the door.

"You see," he explained, "I thought I'd better lock the room up, so that nothing could be disturbed until your arrival —"

"Morning, Kitty, darling," interrupted a voice, the exact counterpart of the captain's, finishing with the unmistakable sound of a kiss; then, "How are you, papa?" in a feminine voice. A moment's reflection convinced me that it was a parrot speaking, and, looking up, I found my surmise to be correct.

"Ah, Poll, old woman," returned the captain; and motioning me to be seated, he began:—

"First of all, Mr. Anderson, my small household consists of six persons — myself, my wife, my daughter Kate, a cook, a general servant, and the driver who brought you here. The three servants have been in my employ for years, and I would trust them with untold gold. Now, then. Yesterday afternoon I received from Messrs H——— and C———, jewellers, of Bond Street, a brooch set with a particularly precious stone — precious to me, and of priceless value by reason of old associations and circumstances connected with it; but I need not trouble you with them. The intrinsic value of the gem may not be more than five hundred pounds, and that of its setting, perhaps another thirty."

"Keep your hair on, old chap," said the parrot.

"S-sh, Poll! Well," continued the captain, "I showed the brooch to my daughter only — for it was to be a surprise gift to my dear wife, on her birthday, and such a gift as she would prefer to anything this world contains, simply on account of the associations I hinted at just now. After hearing Kitty's rapturous expressions as to its beauty, and her assurance that for a similar present on her twenty-first birthday she would be as agreeably surprised as I could desire, I locked up the trinket in a private drawer of that cabinet in the corner. On coming downstairs this morning, the first thing I did was to go to the cabinet, to feast my eyes with a sight of the brooch, for I had been strangely anxious about it up to going to sleep, and had driven myself to dreaming of it, I suppose, by my anxiety; and ugly dreams they were, too, and you would fully appreciate my anxiety if you were acquainted with the history of the gem, and how it has been endeared to us for a quarter of a century. Mr. Anderson" — and his voice quivered — "imagine my dismay, my agony, when on opening the drawer, I found it was empty! The brooch was gone!"

"The brooch, the brooch," muttered the parrot.

"I cannot describe my feelings at my loss, and though I am not a rich man, I will willingly pay five hundred pounds for the recovery of the brooch."

"I will examine the cabinet, with your permission," I said; and as I rose for the purpose of crossing the room the bird broke forth with:—

"Keep your hair on, old boy" (this in the voice of the driver). "Cook, how are we for butter? Pretty Poll!" The last two remarks in the sweet, feminine tones imitated previously; then in a delicious drawl: "For what we are about to receive, the Lo-ord make us truly thankful."

"A very clever bird that," I remarked, casually.

"She is a wonderful talker and mimic," he replied, and was instantly absorbed in my examination of the lock of the secret drawer.

Here the servant entered with a visiting card.

"Tell the gentleman I will be with him immediately," and as the servant left the room the captain said:—

"It's Holmes, so perhaps you'll excuse me for a short time. I'll explain things to him, and bring him in to you; in the meantime, make whatever examination you like."

He had no sooner gone than I made a complete and exhaustive examination of all that I considered bore on the case, but without result.

"Keep your hair on, old boy! Ain't it 'ot? Woa!"

All this was in the driver's voice, rendered with phonographic accuracy, even to the slight cockney accent, and as I looked up at the bird, and saw its head on one side and its eye fixed upon me so comically, it flashed across me all at once that it might possibly know something of the brooch.

I was lost in admiration of the parrot when Captain McDonald came into the room with Holmes, whom he introduced to me. Holmes was dressed in boating flannels and looked more like a middle-aged tradesman out for the day than one of the smartest detectives in London.

"I have given Mr. Holmes the particulars I have given you," explained the captain, as Holmes went to the cabinet and repeated my performance. "Is there anything you would like to know before I leave the room?"

"Nothing just yet," said my colleague.

"Just two questions," I put in; "first, was the parrot in the cage when you were putting the brooch away?"

"Oh, yes," answered the captain. And Holmes smiled.

"Did you leave the room for a single moment?" I asked.

"No, I simply opened the two drawers, deposited the brooch, locked them up, and went straight to bed."

"Thank you," I said, "that is all I require," and as he left the room I turned to see what Holmes was doing. He had done with the locks of the drawers, and was engaged at the window, and looking mighty puzzled, I can tell you, when the parrot asked:—

"What're you staring at?"

"Ah, Mademoiselle Psittacus Erithacus," said Holmes, "you are very inquisitive this morning."

"And very insulting, too," I remarked; "she called me stupid just now."

"She is a very intelligent bird," he returned, sarcastically.

"All right, my friend," I thought, "we shall soon see who is the stupid party. If you can come to any different conclusions cleverer than I give you credit for being."

Holmes was on the floor looking for footmarks on the velvet pile carpet; but his microscope showed none. Then he took a good look at every inch of the apartment. He walked to the fireplace, then to the door, and finished by re-examining the two locks of the drawers. After this he opened his pocket-knife and began trimming his nails.

"There is a gorgeous simplicity about this affair," remarked Holmes, "and what the captain tells me makes that simplicity colossal in its gorgeousness. Here we are told that a valuable knick-knack has been stolen; we see for ourselves that no entry has been made from outside; we both know, I think, that the thief must be on the premises, and yet we are told distinctly that we are not to suspect them."

"Keep your hair on," screamed the parrot.

"Confound your noise!" cried Holmes, angrily.

"You must remember one thing," Holmes continued, "and that is that his daughter was very much taken up with the bauble, and expressed a wish to possess one like it. There is only one person for it, Anderson, and Miss Kate McDonald is the thief. And here goes. There is the captain pacing the terrace like a caged lion; I'll be back in a jiffy."

I took my head in my hands to have a good, square think before he returned; I went over the simple facts of the case again, but all to no purpose.

The next things I remember were hearing the parrot talking in its cage above me, and the captain and Holmes talking as they came along the hall. The words the parrot said are as indelibly photographed on the tablets of my memory as if it had taken them down in shorthand, with an acid which bit in every syllable.

The parrot said, in the captain's voice:—

"Brooch, precious brooch; safer, wouldn't look there. Safe:

billiard-table pocket; ha, ha! safe — brooch."

"My coachman!" the captain was saying, indignantly; "why, the fellow would lay down his life for me."

"Then there is only one other person for it," said Holmes, decisively, as they reached the dining-room door.

"And that one?" demanded the captain, turning upon Holmes as they entered.

The latter was slightly pale, but cool.

"Captain, the purloiner of the lost brooch is your —"

He got no farther. Up to this point I had listened as in a dream. I heard, but was unable to speak. I was stunned by the lightning flash which laid bare the whole mystery, and the after-clap was still ringing in my ears. But I roused myself in time to save Holmes's reputation!

"Allow me, captain," I hurriedly interrupted, and casting an imploring look at my colleague; "I have made an important discovery since Mr. Holmes left the room. Will you, please, conduct us to the billiard-room?"

I felt instinctively that the mystery would be cleared up there. The parrot could not have uttered those pregnant words without hearing them from some person, nor could it have repeated another person's words in the captain's voice, or vice-versa. It was evident to me that McDonald's uneasiness had caused him to get up in his sleep and — well, I was prepared to go "nap" on the rest.[1] On reaching the billiard-room I said:—

"Mr. McDonald, will you oblige me by feeling in the pockets on that side of the table?"

He did — but it was not there! Had that parrot sold me? I felt like perspiring.

"Feel in the top pocket of this side," I said.

"What the dickens, sir?" he began, after doing so.

"Now the middle one, if you please, captain."

Holmes was excited. My heart almost stood still as the captain inserted his hand; oh, how I watched his face! If it

---

[1] Gambling slang for risking everything on a single card or throw of the dice.

were not there, only one other pocket remained, and — but I was relieved of all anxiety by the wondrous change in the captain's face, as his hand touched the brooch. Such a look of astonishment, joy, and gratitude combined!

"Thank God!" he cried, in a voice of great emotion; and, seizing my hand, he wrung it warmly and long.

"Mr. Anderson," he said, after a short interval, and pulled out his cheque-book, "I never, in the whole of my life, paid money more willingly than I pay this five hundred pounds."

"Excuse me, captain," I replied, "but there is no five hundred pounds due, as there has been no burglary committed."

To say that both he and Holmes were astonished would but faintly describe their condition; they were, in the expressive phraseology of our Yankee cousins, "flabbergasted!"

"But how did you find it, Mr. Anderson? It is so — so — bless my soul, I can't understand it."

"Pardon me, sir, but we never disclose our modus operandi, do we, Mr. Holmes?" and I beamed a meaning smile upon the latter, which went home. "You see, Mr. McDonald, if we detectives and conjurors were to show the public how we did our tricks, we should have the profession crowded in no time, and then—"

"But this discovery was made by no trick."

"Well, well, we have all sorts of little birds telling us things, eh, Mr. Holmes?"

But Holmes did not take me, for a wonder.

"Just one question, captain, before we go: did you ever read *Sylvester Sound, the Somnambulist*, by Henry Cockton?" [1]

A light broke upon them both.

"I have read the book, Mr. Anderson," replied the captain, with a smile of anticipation.

---

[1] English novelist (1807-1853) whose *Sylvester Sound* was promoted by his publisher as "decidedly the most exquisitely humorous Work ever issued from the Press, and as may be well expected, a Somnabulist's midnight wanderings form one continuation of incident and interest from the first page to the last."

"Well, the next time you think of going in for a little sleep-walking, I would advise you to take the same precaution as Sylvester did in attaching himself to his bedfellow," and we all laughed heartily at the recollection of the somnambulist's ruse and its result.

"And," concluded Anderson, "that charming landscape by David Cox,[1] hung in my den at home, was a present from the captain. What did Holmes say? I'll tell you, Ah, it was rich the way I rubbed it in.

"'Anderson,' said he, 'I'm obliged by your kindness — the way you did it was fine; but how did you find out about the old fellow walking in his sleep?'

"'Perhaps, Mr. Sherlock Holmes,' said I, 'you noticed a parrot in the room we were in, or possibly so small a thing escaped your attention?'

"'Go on, old sword of Damocles,' said he.

"'Holmes, old chap,' said I, 'that parrot was, as you remarked, an intelligent bird — a ve-ry intelligent bird.' And I roared at the sight of his perplexity."

I joined my friend in the boisterous laugh he was seized with at the memory of it all. But, while subsequently acknowledging his smartness in taking such ready advantage of so rare an accident, I would not alter my previous estimate of the reception posterity would accord to the chronicled exploits of Sherlock Holmes.

---

[1] English painter (1783-1859), considered a precursor of impressionism for his highly regarded landscape paintings in oils and watercolor.

The Adventures of Chubblock Homes

Jack Butler Yeats

The earliest attempt at turning Holmes into a comic strip was made by Jack Butler Yeats (1871-1957), the brother of the poet William. Chubblock Homes debuted in the Comic Cuts *weekly newspaper on Nov. 18, 1893, and ran until 1897.*

1. The rich man's son was crossed in love — you can spot him a-moping in the garden — and the rich man wanted to find out who was the lady; so he engaged a lady detective. "Why not Chubblock Homes?" you say. Oh! the old man thought a lady would manage the business better.

2. The first place that lady 'tec went to was a Waterated Bread Company's tea-shop, to see if that young man was in love with the attendant! But he wasn't.

3. Then to a ball, to see if the lady who had won his heart was Clementina, the millionaire daughter of Mr. Newcomb Splosh. But he evidently wasn't much in love there, either.

42 | The Best Sherlock Holmes Parodies and Pastiches

4. After that the lady detective went down to the country, to see if that young man was mashed on his country cousin; but she didn't think he was in love there; nor would you if you'd seen the look that young man gave his country cousin when he found she'd sawn the bridge through for him to fall in! He didn't find out till he was in.

5. The lady detective gave up the hunt as hopeless, and started for the London train; but on the way that young man (still wet and muddy) followed her; and then she discovered he'd been and gone and fallen in love with *her!* Then —

6. Then she removed her brain-cover, and it wasn't a lady at all, but our own Chubblock Homes, disguised. "Have a cigar, young man; it will do you good." But the young man was not there, and naught remained where he had been but the muddy marks of his knees.

Sherlock Holmes and the Missing Box

(With apologies to Dr. A. Conan Doyle.)

The exploding popularity of Holmes made it inevitable that advertisers would press-gang the detective without Conan Doyle's permission. This early example appeared in the Nov. 18, 1893, issue of The Family Doctor. Beecham's Pills was a laxative introduced about 1842 by Thomas Beecham (1820-1907). The pills became the foundation of a pharmaceutical empire, and Beecham lives on as a brand name for cold and flu products.

Yes, it had gone! Where and how no one could fathom! Evidently the only thing to be done was to call in my friend Sherlock Holmes whose marvellous detective feats and miraculous deductions in tracing the perpetrators of mysterious crimes had startled the entire civilised world and set them wonderingly twiddling their thumbs while discussing his extraordinary ingenuity.

The box itself was not of much intrinsic value but its contents were absolutely priceless. I had carelessly neglected to secure it in the safe and left it lying on my dressing table — I was confident of this. The servants were closely questioned — I did not care to search their boxes at this stage. They all indignantly protested absolute ignorance of its whereabouts, my wife repudiated all knowledge of it. In my dilemma I wired as follows:—

> TO: Holmes, Baker Street W.
> Come immediately in great distress box and valuable contents missing no clue
> FROM: Watson

> "HOLMES, BAKER STREET W.
>
> "Come immediately in great distress box and valuable contents missing no clue
> "WATSON"

Within a very short period I recognised his characteristic ring at the door.

"Ah! Watson," he said as he rushed into the sitting room, "you were at a banquet last night and stayed till very late, failed to obtain a cab and walked home in the rain along the Strand without an umbrella, smoking a posener clay[1] which you had the misfortune to break.

"How do I know? Nothing so simple; I saw your silk hat in the hall as I came in bearing unmistakeable signs of a recent wetting, if you had taken a cab or had an umbrella it would have been in its usual glossy condition; your boots are covered with tar and cement — the Strand is being relaid, — I recognised fragments of your pipe and favourite mixture, Latakia and navy cut,[2] lying on the step, I know you had a dozen "poseners" specially made for you of a peculiar shape and I see on the table a menu card of last night's masonic banquet: a man with half an eye can see you have a severe bilious attack in consequence of the rich food you partook of. — Now about the box."

"Well," said I laughingly, "you have unwittingly men-

---

[1] A pipe manufactured by A. Posener & Son. The company sold its wares under the A.D. Pierson label. Coincidentally, Leslie Klinger in his annotated edition of the stories identifies an A.D.P. pipe that appears in "Silver Blaze" as a Posener.

[2] Latakia was a tobacco named for the port city in Syria where it was produced. Most smokers prefer to soften its strong taste by mixing it with milder varieties. Watson preferred to use Player's Navy Cut, which uses a mild Burley leaf from Virginia. The Navy cut name was inspired by the sailors who would cure the leaf with a combination of rum, molasses and spices.

tioned the very reason that makes me so anxious to find it. I only paid 1/1½ for it and contents — the latter are certainly worth a guinea: to me at the present moment they are simply invaluable and indispensable; the chemist is closed and if I don't find this box of Beecham's Pills to-night, I shall — with this beastly bilious attack on me — be quite incapacitated for work to-morrow."

"There," said Holmes quietly, "have some of mine, I always carry them with me and to their head clearing qualities I owe much of my success — in fact it is part of my SYSTEM to use them in my SYSTEM."

The Identity of Miss Angela Vespers

"Ka"

This story is unusual by adding a feminine angle to the Holmesian parody. It features the widow of Herlock Shomes, taking up her husband's profession after his death. There were few women writing in the detective field at the time, and even fewer women portrayed as detectives. While we don't know if the author of these stories, known only as "Ka," was a woman, the presence of Mrs. Shomes adds weight to the argument.

"Ka" wrote two stories about Mrs. Julia Shomes: "The Adventure of the Tomato on the Wall" and "The Identity of Miss Angela Vespers." Both appeared in 1894 in The Student, *a journal for university extension students published by Durham University in Newcastle-on-Tyne. University extension programs were designed to make a school's resources, expertise and courses available to non-students in their area.* The Student *usually published articles connected with the university's courses, but, fortunately for us, also found room for Mrs. Shomes.*

It's also worth noting this story inspired a feminist critic to write that Mrs. Shomes' habit of kissing a man, thinking it was her husband in disguise, only to find "the creature had committed some terrible crime," was a "transgressive hint towards an illicit sexuality" and "a metaphorical incursion into the male detective story."

"I wonder who will be our next visitor," said Mrs. Herlock Shomes. She was in good spirits that afternoon, and had assured me several times that our discovery about the tomato, though galling to the landlord, was quite a feather in our caps.

"We were not at all to blame, my dear," said she, leaning back in her chair and putting her finger-tips together in a judicial manner, "except in underestimating the extreme waywardness of Human Nature. Man is perpetually full of surprises; it is that which makes him so interesting. Once let us thoroughly understand a man; and no matter how much we may admire him, the element of curiosity is lacking, and we are bored."

"Julia," I said, "you talk like a philosopher."

"Who would not," she replied, "who had been the wife of

such a man as Herlock? Life with him was as interesting and as full of the most delightful unexpectedness as a sixpenny raffle. Just fancy sitting waiting for him to come into tea, and never knowing whether a visitor was he or not till he'd been in the house half an hour! I've several times rushed to welcome a man and kissed him, thinking it was Herlock, only to discover afterwards that the creature had committed some terrible crime.

"The life you have led together must have been most interesting," said I, sighing, and wishing that Mr. Wiggins, though a kind husband, had not been so commonplace. In considering the late Mr. Shomes one felt that, as a spouse, Darby himself would have been unsupportable. Why, oh why, should the latter have been "always the same!"

"Oh, very interesting indeed," said Mrs. Shomes, shaking her head pensively; "sometimes a Rough, sometimes a Costermonger, and sometimes a Gentleman! There is not a charm peculiar to any station of life I did not occasionally find in Herlock. And now they are all gone — all."

I thought of Macduff's touching "What! all my pretty ones?"[1] and sighed. Julia was certainly unfortunate in having lost such a man. But after all, was it not better to have had a Herlock Shomes and lost him, than never — "How you must miss them," I said, suddenly recollecting my duty to Mr. Wiggins, "him, I mean."

"I do indeed," said Mrs. Herlock Shomes, "I don't know which of him I miss the most! And never do I miss him more, Lucilla, than in trying to solve the questions brought before us. I seem to feel more and more at every turn the need of his almost supernatural powers of observation."

"Is there no kind of rule that one could go by in solving these mysteries?" I asked, munching a biscuit. We had decided that it would not be professional to have afternoon tea, and I felt famished.

---

[1] In *Macbeth,* Macduff learns that his wife and children were killed and cries out, "All my pretty ones? Did you say all? O hell-kite! All? What, all my pretty chickens and their dam, at one fell swoop?"

Mrs. Herlock Shomes reflected profoundly, and then said: "It seems to me that in trying to clear up a Mystery one can count upon one thing only, and that is, that what at first appears to be the most improbable solution will prove to be the true one." She paced up and down the room as she spoke, occasionally pausing to look out of the window in the street below.

"Aha! here is someone at last," she cried, as a thin young man wearing spectacles came round the corner. He looked up at the numbers on the doors in a short-sighted manner, and after minutely examining our nameplate, rang the bell.

"Have I the honour to address Mrs. Herlock Shomes?" he asked, bowing most respectfully as I opened the door to him.

"You have not," said I, judging it best to keep my own name of Wiggins in the background; "Mrs. Shomes is upstairs, considering her cases, but might spare you a few minutes, I daresay."

"I should be greatly obliged," he said, bowing again, "Mrs. Shomes' success in connection with the famous 'Tomato on the Wall' is not unknown to me."

I ushered him in, and Julia, after gracefully bending her head, eyed him over with the most minute and yet abstracted attention of which she was capable. "Why should you have on your elder brother's clothes?" she asked, letting her eyelids droop over her eyes, and looking at him in rather an ill-used way. The young man started violently, and examined his clothes with misgiving. "They — they are my own, I think," he said, looking up at her again; "but I had an elder brother who was lost in infancy. It is most remarkable that you should know anything about him."

Mrs. Shomes did not reply. She took a ruby-tipped pencil from her pocket, scribbled the following words and handed them to me. "In mercy aid me, Lucilla, and suggest, if you can, why the suit he has on is so big for him."

Of course I made up my mind to do the best I could, but oh, for Herlock! "I should like to know, sir," I said, looking at him with all the intelligent abstraction which I could muster, "why within the last six months you have taken to wearing corsets?"

"Corsets, madam!" repeated the young man, glancing from one of us to the other, with an expression of curiosity tempered with respect; "I-I've seen the name in tradesmen's bills but I'm not quite sure that I can define the term. Pray explain yourselves, ladies."

"It is no matter," cried Mrs. Herlock Shomes — rather too hastily, as it seemed to me, for he might have known the corset by some other name — "It was just a little idea of my friend's, that is all. And now, sir, may I ask you to proceed with your story. "

The young man sighed pensively, groaned once or twice, and then began: "About seven months ago," said he, addressing himself to my friend with an air of the most touching confidence, "I had occasion to change my lodgings. My new rooms were comfortable and the cooking good. Do I make myself clear?"

"Entirely so," said Mrs. Herlock Shomes, folding her hands in her lap. "Your statement is remarkably lucid."

"My landlady was elderly and very plain," went on the young man in a melancholy tone, "she was also not a little mysterious. Even when she personally opened the door to the tax-collector she would sometimes insist that she was 'not at home' and when she went out with her husband, which she did every evening, she always put on a very thick veil. I had only been in the house three days when the servant handed me a playbill. It exhibited the portrait of a lady of remarkable beauty, stated that she was the sensational skirt-dancer, 'Miss Angelica Vespers,' and described in glowing terms a performance in which she had appeared the night before, and which she was to repeat that evening. Madam, I went to that performance, and was at once bewitched by the beauty and agility of the fair Angelica. Attired in a filmy cloud of lace, and seeming rather to hover in the air than dance upon the ground, she appeared to me divinely beautiful, and not above eighteen or nineteen years of age. 'She is my affinity!' exclaimed my heart, enraptured at her charms; 'she shall become my wife,' said I before Angelica had done more than poise herself, and gaily pirouette upon one toe. In all she did I seemed to follow her with my heart as well as my eyes; and when, after lightly vaulting in the air, she leant suddenly back and. three times touched the stage with the crown of her lovely head, a mist floated before my eyes, my breath came in one gasp of admiration, and I vowed that she and none but she, must sit at the head of my table.

"From this time forth I haunted the hall in the hope of seeing Angelica. I sent her bouquets, bracelets, notes, occasionally receiving a few scribbled lines in reply which set my heart aflame. In these messages she stated that she admired my presents and personal appearance; but was averse to matrimony, intended to dance till she was ninety, and could not bring herself to grant an interview. At this treatment, my excitement became intense. I tried to bribe first one attendant and then another to make them divulge by what secret exit Angelica left the hall; but without success. They informed me that my landlord and landlady were the proprietors of the place, that the two scene-shifters who slept upon the premises were their sons, and that none but these four persons were ever permitted to speak to the dancer.

"What was the appearance of the two scene-shifters?" asked Mrs. Herlock Shomes. "Did you ever see them?"

"Frequently," replied the young man; "they were dwarfs, and squinted horribly. They were not above three feet high."

"It never occurred to you that either of them resembled Angelica?"

"It did not."

"Pray continue," said Mrs. Herlock Shomes, noting down these particulars, "you interest me extremely."

"During the next six months I not only spent every penny I could afford on presents for Angelica, but in order to make these as handsome as possible I began to restrict myself as to diet, coming down latterly to two meals a day."

"Ah!" said Mrs. Shomes, looking thoughtfully at his suit of clothes, "I see it all now."

"Madam," cried the young man, "your words fill me with the utmost confidence in your powers! — but I will resume. The waywardness of the fair dancer, her beauty, and the mystery that surrounded her, were driving me frantic, and I went to the hall one evening determined to bring matters to a crisis. The dance which she performed on that occasion was called 'The Devil's Horns.' In it she wore a whirling robe of black and shimmering gauze, which set off her dazzling fairness to perfection. Never shall I forget her as she then appeared with her long robes coiling round and round her lovely form, enveloping her snowy arms, and rising at last to a great height on either side like two demoniac horns. Faster and faster played the music, higher and higher danced Angelica. A weird red light was suddenly flashed upon her from the side. The audience cheered; but as she danced on their faces began to blanch, and sinister whispers of 'witch' and 'demon' could be heard among them. Just as she gave her final pirouette and was about to leave the stage, she turned in my direction and blew a kiss into the auditorium. This was too much for my excited nerves. With one bound I leapt upon the stage; but was immediately followed and held back by several members of the Orchestra. 'Let me see her!' I panted, 'where does she go? I insist on following her!' There was a shriek, a slamming of a door, and all was still. Then a great hubbub arose amongst the audience, the curtain fell, and I was taken by two of the attendants and thrust into the street.

"Well?" said Mrs. Herlock Shomes, as the young man looked at her and paused, "well?"

"From that day to this," he said impressively, "Angelica Vespers has disappeared! Her name is no longer on the bills, other performers are on the stage, and all my enquiries after her have met with no response."

"Have you asked your landlord and landlady about her?"

"Oh, repeatedly; but they profess to be as much in the

dark as I am."

"Do you happen to have a specimen of your landlady's handwriting here?" The young man produced a bill for a week's board and lodging. "Thank you," said Mrs. Herlock Shomes, "and now give me one of Angelica's letters." She carefully compared the documents, and put them into her pocket. "Have you anything more to tell me?" said she.

"There is only one fact more, madam, but it is a most important one. I have twice seen my landlady wearing a bracelet which I could swear was one of those I gave Angelica."

"Ha!" said Mrs. Herlock Shomes, "what sort of woman is this landlady of yours to look at?"

"Very ugly; she is slim and active, but has grey hair, small eyes, a nose to one side, and a complexion of walnut shells."

"That will do," said Julia, affably; "I quite see the whole thing."

"Eh!" cried the visitor, falling back a few steps, "you can find Angelica?"

"I can put my finger upon her at any moment," said Mrs. Herlock Shomes firmly. The young man bowed with an air of stupefaction and took his leave.

"I begin to be afraid of you, Julia," I said, when he was gone. "Where do you think she is? What are you going to do?"

For an answer she went to the bathroom tap and filling a bottle with water placed it upon the table. Then she went to the cupboard, and got out a piece of coarse flannel and a large lump of washing soda. As I looked at these preparations I felt in a state of utter collapse. My hands fell limply by my sides, and I emitted a low gurgle of amazement.

With an unpretending leather bag in our possession we went to the somewhat shabby hall that night and asked to see the proprietress, Mrs. Delaware, on important business. We were taken to a small room where we found her renovating the theatrical wardrobe; and no sooner were we alone with her than Julia pounced upon the key of the door, turned it, and put it into her pocket.

"So you have locked the door have you?" said the lady, pausing in her work. "You seem to be rather an extraordinary person. Why have you come here?"

"I have come, madam," said Mrs. Herlock Shomes, with perfect calmness, "to wash your face."

Mrs. Delaware sat and stared at us both for several minutes. "To wash my face," she repeated musingly, "are you a professional face-washer then?"

"I am not; but I've every intention of removing that mask of yours," said Mrs. Herlock Shomes, getting out the flannel.

"M-mask!" murmured Mrs. Delaware.

"Yes," said Julia firmly. "What looks like your face you know. Don't imagine we are deceived. That hideous mask is merely a cosmetical preparation warranted to ensure all sorts of charms beneath. Your secret, Angelica, is discovered!"

Almost before my friend had finished speaking, the lady went off into violent hysterics, and I had much ado to bring her round. "There, she is better now," said Julia. "You hold her and I will try her face with this."

She had been vigorously rubbing the flannel on the soda, and no sooner did Mrs. Delaware hear the words than she sprang from her chair at a single bound and positively screamed for mercy. "Anything but that," she cried, clasping her hands in supplication. "You terrible person, I am as wax in your hands. Anything but that awful — awful soda!"

"Well then," said Julia, seizing her opportunity, "Are you, or are you not, the lost Miss Angelica Vespers?"

"I Miss Vespers?' returned the lady much amazed. "I the lovely Angelica? Certainly not." She seemed to be still much agitated; and at a sign from me Julia put down the flannel.

"Then what have you done with her?" asked my friend. "Your writing is identical with hers, which should not be. Produce her at once, or I arrest you upon the spot for forgery."

"But Angelica had no education," cried Mrs. Delaware, "I had to write her letters."

"No matter," said Julia, unabashed, "Produce her at once, or

I arrest you for stealing her bracelets, one of which you have on."

"I never knew anyone like you!" said Mrs. Delaware, looking from the bracelet to the face of my friend in uncontrollable agitation. "And must we suffer?" she went on, "and must our little ruse by which we hoped to gain a fortune be exposed to all the world?"

"Ha!" said my friend, looking at me in triumph; "It need not be, if you will produce the lady."

"And will you not arrest me if I produce her?" cried the other.

"Not if she does not accuse you in any way. It all depends on how you've treated her."

With this Mrs. Delaware appeared to be content. "I can and will produce her, quite unharmed," she said. Thereupon she unlocked a large press which stood in the room, and emerged from it bearing in her arms the apparently lifeless figure of a dancing girl. The face and arms were exquisitely moulded, the hair fell in a shower of golden ringlets to the waist, and the whole form was enveloped in black-bespangled gauze.

"Angelica is a perfect triumph of mechanism," said the lady, taking one of the girl's hands in her own, and turning the fingers about in all directions. "She can vault three feet higher than any living lady on the stage, and has danced us out of bankruptcy over and over again. No one ever suspected us," she went on, carefully dusting the face of the figure of a dancing girl with her pocket handkerchief; "but her accomplishments are of the kind that take with men, and they were constantly pining away on her account. Three noblemen and two poets have committed suicide because of her; and as my own lodger was becoming skin-and-bone, and had begun to make things most unpleasant, we did not like the idea of an inquest at our house, and we've agreed to sell her."

"Then she's neither more nor less than a marionette!" cried I.

"And there's our second Mystery cleared up," said Mrs. Herlock Shomes.

Picklock's Disappearance

R.C. Lehmann

Illustrated by E.J. Wheeler

For 150 years, the humor magazine Punch *served as Great Britain's mirror, critic, and jester. During the Victorian era, one of its principal writers was Rudolph Chambers Lehmann (1856-1929), a lighthearted man who lived his life as a gentleman of leisure. A descendant of the Scottish Chambers family who built a fortune in book publishing, Lehmann as a child met literary lights such as Charles Dickens and Wilkie Collins. He studied law at Cambridge, but soon after graduation quit the legal profession to write and indulge in his passion for competitive rowing.*

Lehmann was also one of the more prolific Holmes parodists of the period. His Picklock Holes is a shadier, loopier version of the great detective, and the settings and plots are much more farcical than the norm. Following Conan Doyle's publishing model, he wrote one series of eight stories, followed up with another eight when Holmes reappeared in 1903, and even returned for a curtain call following the appearance of "His Last Bow." All of the stories and more can be found in The Early Punch Parodies of Sherlock Holmes.

This final story in Lehmann's first series, published on Jan. 13, 1894, follows Holmes to Reichenbach Falls, but adds a surprising twist of its own.

Edward J. Wheeler (1847-1933) was a Punch *artist from roughly 1880 to 1910, after which he went on to illustrate childrens' adventure books, plus reissues of works by William Makepeace Thackeray, Frederick Marryat, Henry Fielding, and Laurence Sterne.*

Never in the course of a long and varied experience have I taken up my pen with a heavier heart than that which now beats mournfully within my breast. It has been my enviable lot to follow my hero, my wonderful friend, my arch-prince of detectives through many a strange and startling adventure.

While he with his matchless acumen has been engaged in checking the ambitious designs of foreign despots, in unveiling to the startled gaze of statesmen the criminal plots of secret societies, in foiling coalitions, in unravelling the tangled skeins of murder-conspiracies, in bringing dark deeds of crime relentlessly home to ducal perpetrators, in restoring jewels to bereaved countesses, in convicting baronets of burglary, and generally in putting local constabularies in every part of the civilised world to shame; while he, I say, has been engaged in these and similar undertakings I have been ever at his side, the faithful foil, the admiring companion, the irremovable fly on the wheel of his world-renowned exploits. And now that fate has taken him from me I scarce know whither I am to turn. Surely never again shall I meet in this world so wise, so cold, so impassive, so friendly a sleuth-hound of detection; never again shall I

Picklock Holes disguised.

behold another upon whom my candid flow of irrepressible wonder will pour itself with so small an effect.

"Potson," he would often say to me when I had congratulated him in my impulsive way upon some master-stroke or cunning strategy; "Potson, you are not absolutely clever, but, personally, I do not care for very clever men. They are always wanting to outwit one. The task of course is hopeless, but to counteract it one has to waste valuable time. But you have about you a comfortable non-cleverness, always delightfully ready to burst into admiration whenever I give you an opportunity. Potson, I like you."

"Holes," I replied, overcome by emotion, "you are an extraordinary fellow. I would willingly follow you to the ends of the world."

I remember this little conversation all the more distinctly because, taking place as it did in an unfrequented thoroughfare of the Bloomsbury district, Holes was immediately afterwards able to infer from a large stain of milk upon the pavement in front of one of the houses that a bald and fraudulent solicitor was at that moment lying in a fit on the floor of the dining-room. This was how he proved it:

"Milk," he said, "has been spilt here. To spill milk is a blunder which is often worse than, and, therefore, *at least equal to*, a crime. We have therefore got the certainty of a crime. A solicitor has to deal with crimes. We thus get the fact that we have here a solicitor who has committed a crime. Now fraud is a crime. Therefore, substituting fraud for crime we obtain a solicitor who has committed fraud. I said a moment back that this solicitor was not only fraud but baldulent—"

"Pardon me," I ventured to interrupt, "pardon me, my dear Holes, you mean bald and fraudulent."

"Of course," he retorted, without moving a muscle; "I said so, bald and fraudulent. Now mark how beautifully it works out. A detected criminal is invariably angry. This man has been detected by me. To be angry is merely another way of saying that one has lost his hair. He is, therefore, proved beyond possibility of doubt to be bald. With regard to the fit, the process of induction is no less delicate and convincing. A solicitor wears clothes which fit him, whether well or badly matters not. He has, therefore, a fit. Have I proved my case?"

"Holes," I said, "you are a wonderful fellow."

We informed the neighbouring policeman, but I cannot now remember if matters proceeded to a conviction. The incident, however, remains in my mind as one of the most remarkable proofs of my friend's almost superhuman powers.

And now, as I said, I have lost him, and must proceed as best I can to give some account of his disappearance. We were engaged in investigating the mysterious circumstances connected with the theft of one of our best-known public monuments. I do not care to be more precise, though some day in defence of my friend I may have to tell the story in detail. But at present the honour of a great family is involved, and I prefer to mention no names.

I had noticed that Holes had been even more taciturn than was usual with him during the course of his investigations, but at the time I attributed little importance to this.

One night he came quietly into my rooms, and after removing from my coat a speck of dust, which proved, he said, that I had been assaulted by a ticket-of-leave

"Dropping an H."

man[1] in Southampton Street at 5.45 that very afternoon, he sat down opposite me in an armchair.

"Potson," he said, "there is something in this business which is out of the common. At every turn I encounter a hidden force. I walk in Piccadilly and am splashed with mud by a passing hansom; I turn into Regent Street, and a Music Hall singer — I knew him by his prosperous, well-fed appearance — insists on shaking hands with me. Discouraged by these accidents I stroll into Jermyn Street, when a regiment of Life-Guards charging up Bury Street all but tramples me under foot. There is more in all this than meets the eye. Potson, I am being pursued."

"But surely," I said, "they know you too well. Who would venture to pursue you? Would anyone venture to fly in the face of the public and of probability by tracking one who has always been himself the tracker?"

But my words were unavailing. He insisted upon it that he was being shadowed, and left me with this impressive warning: "If I do not return to you to-morrow before six o'clock you will know that I am somewhere else. Do not look for me in the Serpentine."[2]

On the following day I awaited the arrival of six o'clock with a feverish impatience. As the hour struck the door did not open, but a scrap of torn paper came fluttering down from the ceiling. I grasped it convulsively, and read these words:

> "MY DEAR POTSON, — It has been a duel to the death, and both of us perished. By the kindness of my late opponent, Mr. Sherlock Holmes, I have been permitted to expire after him, and to use the few remaining seconds of life that remain in me in writing to you. I knew I was pursued, and I knew it was Sher-

---

[1] An early version of parole in Australia, consisting of a document issued to convicts giving them the right to live and seek work in a designated district for a period of time.
[2] A 40-acre artificial lake — its snake-like shape inspired its name — that forms the western border of Hyde Park in central London.

lock who was dragging me to my doom. I have killed him, but at the penalty of my own life. If you wish to know more do as I should have done under the circumstances. Commend me to Mrs. Potson, and believe me yours inductively,

"PICKLOCK HOLES."

That was all. The blow was a terrible one, but when I recovered in a measure I set to work immediately to do what I thought Holes would have done. I assumed a meditative air, I conducted chemical experiments, I despised the police, I picked up clues in unsuspected corners, I proved beggars in rags to be Cabinet Ministers in disguise — but all my efforts were fruitless. My friend's last behest is to me a sacred command. Some other — not I — may search the depths of the Serpentine and discover there the secret which I have sought in vain.*

The End.

[* We've got the very man to do it, and when either "Sherlock Holmes" or "Picklock Holes" may be "wanted," we undertake to produce both or either of them. — Ed.]

R.C. Lehmann

Mrs. Dr. Sherlock Holmes

Anonymous

This sketch of a conjecturing, strident interrogation ratcheted as high as it can go appeared in the Feb. 9, 1895, issue of Tit-Bits.

All of a sudden, she turned to the man in the tramcar on the left, and said:—

"You were putting down an ingrain carpet[1] at your house this morning. Don't attempt to deny it, for I have most conclusive evidence."

"How do you know?" he stammered, in surprise.

"There is lint on your knees, sir, showing the kind of carpet, and your thumb is done up in a rag to prove that you hit it with a hammer. You have a bunion on your left foot. Deny it at your peril!"

"Yes, I have a bunion; but—"

"I knew it, because you can't keep that foot still, now and then you utter a cuss word below your breath. You are living with your second wife. Admit the truth of what I say, or take the consequences."

"How on earth can you tell that?" he asked, as he began to turn pale round the mouth.

"By the hairs and dandruff on your coat. Your first wife always brushed you before you went out. Now, you have a small child at home."

"Yes, a boy three years old; but—"

"I knew it, because he shoved that jumping-jack into your pocket while you were playing with him just before you came out. You are also an absent-minded man. Denial will be useless, and may get you into serious trouble."

---

[1] A flat-pile wool floor covering produced with an elaborate geometrical or floral pattern. Because they have no pile and the design was shown in reverse on the other side, the rug could be flipped when it became worn or soiled. Because they were machine-made, they could be produced at a lower cost and proved popular with middle-class buyers.

"I — I—"

"If you were not an absent-minded man you would not have pocketed that table-napkin handkerchief, nor come out with your old hat on. While your first wife has been dead for several years, you have not placed a tombstone at her grave. Don't try to bluff me, sir!"

"You are right, but—"

"Of course I am. When we passed that marble shop you gave one look at the tombstones and placed your hand on your wallet. Your present wife is not domestic."

"No, she is not; but how on earth can you tell?"

"The moths have eaten your coat, there are two buttons off your vest, and from the way you wriggle that right foot I'm sure you have holes in your stockings. Think not to deceive me."

"Great lands, woman!" he gasped, as the perspiration stood out on his forehead, "but you must be—"

"Mrs. Dr. Sherlock Holmes, sir," she finished. "I have to get out here to solve a mystery in a butcher's shop. Blood has been found on a cleaver, the butcher's wife has got a new sealskin jacket, and the errand-boy has a boil on his leg. 'Sdeath!'[1] I will unravel the whole affair in five minutes and spot the murderer! Good day, old man."

---

[1] A mild oath that's a shortened form of "God's death." Taking the Lord's name in vain is blasphemous and even illegal at this time, so many curse words were created to avoid committing that sin.

The Reappearance of Sherlock Holmes

Roy L. McCardell

Roy Larcom McCardell (1870-1940) was an American journalist and humorist. He was a staff writer for Puck *when this story appeared in the Sept. 25, 1895, issue. Two years later, he became a screenwriter and wrote more than a thousand scripts for the silent movies.*

❖   ❖   ❖   ❖

Note. — Dr. Conan Doyle claims that, having let his great detective fall over an abyss, he can not see how to make him reappear again alive and well. The present writer in the following tale, kindly helps the doctor out of his difficulties.

THE END INEVITABLE.

After that awful, unseen tragedy at the Falls of Reichenbach, when my friend had gone over the sheer and horrid precipice, clasped in a death struggle with Moriarty, as the traces of that awful combat showed too well, I returned to England a broken man.

The dreadful death of Sherlock Holmes preyed upon my mind so much that, in the following Spring, I gave up the room in Baker Street and sailed for New York.

Here I hung out my shingle, hoping that the change of scene and the newer faces and occupations would drive from my memory that awful scene of the death struggle ever in my mental eye.

In some slight measure I was successful. That is, I had gotten so I could review the thing more calmly and still cherish that faint, trembling hope that Holmes was not dead.

I was sitting in my office one Summer evening, turning the matter over in my mind. The image of my friend, discreet, cautious, resourceful, rose before me. Unconsciously, I spoke aloud, "Suppose, after all, Holmes was *not* killed?"

"Well, let us suppose it." As the words in answer to mine rang out, I sprang, faint with fright, to my feet, and clutched my study table for support. For there before me stood Sherlock Holmes *in the flesh!*

"You? You?—"

I gasped, but could say no more.

"Yes, Watson." It was the same careless yet incisive voice of old. "It is I. Have a cigar?" And my friend coolly sat down and pushed his pocket case toward me.

"But — but, the Falls of Reichenbach, man?" I stammered.

"Watson," Holmes looked at me, smiling calmly, "I'll admit that circumstances did look as if I had gone over that dizzy height, into the boiling torrent below, in company with our extremely versatile friend, Professor Moriarty, and so I did. But, Watson, how often have I told you to deduce?" Here Holmes bit off the end of his cigar.

"But you say you and he went over the falls. How—"

But Holmes broke in.

"Watson, am I not a man of resources?"

I nodded.

"Well, you remember that I wore a cloak when you last saw me?"

"Yes, yes; but—"

"Now, don't interrupt. I had expected that meeting wish the Professor. I had a portable parachute under that cloak. After we fell over the cliff in our struggle, we let go our holds, and I opened the parachute and drifted down."

"And the Professor was dashed to death?" I asked, eagerly.

"No," Holmes flicked the ash from his cigar; "the Professor is also a man of resources. He had a parachute, too."

I was too much surprised to speak, and Holmes continued:

"The long and short of it is, that we struck the water safely; but in the boiling mist I lost the Professor. I swam down the torrent to the next canton, and, after a few days' rest, resumed my search for Moriarty. But again he had been too much for me. I had the pleasure some weeks after, to read the very nice notices of my life, deeds and death, in the English papers. For once the jealousy of Scotland Yard was abated, and I got my due measure of praise. De mortuis nil nisi bonum, you know.[1] So I thought I would let them think me dead. But Moriarty knew better, and fled to America. He is here, somewhere in New York, now. But he, the arch plotter, the head and brains of organized, educated crime can not escape me. His capture is but a question of time, and I shall have him"

"But how?" I asked. For the old, calm, confident manner of Holmes, his old self, sitting there, had almost brought me to the belief that his struggle and his disappearance were as a dream.

Holmes looked at me calmly.

"Yes," he said; "he can not escape me. I shall stand on the corner of the Boulevard and Sixty-sixth Street, and catch him when he comes by on a bicycle!"

Roy McCardill

---

[1] Latin for "don't speak ill of the dead."

The Adventure of the Child's Perambulator

"Another Conan Doyle" (Charles Loomis)

This story from the April 1895 issue of Puck *might have been inspired by the Berners Street prank of 1810. Someone had sent hundreds of letters — to tradesmen, greengrocers, even the Lord Mayor — asking them to come to 54 Berners Street at the same time. The result was a day of chaos and pandemonium as everyone vied to reach the home. "Perambulator" is also noteworthy for its clever exploitation of Holmesian tropes and the witty dialogue that begs to be read aloud.*

I had not heard from Sherlock Holmes for some time, when one day I received a post card, with no date or signature, bearing the single word. "Come!"

I knew that I was wanted on a dangerous and delicate mission, so I put an American bowie knife, a dark lantern, a brace of revolvers, a bottle of smelling salts, and a ham sandwich in my grip. Then I kissed my wife goodby telling her I might be back in a six-month, next day or never, and bidding her to tell my patients to keep stout hearts and to continue to take whatever I had ordered until I returned. I hurried off to the station, and in two hours had reached the lodgings of Sherlock Holmes, in Baker Street, and knocked on the door which he at once opened.

"Ha! Watson, you've come," said he. I couldn't deny the fact although I did not know by what subtle processes he had arrived at the conclusion.

"Well," said I, "what's in the wind today?"

"Do you value your life?"

"Not a ha'porth," said I.[1]

"Good, neither do I. I have got a murder mystery on my hands besides which that of the Boscombe Valley sinks into

---

[1] A half-penny's worth, a small amount indeed. The word is also slang in the north of England for a silly or stupid person, such as a "daft ha'porth."

insignificance. But, hark! what is that? I hear a footstep. Ten to one, it's Lestrade of Scotland Yard. I never mistake the cocksure gait of his. He's coming to consult with me."

I went to the window and looked out. For once, Holmes was mistaken. The noise he had heard was caused by a tally-ho and six[1] that dashed by at a furious rate. Not a soul was in sight. The tally-ho stopped at the corner and a man alighted. The next minute he was knocking at our door, and a voice shouted: "Phair the divvle does Sherlock Holmes keep himself?"

"Walk in," said the great unraveler, and a red-headed man in a smock and overalls entered the room.

"You are an English gentleman, are you not?" asked Holmes.

"Phwat make ye think so?"

"Your disguise and accent."

"Can your friend be trusted?"

"Certainly, he is my colleague, Dr. Watson."

I WENT TO THE WINDOW AND LOOKED OUT.

"Then behold me, Sir Edward Percyvale Vere Bermondsey-on-Trent Boggs," and with that he shed his smock and overalls, pulled off his wig and beard, and stood revealed as a slim, aristocratic-looking fellow, whose ancestors, according to Burke's peerage, which Holmes at once consulted, turned

---

[1] A carriage drawn by six horses. Inspired by the name of a fast coach that traveled between London and Birmingham in the 18th century.

up their noses at William the Conqueror.

"Sir Edward, take a sofa. We are at work at a little murder mystery, but we can let it stand for awhile. Please give me the smallest particulars of the mystery you want unraveled."

Sir Edward spread himself over the sofa, and, taking out a copy of the *Times*, said: "Yesterday's *Times* contains the following advertisement: 'If the finder of the child's perambulator that was mislaid somewhere between Charing Cross and Seven Dials will return same to Edward Percyvale Vere Bermondsey-on-Trent Boggs, 27 Henrietta Street, third bell, he will be handsomely rewarded, as the perambulator contained nothing save a child, of no value to any one save the owners.'"

"My wife is lying ill at my house in Henrietta Street, and the doctor has prescribed absolute quiet; but since early dawn yesterday the street has been filled with perambulators, containing all sorts and conditions of noisy children, and the bell has not ceased ringing. My wife and I are perfectly childless, and I am at a loss to conceive who could have put us to this great annoyance. This morning my wife's illness has taken a turn for the worse, in consequence of the ceaseless clamor, and if you can help me to find the man who inserted the advertisement, I promise you that I will furnish a murder with no element of mystery in it."

"This is a very lucid account of which promises to be the most interesting case I ever undertook. Pardon me if I ask a few questions that may appear to be trivial, but which nevertheless, may have a direct bearing on the subject.

"Was your wife ever married before?"

"She was not."

"Ha! That is very important, and now may I ask whether you have had in your employ a Pole at any time in the last six years?"

"No sir, I employ none but English."

"And quite right. Now one more question. What was the maiden name of your wife's mother?"

"Saunders."

"Enough, come here to-morrow at this time, and I will show you the busy-body who inserted the advertisement, or my name is not Sherlock Holmes."

During the whole interview, Sir Edward was smiling in a very peculiar way, and he now took his departure still smiling.

When he had gone, Holmes said, "It will not take long to clear up that mystery, though it is a very pretty one. Then we will make up for lost time on the murder case. In the meantime, let us forget that such things as mysteries that need ferreting. Hand me my violin, and I will play you seven variations of 'After the Ball,' by Grieg."[1] For the next half hour he played for me in a manner to make the great Sarasate[2] himself blush, and then he said, "Come we have idled enough. I will disguise myself, and you take this business directory and hunt up all the firms engaged in the manufacture of perambulators."

HE PLAYED FOR ME IN A MANNER TO MAKE THE GREAT SARASATE HIMSELF BLUSH.

---

[1] The piece by Edvard Grieg (1843-1907) is "Love's Dream after the Ball," opus 356.
[2] Pablo de Sarasate (1844-1908) was a Spanish violinist and composer, famous for his performing style which, as George Bernard Shaw wrote, "left criticism gasping miles behind him."

In a few minutes I had prepared a list of the perambulator manufacturers in the United Kingdom. Before I had finished, however, Holmes had stepped out of his bedroom, disguised as an unmarried Baptist preacher of Pennsylvania, U. S. of A. Not a person could have guessed what he represented, so cleverly was he made up. I, who am comparatively unknown, did not need a disguise; but Holmes suggested I carry my revolvers, as he might have to place me in a dangerous position.

On leaving the house we jumped into a cab, and, after giving directions to the cabman to take us to Hogg & Chichester's, the leading manufacturers of perambulators, Holmes dismissed all thoughts of business from his mind, and, taking out a jews-harp, played the "Spanish Rhapsody" in a manner that I have rarely heard equaled.[1]

HOLMES HAD STEPPED OUT OF HIS BEDROOM, DISGUISED AS AN UNMARRIED BAPTIST PREACHER.

---

[1] *Jews-harp:* Also called a mouth or jaw harp, the instrument consists of a horseshe frame with a bamboo or metal tongue. The harp is placed in the mouth and plucked to produce a note. *Spanish Rhapsody* could be a solo 1858 piano piece by Franz Liszt (1811-1886) or an orchestral piece written by Maurice Ravel (1875-1937) between 1907 and 1908. Either would no doubt sound peculiar on a Jew's harp.

Arriving at the warehouse, Holmes asked to see the foreman, and that worthy soon came into the room.

"Have you among your workmen a Pole?"

"No sir, we have not a Pole."

"Quite so. Kindly let me see the man who is not a Pole."

A young man with auburn hair and a pug nose came to us in a minute.

"Are you the young man who is not a Pole?"

"I am."

"Is your name Saunders?"

"It is not."

"Do you ever see the *Times*."

"No, sir, the pink 'un[1] is the only paper I ever read."

"What do you think of this affair."

"Nothing. Didn't even know there was an affair."

"Just so. That is all."

When we had regained the street, Holmes said, "This mystery is prettier than I first gave it credit for, still I have a clue. I consider it very auspicious that that young man is not a Pole. If he is not the man who inserted the advertisement, then we must go to the Isle of Wight for him."

"Why the Isle of Wight?" asked I.

"Wait," said he oracularly.

Just then we passed a restaurant. "How long since you ate?" asked he.

"Breakfast was my last meal," I replied.

"Do you know I haven't thought to eat for the last five or six days. Suppose we go in."

When we were seated, he ordered six hot, hard-boiled eggs, which when brought, he ate, shells and all. "I need the lime," he said. I looked with admiration at this remarkable man, who had the stomach of a camel and a Vidocq[2] combined.

---

[1] A reference to *The Sporting Times*, a weekly newspaper particularly devoted to horse racing. It was known as "The Pink 'Un" for its pink newsprint.

[2] A reference to the thief-turned-detective Eugène Francois Vidocq (1775-1857) who founded the French national police, the Surete.

Suddenly the door of the restaurant was opened by no less a person than Sir Edward Etcetera Boggs.

"Ha!" said Holmes. "You are the very man I wanted to see. Have an egg."

Sir Edward, with the smile of the morning still lingering upon his face, declined the delicacy, but seated himself at our table, where he ordered a b. & s.[1] and a cup of tea.

"Sir Edward, have you relatives in the Isle of Wight?"

"I have not."

"Do they spend the summer there?"

"They do not."

"H'm. Have you ever happened to drop a hint that your wife hated to have people answering advertisements for lost perambulators when she was sick?"

"No, I didn't know she did hate it until yesterday. Now let me ask you a few questions: Aren't you almost omnipotent?"

"Almost."

"Well, do you know yet who inserted the advertisement?"

"No."

"Isn't all this Isle of Wight business a bluff to give you time to chance on a clue?"

"Yes."

"Well then. I've won my bet with Watson. I inserted the advertisement myself, and bet him that you couldn't find out who did it before we met again."

"You bet with Dr. Watson? — Who the devil are you?"

To the everlasting discomfiture of Know-it-all Holmes, Sir Edward pulled off the whole top of his smiling face and disclosed inside of the papier mache head

The well-known features of Lestrade, the Scotland Yard detective!

---

[1] A brandy and soda.

The Adventure of the Pink Pearl

Anonymous

When Conan Doyle went to South Africa to assist the British effort in the Boer War, it made sense to send Sherlock there as well. This story was one of eight featuring spy-hunting Sherlock Gnomes and army doctor Totson that were printed between March and May in Scraps *magazine.*

"Good gracious, major, you never brought it with you! What a risk!"

These words fairly bounced from Gnomes, so hotly were they uttered. It was seldom, indeed, that he allowed himself to express surprise, and rarer still did excitement get the better of his imperturbable dignity, but the incident which drew forth such energy certainly justified it.

We had arrived the evening before at Bloemfontein,[1] and having spent the night in fairly comfortable quarters, Gnomes and I, being unoccupied during the morning in question, had been engaged in observing the manners and customs of the inhabitants of a capital which had recently surrendered to an invading army. When breaking the journey, so to speak, for refreshments at a hotel in Market-square, we got into conversation with Major Spark, of Omdurman repute,[2] who, in relating an occurrence at the battle of that name, had called forth the astonishment of my friend.

"You seem to think the pearl is valuable," said the major as we strolled down the somewhat crowded thoroughfare.

---

[1] The capital of the Orange Free State Republic (1854-1902). It was captured in 1900 during the Second Boer War.
[2] A city in the Sudan that was the site of an 1898 battle between the British army and Muslim forces commanded by Mahdi Abdullahi ibn Muhammad. The British capture of the city toppled the Mahdi's government and re-established control over the country. This was one of the many, many "little wars" of the Victorian era.

"Valuable!" repeated Gnomes. "If it is a pearl of great size, as you say it is, and likewise pink, it is about the rarest thing on earth, and would bankrupt more than a merely wealthy man to purchase. But although you have told us that you brought it over when you came from Egypt with Kitchener's staff,[1] instead of placing it in safety, you have not recounted how it came into your possession."

"Well, it was this way," said the major. "When we — you will, no doubt, remember the charge of the 21st Lancers[2] — cut through the Khalifa's army, our fellows made for shelter in a hollow, but I, having had my horse shot under me, was left somewhat in the rear.

"I moved slightly round to the right in order to effect a junction, and came upon several emirs[3] that were lying in a heap behind a sand-hill, all dead excepting one, who was in a very bad way.

"Seeing me approach, he made a motion as if for a drink of water; so I took out my flask and gave him some diluted with a little brandy. He appeared very thankful, but could not express himself; as neither of us understood the language of the other. To show his gratitude, however, or perhaps in appreciation of my bald head and Mohammedan forelock,[4] he gave me the pearl in a small cedar box, which, as I have said, I have with me here, or rather at my diggings, and which I shall be very pleased to show you, provide you take the trouble to come so far."

---

[1] Herbert Kitchener (1850-1916) was the army commander and colonial administrator who played key roles in the Sudan invasion, the Second Boer War, and the first half of World War I. He drowned in the sinking of the HMS Hampshire.
[2] Cavalry regiment that fought in the Battle of Omdurman (2 September 1898) in the Sudan. The 400-man cavalry regiment charged 2,000 Dervish spearmen and routed them. For their gallantry, four soldiers were awarded the Victoria Cross.
[3] A Muslim military commander or local chief.
[4] Shaving the head has several meanings in Islam. In this case, the emir saw Sparks' bald head as a sign of his devotion to God.

This recital was followed by Gnomes with great interest, and as it promised something quite out of the ordinary we very willingly accompanied the major to his "diggings," which, upon arrival, we found to be an unoccupied cottage of three rooms, all upon the ground floor, and with a small garden abutting at the back, situated upon the extreme outskirts of the town. We passed in safety the muddy garden path, which had been converted into an unpleasant bog by the heavy thunderstorm of the early morning, and shortly afterwards entered the little bedroom occupied by the major.

"Now," said the latter, advancing towards a rough wooden slab over the fireplace which answered the purpose of a mantelshelf, "you shall have a look at this — Good heavens, it is gone!"

"Stolen?" added Gnomes.

"I fear so; it was there not three hours ago in the cedar box."

"Did any one know of your remarkable gem?" queried my friend.

"Only two persons that I'm aware of," replied the major; "one a private named Jenkins, whom we left at Kimberley[1] (he came across from Egypt in the same transport, and I showed him the pearl while we were stopping at Cairo); and the other a young fellow belonging to the Cape Rifles,[2] who has shared this place with me since we have been here, but who is now on outpost duty. It must be the latter. I'm awfully sorry, as I had taken a great fancy to him."

---

[1] A South African city about 165 kilometers (100 miles) west of Bloemfontein. When war broke out in 1899, the Boers surrounded the city. Despite being caught unprepared, the British held out for four months before being relieved.

[2] The Cape Town Rifles is an infantry regiment established in 1855. It received its nickname as the "Dukes" (for "Duke of Edinburgh's Own") in 1867 after it served as a guard of honor for him during a visit to Cape Town. It fought during the first Boer War, but during the second detachments were formed to occupy outposts and blockhouses in the northern Cape area. It still exists as a reserve unit in the South African Army.

"Did he ride a bicycle with a red Seddon tire on the front wheel and a Clincher[1] on the back?" said Gnomes, with his usual directness.

"No; he does not ride a machine at all," the major answered. "Whatever made you ask that question?"

"Because the man who stole the jewel this morning during the time you were out arrived and departed upon those tires," returned my friend.

"What an extraordinary thing!" exclaimed the major. "Now you mention it, Jenkins, who came with me from Omdurman and remained behind at Kimberley, is a scout. I remember seeing him on his bike, and the front tire was red. However did you arrive at all this?"

"By the wheel-marks on the garden path," replied my friend sharply. "I observed as we came in the arrow-heads of the Seddon and the straight furrows of the non-slipping Clincher plainly indented in the mud. He must have been here this morning, or the impressions would have been washed away by the thunderstorm."

"But the bike and the man are in Kimberley."

"The bike and the man, together with the pearl, are on their way to Delagoa Bay,[2] and will probably get to Germany if we don't make haste," said Gnomes, with a suspicion of savageness in his tone. "What was Jenkins like?"

"Fiery red hair, clean shaven, and a long, thin nose," replied the major.

"Come, Totson," said my friend, "we will see into this."

Wishing our companion good morning, we left him with a most bewildered expression on his countenance, and walked rapidly back to the town. Without a word my friend led me

---

[1] The type of tire used today, consisting of a rubber shell in which the tube is inserted and shaped to grip the metal rim. The alternative is to use a tubular wheel in which the tube is stitched into the casing and glued onto the rim.

[2] An inlet on the coast of Mozambique about 450 miles northeast of Bloemfontein. It is now called Maputo Bay.

into a bicycle store and selected two machines.

"Now, then, we can both ride well, and don't mind a skid when it's for a good cause," said Gnomes, as he mounted.

I followed suit, and we proceeded to the end of the lane which led to Major Spark's location. Here we picked up the trail and sprinted away merrily.

"It is impossible to say exactly how long a start our red-headed friend has had. Anything under three hours; probably not more than one, as the marks were very fresh," said Gnomes, some time later. "You see, he will make for the railway to Lorenco Marques,[1] and get in the train when he can do so in safety."

"That will not be until he gets over the Transvaal border," I added.

"Hullo!" shouted Gnomes, "we're on the right track. Here's the cedar box."

We both dismounted, and my friend, running a few yards aside his bicycle, plucked the missing article from among the leaves of a thick bush. Needless to say, it was empty.

We continued our journey for about twenty miles without further incident until we came to the banks of a river, thickly fringed upon the margin with tangled shrubs and tall reeds. We rode gently along, and at its side, when, coming to a break in the vegetation, we observed a figure in the water bathing.

"Clean shaven, long nose, and red hair," muttered Gnomes, seizing me so suddenly by the arm that we both fell off, fortunately without making a sound.

Immediately in front of us upon the ground was a heap of clothes and a bicycle with a red front tire.

Noiselessly my friend crawled to the bather's wardrobe, and I watched him as he went through the pockets of every article. Finally, he felt them all over carefully, and came back

---

[1] The capital city of Mozambique, named for the 16th century Portuguese trader and explorer. Marques explored the area and lived there with his African wife. It was renamed Maputo upon the country's independence in 1975.

looking considerably crestfallen.

"It's not there," he said. "We must introduce ourselves and await events."

Shortly afterwards the bather appeared, and we made his acquaintance, chatting affably while he dressed.

"Your bicycle appears rather over-inflated in the back wheel," observed Gnomes to our quarry.

The reply, "that he liked his tires hard," was, I thought, given in rather a startled manner to so simple a question, and I saw that my friend noticed it as we all three mounted abreast.

Before we had gone a dozen yards, I, who was riding upon the right side of the stranger, and level with his back wheel, was startled by a report as of a pistol, and feeling a sharp blow in my left ear, clapped my hand upon it and retained what I thought was a bullet.

Abruptly jumping off, I turned and saw our companion lying on the ground, with Sherlock Gnomes sitting on his chest.

His machine lay upon the grass, and pointing to a large rent in the inner tube, which protruded over the rim of the back wheel, the latter said:

"It was fortunate you were in the way just then, Totson, or the gem might have been lost. I guessed that it was hidden in the tire, but confess I did not expect it would reveal itself so energetically."

My surprise at these events was so great that I had not thought to unclose my hand and inspect the missile. Doing so now, I unveiled an enormous pearl which emitted a beautiful pink radiance in the strong sunlight.

Notes of a Bookman

James MacArthur

The same month that The Hound of the Baskervilles *began running in* The Strand, *the return of Holmes was celebrated in James MacArthur's "Notes of a Bookman" column in the Aug. 31, 1901, issue of Harper's Weekly. MacArthur (1866-1909) also worked as a playwright and consulting editor for several publishing houses. In his introduction to the Harper editions of* A Study in Scarlet *and* The Sign of the Four *in 1904, he predicted that "it is doubtful whether Dr. Doyle will ever surpass himself in the stories which are gathered in these three volumes. They represent not only the best of his work but the most masterly detective stories which have ever been written."*

The resuscitation of Sherlock Holmes is an accomplished fact — *vide* the August *Strand.* In view of the reappearance of this distinguished character I submit the following documents and correspondence in the case:

From the London Daily Mail, *19th July*

Zermatt, Friday.

An extraordinary rumor is circulating here that Mr. Sherlock Holmes, the eminent criminal investigator, whose tragic death in a crevasse was reported circumstantially several years ago, creating a great sensation all over the world, has recently been seen in Zermatt.

A well-known guide, Andrew Breen, has made an affidavit before a notary that on Thursday last he saw Mr. Holmes in a café. [text is unclear] maintains that there could be no mistake about his identity, though he was obviously taking every precaution to keep himself as much out of the public gaze as possible.

It may be remembered that when Mr. Holmes and Professor Moriarty were first reported to have fallen into the crevasse, the story was received with incredulity, and the suggestion made that it was merely a ruse on Mr. Holmes's part with some ulterior object. This was denied at the time, but Breen's story now justifies the scepticism of several years ago.

From the London Daily Express, 20th July.

As our Mr. Hesketh Pritchard has just returned from his search for the Giant Sloth, which he was unfortunately unable to discover, though he met with indubitable traces of its existence, we have determined, regardless of expense, to despatch him forthwith to Switzerland, where the reappearance of Sherlock Holmes is reported. Holmes is said to have been seen as late as last week at Zermatt.

We always suspected that he was not really dead, and venture an hypothesis that he did not fall to the bottom of the precipice when he fell over the ledge with Professor Moriarty. He was doubtless caught by a clump of trees twenty or thirty feet below, and, fearing pursuit from some other members of the Moriarty gang, he allowed the report of his death to go unchallenged, hiding himself for that time under another name in one of the Cantons.

If our Mr. Pritchard is as successful as he hopes to be, he will bring the Great Investigator back to London to score greater triumphs than ever in the interest of truth and justice.

From Le Journal de Geneve, 19th July.

What we maintained in face of the whole world's press some years ago has at last been proved correct, and the notorious Sherlock Holmes is proved a greater liar and fraud than even we ventured to suggest he was. It will be remembered by our readers that Holmes, while on a wild-goose chase over the Continent, found his way to Switzerland, and was stated (with many plausible details) to have fallen from the ledge of an Alpine pass, along with a scoundrel of the Dynamite English party named Moriarty.

The story was circulated everywhere, and the result was that Alpine-climbing was rendered very unpopular for two seasons. From the very first we disbelieved the story, which had many suspicious elements in it. The only witness of the extraordinary and inexplicable accident whereby the two men were said to have lost their lives was one Watson, a friend of Holmes, who, so far as we have been able to ascertain, earned his living by narrating the exploits of Holmes. That Watson was in a state of intoxication when he returned from the mountain to ask for a search expedition was well known at the time, though delicacy prevented us from mentioning the fact.

The search party, consisting of nineteen guides, went all over the pass, and left not a yard of it unexplored, but they failed to find a scrap of evidence in support of Watson's story. This of itself would have been sufficient to throw grave doubts upon the story, but two days later, Watson, pretending to go out for a toothbrush, eluded the vigilance of the genial proprietor of The Bear of Berne Hotel (whose advertisement will be found on page 4), and decamped from the district, leaving his bill unpaid.

Influenced by the serious injury which was done to the popularity of mountaineering by the narratives of Holmes's death, we boldly expressed a doubt of the whole affair, and were threatened with an action for damages by the English canon named Doyle, who appeared to be a relative either of Watson or Holmes.

At the time we apologized to Canon Doyle for suggesting that the story was false, but now we withdraw our apology, and brand Holmes and Watson as unprincipled ruffians. We hope soon to be able to lay bare the plot whereof this cock-and-bull story was an essential part.

Letter from Holmes to Watson.

Zermatt, 5th May.

Don't you think it is about time I was permitted to leave this confounded place? I'm sick of it. It is all very well to maintain that the longer I stay away the keener will be the interest in my return to active work again; but I am not blind to the possibilities of a generation rising "who know not Joseph."[1] I hear about a new fellow called Captain Kettle,[2] who seems to be a little in our line. I hope you are not ass enough to let him get a position we cannot easily bounce him out of. But, first and last, I'm sick of this d — place. And the fleas!

From Watson to Holmes.

London, 8th May.

On no account venture into the open for a while yet. Doyle's far too busy to have anything to do with us at the moment, for he's over head and ears in the war movement.[3] There's nothing at all in the Kettle story. Kettle is simply a low, maritime bully, who could not maintain the regard and affection of the British for more than six months. Besides, he's given up that business and has been cavorting in *The Messenger Boy*[4] at the Gaiety for a year back. I believe he has started farm somewhere about Hythe[5] lately.

There was never the slightest danger that Kettle would interfere seriously with your position. Why — you are unique, my boy, unique! There has been nothing like you since old

---

[1] A phrase from Exodus 1:8: "Now there arose up a new king over Egypt, which knew not Joseph."

[2] Also mentioned in "The Book of 1900," above, Captain Kettle was the creation of C.J. Cutcliffe Hyne (1866-1944), who modeled his anti-hero on a sea captain he knew from South Shields, Davey Proffit.

[3] The year before, Conan Doyle had spent six months in South Africa supervising a field hospital treating the wounded. He also wrote a history of the war and a pamphlet defending the British against atrocity charges.

[4] A popular musical comedy about two men competing for the same woman that ran in London and New York. The show was produced by George Edwardes (1855-1915), whose habit of casting pretty girls in his productions was so notorious that he was credited with creating the trope of "Stage Door Johnnies" waiting for chorus girls outside the theatre with matrimony and other goals in mind.

[5] There are at least three Hythes to choose from, in Essex, Hampshire, and Kent. Hythe is from the Old English word for haven or landing place.

Lecoq,[1] and if you stayed away ten years you would be hailed like an emperor on your return. But make no mistake; if it is "oof" that is wanted I will send it.

I can't see that the work of waiter at a Swiss hotel is any harder work for you than investigating, and if you continue to wear the false whiskers you'll never be discovered. In any case, it's not the time to come back here. We're all in a mess over the war; money is tight, and our particular form of entertainment would scarcely go, I fear.

From Holmes to Watson.

Zermatt, 3d June.

False whiskers! That's the confounded thing. The boss of this place insists on my shaving, and if my hirsute adornment goes it's all up with us, for I'll be spotted, sure. And you say I'll "never be discovered." I begin to fear that is what you want. Why, man, I long to be discovered. Discovery, let me remind you, Watson, was my business. It is all very well for you and Doyle to live like lords on the strength of my alleged reputation, but I'll be hanged if I stay here any longer waiting on Cook trippers[2] and hunting Swiss fleas. Unless you send me

---

[1] A fictional amateur detective created by Émile Gaboriau (1832-1873) and based on the thief-turned-detective Eugène Francois Vidocq (1775-1857).

[2] Travelers participating in a tour organized by Thomas Cook & Son. The elder Cook (1808-1892) took advantage of the expanding railroad network to organize tours that included discounted train fares and food. "Cook's trippers" were looked down on as vulgar tourists being herded about to gawk at the natives and scribble graffiti on ancient sites.

For example, a writer about the Irish festival in Killarney for *The Leader* observed with distaste that "the Cook's trippers and other tourists flitted to and fro. The feelings they inspired were somewhat different in 1905 to those they aroused in, say, 1898. In the latter time they made a thoughtful Irishman feel savage as he watched the procession going by, the angels of mongrel Anglicisation passing unchallenged amidst a volley of 'Yer honers' to the Gap; in 1905 at least they are challenged — streamers with Irish inscriptions spanned the streets and under them they had to go; a couple of British tourists even strolled into the Irish play on Wednesday night and it was their turn to feel savage; they didn't like George Swiggins [the play's villainous

enough money to get back to London comfortably, I shall blow the gaff. That's flat!

Telegram — Watson to Holmes.

5th June.

For Heaven's sake don't! Will see what Doyle says. Newnes[1] encourages the idea, but I think it suicide.

Telegram — Holmes to Watson.

5th June.

I'm off. Will be in London this week.

Extract from Letter by Lord Rosebery[2] to the London City Liberal Club.

The paralysis of Liberalism is due to a fundamental and incurable antagonism of principle with regard to the Empire at large and our consequent policy. More vital than that is the fact that we want a Man — a Mind sufficiently strong to influence the warring elements of party; to placate the Opposition, now howling like wolves out of all harmony.

In the great crises of history the hour has almost invariably brought such a Man, and I need scarcely recall to you the case of Napoleon, who took the scraps of Empire and welded them to his mighty purpose, But where are we to look for such a Man? I have in my mind at the moment the name of one who, it seems to me, is alone able to save the party, whose name some years ago was on every lip, though since then

---

English planter], and vowed that they would warn the would-be trippers at the other side of the violence that was done to their imperial souls."

[1] George Newnes (1851-1910), the publisher of *The Strand* magazine and *Tit-Bits*.

[2] The fifth Earl of Rosebery, Archibald Primrose (1847-1929) was a politician with a gift for oratory but no experience in the day-to-day workings of government. His disastrous stint as prime minister (1894-1895) after William Gladstone fatally weakened the Liberal Party.

there has been an interregnum of mysterious silence. Need I say that I allude to Mr. Sherlock Holmes?

If there is one in Europe to-day who could discover the mind of Liberalism, who could see what lies at our hearts as a party, it is this great and world-eminent investigator. It could not fail to gratify many of you to learn that Mr. Holmes, whose death in Switzerland some years ago we were led by some as yet inexplicable events to deplore, has within the past fortnight been reported alive and well.

If that is so — and there is every reason to believe it is so — we have in Mr. Sherlock Holmes the Man and the Mind. I myself shall never, voluntarily, return to public life associated with the party; but I have the utmost confidence in recommending Mr. Holmes to your notice.

From the Agony Column, London Times.

20th July.

SH-RL-CK H-LM-S. — If you are in town, come to us at once. All will be forgotten and forgiven. — W-ts-n.

30th July.

W-TS-N. — Rats! Simply Rats! It's all over between us. Have seen Sir George and C.D., and we propose to leave you out of the show altogether. — The Ex-Waiter, Soho.

From the London Star, *1st August.*

Sherlock Holmes is said to be back in London again, and residing in Soho. He is described as looking younger than ever, and we see, indeed, little reason why the suggestion of Lord Rosebery should not be followed, and Mr. Holmes be intrusted with the discovery of the Liberal party.

Dr. Doyle Interviewed. From Literature, *2d August.*

"So it really is the case that Mr. Sherlock Holmes has been discovered alive?"

"I do not commit myself in any way upon that point," said the distinguished author. "You have seen, doubtless, as much of the evidence as I have. I know that my friend Mr. Watson is a most trustworthy man, and I gave the utmost credit to his story of the dreadful affair in Switzerland.

"He may have been mistaken, of course. It may not have been Mr. Holmes who fell from the ledge at all, or the whole thing might be the result of hallucination. I confess the stories now being published seem circumstantial enough, and that Holmes may be alive. But I have not seen him. There has been an advertisement in the *Times* suggesting that I have, but it is not true; I have never seen Holmes.

"Watson, however, lately came on certain old documents dealing with a part of the career of Holmes early in life, and I propose to publish these. They may be interesting; they may, indeed, induce Holmes, if he is really alive, to manifest himself again."

Cigarette card, 1901

Mr. Homes Solves a Question of Authorship

John Kendrick Bangs

John Kendrick Bangs was the most prolific American author of Holmesian pastiches during Conan Doyle's lifetime, penning both humorous crime stories ("The Mystery of Pinkham's Diamond Stud" and "Sherlock Holmes Again") and fanciful fantasies set in Hades ("The Stranger Unravels a Mystery" chapter from Pursuit of the House-Boat*). He even paired Holmes and gentleman burglar Raffles — sort of — by writing stories about a descendant, Raffles Holmes.*

In 1903, he returned to Hades, writing 10 stories for U.S. newspapers in which Shylock Homes opened a detective agency there. Without a Watson by his side, he contacted Bangs by knocking on his radiator in Morse code and dictated The Further Recollections of Shylock Homes.

This story refers to the Baconian theory, which arose in the mid-19th century. It was proposed that Sir Francis Bacon had written the plays and used Shakespeare as a front. To prove his authorship, the theory goes, Bacon inserted enciphered messages in the text. Although very few people believe Bacon wrote Shakespeare's plays, many have attempted to find alternative candidates, refusing to believe that a commoner could create works of lasting value.

There had been some acrimonious discussion at the last session of the Cimmerian Branch of Sorosis[1] over the authorship of the works of William Shakespeare. Cleopatra had read a paper of some cleverness, which proved to its fair author, at least, that the plays that have come down to us from the Golden Age of Letters were from the pen of a syndicate, of which Shakespeare was the managing director. Xanthippe, in a satirical philippic, demonstrated beyond peradventure that they were written by Guy

---

[1] The first professional women's club in the United States, founded in 1868 in New York City. The name is probably related to the Latin *sororitas* for sisterhood. *Cimmerian:* A mythical people in Homer's *Odyssey* who live at the edge of the world and at the entrance of Hades. They bear no relation to the ancient people who lived north of the Caucuses as early as 1300 BC.

Fawkes; Queen Elizabeth was strong in the debate in the affirmation of Bacon's responsibility for the works; Mrs. Noah proved an alibi for her husband, and Anne Hathaway, when called upon to speak, observed that she had never heard of them at all.

The discussion waxed so fast and furious that in order to prevent the disruption of the society, a committee of three, consisting of Lucretia Borgia, Madame du Barry, and Portia, was appointed to wait upon myself with the request that I solve the mystery on behalf of the club, promising to abide by whatever decision I might render. The ladies mentioned did me the honor to call at my office, where they laid the whole question before me.

"We shall be glad to lay before you any evidence at your disposal," said Portia. "I, for one, have worked out a cipher which seems to me conclusively to prove Bacon's authorship, but, of course, you can take it or reject it, just as you please."

Thereupon she handed me a slip of paper, upon which the following was written:—

Title	Letter		Count
Two Gentlemen o	F	Verona	14
Hen	R	y V.	4
Merch	A	nt of Venice	6
Much Ado About	N	othing	13
Ri	C	hard III.	3
K	I	ng John	2
A	S	You Like It	2
Mac	B	eth	4
T	A	ming of the Shrew	2
	C	omedy of Errors	1
Cori	O	lanus	5
Timo	N	of Athens	5
Total			61

I glanced the acrostic over with interest, and then I asked:—

"But what does this prove?"

"Bacon was born in '61," replied Portia, "which number is the sum total of the letters that spell out his name in the plays I have put down there. Certainly such a coincidence, Mr. Homes, is not without significance."

Lucretia Borgia sneered.

"I have a penchant for that," she said, and she, too, handed me a slip of paper, upon which I read as follows:—

A	N	thony and Cleopatra	2
T	I	tus Andronicus	2
	T	empest	1

Total 5

"You think you're clever, don't you?" retorted Portia, as she read the pendent acrostic, "Nit," "but I fail to see its significance."

"On your own plan," said Lucretia Borgia, coldly. "The sum total of the numbered letters proving it is five, which, when added to your sixty-one, makes sixty-six."

"Well?" asked Portia.

"Bacon died in his sixty-sixth year — that's all," said Lucretia Borgia.

"You absurd creature—" began Portia.

"Ladies, ladies! I beg of you!" I interjected, foreseeing a row of stupendous proportions. "Pray do not quarrel. Your evidence — that of both of you — interests me hugely, but I must look into the situation a little more carefully before I decide between you, and, since you both seek only the truth, you should not be angry if the theories of one or the other, or even both, are overthrown. Now, I'm something of a cipherologist myself, and I should like to see what I could prove to you in the same line. Suppose we try this arrangement," and I wrote out the following:—

Mer	C	hant of Venice	4
As You	L	ike It	6
Henr	Y	IV.	5
Mi	D	summer Night's Dream	3
M	E	asure for Measure	2
Twel	F	th Night	5
K	I	ng John	2
	T	imon of Athens	1
	C	oriolanus	1
	H	amlet	<u>1</u>

Total 30

"You see, Mr. Clyde Fitch[1] is thus proved to be the author of Shakespeare's plays, which is preposterous, since he was not living at the time. Nevertheless, he was thirty years old when he had his first great success; he writes thirty plays a year, and each act is about thirty minutes long. Some of his characters look like thirty cents, and so on, and so on. Thirty is his magical number. You perceive the fallacy of your own method of proving by a course of acrostical reasoning that Bacon either did or did not write Shakespeare's plays," I continued.

"Oh, well," said Portia, a bit perplexed, "it only happens that way in this particular case."

"Let's see about that," said I. "Here is another cipher for your consideration."

And I worked out the following:—

---

[1] From 1890 until his death in 1909 — from blood poisoning after an appendicitis operation — he was America's most popular playwright. At one time, five of his plays were running on Broadway.

Ti	**M**	on of Athens	3
Me	**R**	hant of Venice	3
Much A	**D**	o About Nothing	6
King J	**O**	hn	6
C	**O**	riolanus	2
Ju	**L**	ius Caesar	3
Rom	**E**	o and Juliet	4
Henr	**Y**	V.	5

Total 32

"Well," sneered Portia, in that freezing tone of hers, "what of it?"

"Only that the numbered letters of the cipher foot up to thirty-two, which is Mr. Dooley's[1] age, his books are all 32mos[2] and for two years he has been getting thirty-two cents a word for all he writes," I explained. "My dear ladies," I added, rising, "these things are interesting, but they prove nothing. By them you can prove that almost anybody, except Sienkiewicz,[3] wrote Shakespeare's plays — aye, even Hall Caine and Marie Corelli."[4]

"Why not Sienkiewicz?" asked Portia, icily.

"Because, as you will observe from a glance at the backs of the immortal bard's works, there is no 'z' in any of Shakespeare's titles, madam," I replied.

"How about 'Julius Caesar'?" she demanded, hastily.

"A good play, madam," I replied promptly, "but spelled

---

[1] A reference to Martin Dooley, a character created by Finley Peter Dunne (1867-1936). Dunne was a newspaper reporter who wrote columns about the saloon-keeper who delivers humorous opinions in a thick Irish accent.
[2] Abbreviation of thirty-twomo, a sheet of paper large enough to be folded into 32 leaves to create a 64-page book.
[3] Henryk Sienkiewicz (1846-1916), a Polish journalist and novelist who won the 1905 Nobel Prize in Literature. He is best known for his Roman epic *Quo Vadis*, which has been filmed several times.
[4] Two of the most popular novelists of the time.

with an 's,' as you would note at once if you had ever glanced at one of Mr. Mansfield's[1] programmes."

And then I entered upon the enterprise which, I must confess, startled even myself in the manner of its ending. The first thing I did was to call upon Sir Francis Bacon. He received me in the library of his villa at Noxmere, and I found him a most interesting personage.

"What can I do for Mr. Shylock Homes?" he asked, after we had exchanged the civilities of the moment.

"Well, Sir Francis," I replied, "I have a somewhat delicate mission. I would like to make use of your keenly critical mind to solve a disputed authorship."

"Aha," he cried, betraying no little nervousness. "You are not taking up literary detection, I hope?"

"Yes, I am, Sir Francis," I answered, "and my reputation is at stake. I wish to save it—"

"And cause me to lose mine by so doing!" he cried, impetuously, rising and pacing the room like a caged tiger.

"I don't understand you, Sir Francis," I said. "I certainly would not have you lose your reputation to save my own. Are you under suspicion in any literary controversy?" I added, innocently.

Bacon eyed me narrowly, and then sat down.

"Not that I am aware of," he said, with a sigh of relief, "although — well, never mind. What is the mystery you wish to solve?"

The action had begun sooner than I had expected. It was clear that his lordship was much perturbed at the intrusion of myself into his affairs, and so, to throw him off the scent, instead of asking him frankly the question, "Did you, or did you not write Shakespeare's plays," as I had come to do, I an-

---

[1] Actor-manager Richard Mansfield (1857-1907) — after a successful run as Beau Brummell in Clyde Fitch's play — went on to introduce to America plays by George Bernard Shaw and Henrik Ibsen. He was best known as a Shakespearean actor, having played Richard III, Henry V, Brutus in *Julius Caesar*, and Shylock in *The Merchant of Venice*.

swered, choosing my words by the merest chance, "That of Dr. Jekyll and Mr. Hyde."

If I had thrown a bomb into the middle of the library, the effect could not have been more dramatic. Bacon jumped up as if he had been shot, but I paid no attention, going on with my question calmly.

"Was that story romance or realism?"

"You have the subtlety of the serpent, Mr. Shylock Homes," he answered, with difficulty regaining his composure. "Why do you ask me, of all men, that question?"

"Because," said I, a great light dawning upon my mind, "I thought you, of all men, could tell me."

"But why? Why? Why? Why?" he cried, the reiterated "whys" rising in inflection until they ended in a shriek.

Unconsciously, I had struck a vein of rich ore, and my future course revealed itself to me on the instant.

"Because," I said, "because you, of all men, should know — having tried the same scheme yourself."

The pallor that spread over his countenance was deadly, and he sank back limp in his chair, but, as with a sudden resolve, he straightened up again and became strong.

"Great Heavens, Homes, where have you heard this?" he implored.

"Oh, just a little coterie to which I belonged in London used to take that theory," I lied, "and it found so general an acceptance among us that our friends and our friends' friends that I had supposed that by this time it was all over."

"You are retained by?" he queried.

"Sorosis," said I.

"And your fee — I will double it, Mr. Shylock Homes, if you will call off."

"I am incorruptible, Sir Francis," said I, rising, with a mock show of anger, "and I bid you good evening."

"Don't leave me in anger, Mr. Homes," he pleaded, holding out his hand, "I have long admired you and your work, and was frankly delighted when I received your card. My unfortunate suggestion as to your fee, I deeply regret. I, of course, know that you could not be corrupted, but I so deprecate the prolongation of the controversy as to my connection with — er — Shakespeare's works, that I forgot myself."

"Don't mention it, Sir Francis," I replied, accepting his proffered hand. "I understand. And to show you that I have no ill feelings, I wish you would take luncheon with me next Wednesday."

He fell into the trap at once. "I shall be delighted," he said.

"And to set forever at rest this absurd theory as to you and Shakespeare being another case of Jekyll and Hyde, I'll ask him, too. If you are both there, you cannot, of course, be the same man, you see."

Bacon tottered and almost fell as I spoke, but he soon recovered his equilibrium.

"I — I will see that he accepts," he said huskily.

"Thank you," said I, and took my departure.

Upon my return to my office, I dispatched a note to Shakespeare bidding him to the feast of Wednesday, and was somewhat taken aback, in view of my theory, to receive an immediate acceptance. When I left Lord Bacon, I was morally convinced that I had fallen upon the right solution of the mystery, but if this were so, how could both Shakespeare and Bacon be present at my luncheon simultaneously?

It perplexed me much, and, seeing no way out of the mystery, I dismissed the whole matter from my mind and sat down to await developments.

Wednesday came, and at the appointed hour both guests arrived, walking in arm in arm and chatting away as amiably as if there had never been a fierce battle raging between their followers for the greatest literary honors the world has to bestow. I was more than ever puzzled, when I shook them by the hand and made them welcome at my table, but it was none the less clear that there was some mystery to which they were both a party, for Bacon was excessively nervous all through the luncheon, and Shakespeare perspired as freely as though he were

Damocles[1] sitting beneath a suspended sword.

Moreover, Bacon was loath to let Shakespeare open his mouth, save to take in food and drink. He talked incessantly, and, at times, so vigorously that I wondered if he were in his right mind. Nor was there about Shakespeare any of the bonhomie that I had heard was so characteristic of the man, and, when the luncheon was over, instead of feeling that I had known him all my life, I really felt as if I knew him less well than when we had first sat down at table.

Still, there they were, both of them, and my theory must fall in the face of the fact, unless! Ah! That unless! It saved the day for Shylock Homes, for it bade me pursue the same line of inquiry even in the face of certain defeat.

Turning the conversation upon certain political schemers and their plans, I ventured the Shakespearean quotation:—

"Excellent! I smell a device!"

Bacon was about to respond, when Shakespeare growled.

"You don't smell advice, do you, Mr. Homes? Your English language is so—"

Bacon upset his coffee in Shakespeare's lap, to divert the bard, and set his tongue wagging on other lines, with which subterfuge I fell in most readily, but it was too late. Evidently there was something wrong with this Shakespeare who protested against his own periods and ventured the beginnings of an assault upon his own language. I did, indeed, smell a device but for the moment pursued it no further.

"I must lull them into a sense of security," I thought, "and maybe then all will become clear."

---

[1] Damocles was a courtier in the court of King Dionysius II (c. 397-343 BC). When he flattered the king by telling him he was fortunate to be a great and powerful ruler, Dionysius offered to change places so that he could experience it for himself. Damocles accepted and found himself on the throne, treated like a king, underneath a large sword held in place by a tail from a horse's hair. In his fifth *Disputation*, the Roman orator Cicero used the story to teach the moral that virtue is all a man needs to lead a happy life, asking us to consider if "Dionysius . . . made it sufficiently clear that there can be nothing happy for the person over whom some fear always looms?"

Bacon Was Nervous and Shakespeare Perspired Freely.

How well I did so is evidenced by the fact that when we parted it was with the distinct promise that Shakespeare and I were to spend the following Sunday at Noxmere with Bacon. I was glad, indeed, of the invitation, for my suspicions were becoming so great that all the powers of Hades could not now have diverted me from the mystery I had undertaken to solve. Entirely apart from the interest I was beginning to take in it, it would never do, even from a professional point of view, to give up now or to let Bacon deceive me as he appeared trying to do, and, as I looked back upon the luncheon and recalled several seemingly insignificant little details, I felt pretty certain that there was something very strange about Shakespeare. He preferred absinthe to ale, for one thing; he questioned the use of terms in one of his own phrases; had no good stories to tell, and was very far from being the roystering companion his friends had cracked him up to be. A day in the country might reveal the true inwardness of certain things that just now baffled me, and I accepted with alacrity. Not so Shakespeare, who betrayed considerable reluctance to be one of the party, but, partly by persuasion, and partly, I could see, by intimidation, he was won over.

The next day I called upon my friend, Henry Jekyll, with whom I had been on intimate relations in London the year he and I sprang almost simultaneously into our enviable notoriety. I told him frankly the position in which I was placed, and what I suspected, and adjured him, if he were my friend, to give me the prescription by which he transformed himself into Hyde, and then from Hyde back to Jekyll again.

At first, he refused me point-blank.

"You will use it on yourself, Homes, and if you do, it will ruin you," he said.

"I swear to you that I will not, Jekyll," I replied. "You know the value of my word."

"But—" he persisted.

"Do you want me to be made the laughing stock of all Hades?" I cried. "As I surely shall be if I fail in this enterprise."

"I know, Homes," said he. "But—"

"It is the only favor I have ever asked of you, Henry Jekyll," said I. "And I beg to recall to your mind that I knew the truth of your double existence in London when Hyde murdered Sir Danvers Carew. Did I betray you when your betrayal would have made my fortune?"

"It is yours," he cried, as, seizing a prescription blank from the table, he wrote down the required formula.

I had the powder in my pocket the following Sunday upon my arrival at Noxmere. The day passed pleasantly, and Shakespeare proved a charming companion — rather too much given to reciting lines from his own works, perhaps, but full of geniality and quite like the man I had expected to find him. Indeed, had his manner at the luncheon been the same as that which he displayed at Noxmere, I should have pursued the Jekyll and Hyde theory no further. But now I refused to cast suspicion aside without the supremest test of trying Jekyll's powders on Bacon.

All day long, I avoided allusion to my professional work, and by nightfall both Bacon and Shakespeare were so thoroughly convinced that they had thrown me off the scent that they became frankly and facetiously jocular. I bided my time until the nightcap hour came, and then, in order to put my plan into operation, suggested that I be allowed to mix a cocktail for the company.

"I learned the art from an American friend," I said, "and I assure you, my Lord, and you, too, William Shakespeare, when you have swallowed your first Martini you will say that you've never had a drink before."

"Wassail to the Martini," cried Bacon joyously.

"All hail the queue de coq,"[1] roared Shakespeare jovially — a remark which caused Bacon to frown and Shakespeare to turn pale. What had the "Bard of Avon" to do, indeed, with the French language? I said nothing, whatever, proceeding at once to the making of the mixture, and into Bacon's glass I slipped the powder Henry Jekyll had given me. And we all drank, and then —

Do you remember Dr. Lanyon's narrative in Stevenson's stirring account of Jekyll's fall, in which he describes what happened to Mr. Hyde when he had swallowed the potion? His words, as I remember them, ran as follows:—

"He put the glass to his lips and drank at one gulp. A cry followed. He reeled, staggered, clutched at the table and held on, staring with injected eyes, gasping with open mouth, and as I looked there came, I thought, a change — he seemed to swell,

---

[1] French for "tail of the rooster."

his face became suddenly black and the features seemed to melt and alter, and the next moment I had sprung to my feet and leaped against the wall, my arm raised to shield me from that prodigy, my mind submerged in terror.

"'Oh, God,' I screamed, and 'Oh, God,' again and again, for there, before my eyes pale and shaken and half fainting, and groping before him with his hands, like a man restored from death, there stood Henry Jekyll!"

The same scene was enacted in the study of Francis Bacon. He, too, like Hyde, drained the contents of the glass at a gulp. He, too, reeled, staggered, and clutched and held on to the table, staring with injected eyes, and gasping with open mouth. And over him, also, came a change in which his face turned suddenly black, and the features melted and altered.

Francis Bacon, Lord Verulam, faded in a mist of horror, and out of it emerged, pale, palsied and shattered for the moment, no less a person than William Shakespeare himself, while, seated opposite, gaping in horrified wonderment sat another Shakespeare, who gasped, and choked and gripped and groaned, staring the real in the eye and powerless for the instant to move. I stood back in the shadow of the mantel, watching both, when suddenly the spurious Shakespeare, with a shriek, sprang madly to his feet and plunged toward the door. By a quick move I intercepted him.

"We have solved the old mystery — now for the new!" I cried. "Who are you?"

"I beg of you," he began, whereupon I seized him by the goatee, which, being false, came off in my hand, and with it the rest of the disguise, wig, mustache and all.

It was M. Lecoq.

"I — I paid him for this, Mr. Homes!" gasped Bacon, or, rather, Shakespeare, as he now was. "Do not blame M. Lecoq for this—"

"He may go," said I, "I have only to deal with you."

And Lecoq shrank from the room and disappeared into the night.

"Well, Lord Bacon," said I, addressing the poor creature before me. "I have discovered the secret of the centuries. It is you who are the author of Shakespeare's plays."

"In a sense — as Shakespeare I — I — wrote them, yes."

"So that I may report—"

"I do not know!" he moaned. "I am broken, Mr. Homes, absolutely broken, in spirit. To have this known—"

"It never will be, Lord Bacon," said I. "At least not here. I shall publish my report only in the upper world, and the books of that sphere have no circulation in this."

"And you will conclude?"

"There is but one conclusion, Lord Bacon. William Shakespeare wrote his own works. You backed him. I shall so report to Sorosis, and the ladies may take it as final or leave it."

And so I left him. True to my promise, this story had not been circulated in Hades, and I rejoice to say, that, based upon my report to the committee, the Society of Sorosis of Cimmeria has voted by 369 to 1 that Shakespeare wrote Shakespeare.

The negative vote was cast by Anne Hathaway, who observed that she did not wish to incriminate her husband until she had seen the stuff.

John Kendrick Bangs

The Adventure of the Missing Bee

P.G. Wodehouse

P.G. Wodehouse (1881-1975) was a lifelong fan of Conan Doyle and Sherlock Holmes in particular. Soon after embarking on a career as a writer, he interviewed Conan Doyle for a magazine and the author, in return, befriended the young man. This led to Wodehouse being invited to join Conan Doyle on J.M. Barrie's amateur cricket team, the Allahakbarries.

But he wasn't above making fun of Sherlock. He wrote several parodies for Punch *magazine — found in* The Early Punch Parodies of Sherlock Holmes *— as well as this one for the December 1904 issue of* Vanity Fair.

This story appeared the same month that "The Adventure of the Second Stain" appeared in The Strand, *and therein lies a connection. In the story, Watson informed us that Holmes "has definitely retired from London and betaken himself to study and bee-farming on the Sussex Downs." The presence of bees in both stories leads one to believe that Conan Doyle might have tipped his cricket teammate about what was coming.*

(Sherlock Holmes is to retire from public life after Christmas, and take to bee-farming in the country.)

"It is a little hard, my dear Watson," said Holmes, stretching his long form on the sofa and injecting another half-pint of morphia with the little jewelled syringe which the Prince of Piedmont had insisted on presenting to him as a reward for discovering who had stolen his nice new rattle; "it is just a little hard that an exhausted, overworked private detective, coming down to the country in search of peace and quiet, should be confronted in the first week by a problem so weird, so sinister, that for the moment it seems incapable of solution."

"You refer—?" I said.

"To the singular adventure of the missing bee, as anybody but an ex-army surgeon equipped with a brain of dough would have known without my telling him."

I readily forgave him his irritability, for the loss of his bee had had a terrible effect on his nerves. It was a black business.

Immediately after arriving at our cottage, Holmes had purchased from the Army and Navy Stores a fine bee. It was docile, busy, and intelligent, and soon made itself quite a pet with us. Our consternation may, therefore, be imagined when, on going to take it out for its morning run, we found the hive empty. The bee had disappeared, collar and all. A glance at its bed showed that it had not been slept in that night. On the floor of the hive was a portion of the insect's steel chain, snapped. Everything pointed to sinister violence.

Holmes' first move had been to send me into the house while he examined the ground near the hive for footsteps. His search produced no result. Except for the small, neat tracks of the bee, the ground bore no marks. The mystery seemed one of those which are destined to remain unsolved through eternity.

But Holmes was ever a man of action.

"Watson," he said to me, about a week after the incident, "the plot thickens. What does the fact that a Frenchman has taken rooms at Farmer Scroggins' suggest to you?"

"That Farmer Scroggins is anxious to learn French," I hazarded.

"Idiot!" said Holmes, scornfully. "You've got a mind like a railway bun. No. If you wish to know the true significance of that Frenchman's visit, I will tell you. But, in the first place, can you name any eminent Frenchman who is interested in bees?"

I could answer that.

"Maeterlinck," I replied. "Only he is a Belgian."[1]

"It is immaterial. You are quite right. M. Maeterlinck was the man I had in my mind. With him bees are a craze. Watson, that Frenchman is M. Maeterlinck's agent. He and Farmer Scroggins have conspired and stolen that bee."

"Holmes!" I said, horrified. "But M. Maeterlinck is a man of the most rigid honesty."

---

[1] Maurice Maeterlinck (1862-1949) was a Belgian playwright and poet and author of *The Life of the Bee* (1901). He received the Nobel Prize for literature in 1911.

"Nobody, my dear Watson, is entirely honest. He may seem so, because he never meets with just that temptation which would break through his honesty. I once knew a bishop who could not keep himself from stealing pins. Every man has his price. M. Maeterlinck's is bees. Pass the morphia."

"But Farmer Scroggins!" I protested. "A bluff, hearty English yeoman of the best type."

"May not his heartiness be all bluff?" said Holmes, keenly. "You may take it from me that there is literally nothing that that man would stick at. Murder? I have seen him kill a wasp with a spade, and he looked as if he enjoyed it. Arson? He has a fire in his kitchen every day. You have only to look at the knuckle of the third finger of his left hand to see him as he is. If he is an honest man, why does he wear a made-up tie[1] on Sundays? If he is an upright man, why does he stoop when he digs potatoes? No, Watson, nothing that you can say can convince me that Farmer Scroggins has not a black heart. The visit of this Frenchman — who, as you can see in an instant if you look at his left shoulder-blade, has not only deserted his wife and a large family, but is at this very moment carrying on a clandestine correspondence with an American widow, who lives in Kalamazoo, Mich. — convinces me that I have arrived at the true solution of the mystery. I have written a short note to Farmer Scroggins, requesting him to send back the bee and explaining that all is discovered. And that," he broke off, "is, if I mistake not, his knock. Come in."

The door opened. There was a scuffling in the passage, and in bounded our missing bee, frisking with delight. Our housekeeper followed, bearing a letter. Holmes opened it.

"Listen to this, Watson," said Holmes, in a voice of triumph:

"'Mr. Giles Scroggins sends his compliments to Mr. Sherlock Holmes, an' it's quite true, I did steal that there bee, though how Mr. Holmes found out,

---

[1] A tie that is sold permanently knotted that is attached to the shirt either by a hook or a band that goes around the neck. The earliest version was patented in 1875.

Mr. G Scroggins bean't able to understand. I am flying the country as requested. Please find enclosed 1 (one) bee, and kindly acknowledge receipt to

'Your obedient servant

'G Scroggins

'Enclosure.'"

"Holmes," I whispered, awe-struck, "you are one of the most remarkable men I ever met."

He smiled, lit his hookah, seized his violin and, to the slow music of that instrument, turned once more to the examination of his test tubes.

❖ ❖ ❖ ❖

Three days later we saw the following announcement in the papers: "M. Maeterlinck, the distinguished Belgian essayist, wishes it to be known that he has given up collecting bees and has taken instead to picture postcards."

Maurice Maeterlinck seeking inspiration from his hive.

The Last of Sherlock Holmes:
The Mystery of the Governor's Message and the Missing ————.

A.B. "Banjo" Paterson

Illustrated by Lionel Lindsay

Late on the night of Jan. 20, police in Perth, Australia, received an urgent telegram from Sir Harry Rawson (1843-1910), the governor of New South Wales. Two reliable officers were ordered to meet the train from Moss Vale, where the governor was summering, and meet someone who would order them to keep an eye on two unnamed individuals. Word of the mysterious telegram spread quickly, and news reports fueled speculation. Several days later, the government explained that Rawson had given a messenger negotiable debentures to raise a £2 million loan and was concerned for their safety. Eventually, the truth surfaced: Two Russian agents had been negotiating with a shipping company to buy one of their vessels and the government became alarmed after learning of their presence in the country.

Little more than a week after the story broke, this parody appeared in at least two Australian newspapers—The Evening News *of Jan. 28 and* The Daily News (Perth) *of Feb. 16. No byline was printed, but a compiler for Project Gutenberg Australia identified its author as Andrew "Banjo" Paterson (1864-1941), the reporter whose poems of Outback life including "Waltzing Matilda," "Clancy of the Overflow," and "The Man from Snowy River" would shape Australia's self-image. His portrait appears on the Australian ten-dollar bill. Lionel Lindsay (1874-1961) was beginning his career that would see him as one of the country's most popular artists.*

Those who have followed the career of the marvelous detective Sherlock Holmes, and his assistant, Dr. Watson, will remember that the final exploit of the great Sherlock, as recorded by Conan Doyle, was the recovery of a missing despatch box[1] by the Prime Minister of England. This adventure is sup-

---

[1] As told in "The Adventure of the Second Stain."

posed to have closed the history of the great detective so far as English readers are concerned; but such a mastermind could not remain unoccupied; such a genius must find an outlet for its energies; and there are indications that various mysteries now puzzling Australians—such as why Pye was left out of the Australian Eleven, [1] and The Missing Diamonds, or the Mystery of the Mont-de-Piete, will before long engage the attention of his giant intellect; in other words, Sherlock Holmes is in Australia.

If any confirmation were wanted of this statement, it would be found in the solution recently worked out of a labyrinthic mystery which Sherlock Holmes and Company alone could have successfully solved.

Suppressing, for obvious reasons, the real names of the parties, let us proceed to narrate how Sherlock Holmes unraveled the mysterious telegram sent by one whom, for the purposes of the story, we shall call Sir Tarry Hawser, the Governor of New South Carolina.[2]

❖   ❖   ❖   ❖

It was midnight of a sweltering Sydney summer night. The

---

[1] Leslie W. Pye's omission from the Australian Eleven to play against England ignited much arguing in the region's newspapers. Sources for the other mysteries could not be found.

streets were quiet, except for the usual crowds around the betting shops, and Sherlock Holmes, disguised as an Officer of Detective Police, paced restlessly up and down his official sitting-room, holding in his hand a telegram. From time to time he glanced restlessly at the door. A step was heard without, and three knocks were given. The door slid noiselessly into the groove in the wall, admitting Sherlock's old and true friend, Dr. Watson, now disguised as a policeman. Without looking round, Sherlock motioned him to a chair, saying, "Sit down, Watson. I have a small matter in hand."

"How did you know it was me?" said Watson, gazing admiringly at the back view of the greatest detective the world has ever known. "I never spoke nor gave my name to a soul."

"My dear fellow," said Sherlock, with calm superiority. "I knew it was you the moment that you started to come up the stairs. I knew it was you by the heavy way you put your feet down. When I heard the sound on the stairs, I said, 'This is either Watson, or a draught horse,' and as no draught horse could get round the angle in the first landing, I knew it was you the moment you had passed that point. But there is a small matter, a mere official trifle, which is likely to afford us a little work. It is a matter which, as a rule, I would hand over to the traffic constables, with instructions to inquire whether any strangers had been seen in town lately. But as our old friend, Sir Tarry Hawser, is concerned in it we must attend to the matter ourselves."

So saying, he tossed to Watson a telegram timed 11 p.m. and bearing the Hoss Valley[1] telegraph stamp.

Watson held it up to the light, and read it aloud: "'Hawser, Hoss Valley, to Sherlock, Sydney. Have just come home from amateur races. Very hot. Have lost—' what's this he has lost?— 'exiguous co-ordinate?'"

"That's where the difficulty is," said Sherlock. "That part is in cipher, and we have lost the key. It is evident he has lost something. I deduce that from the fact that he goes on: 'send two detectives at once.'"

"And what do you think he has lost?" said Watson.

Sherlock smiled his inscrutable smile and threw himself into an easy chair.

"I think I recognize the hand of Moriarty in this," he said.

"Do you mean Moriarty, the Crown Prosecu—"[2]

"No, I mean Moriarty, the great chief of crime, the Napoleon of iniquity. See here, Watson," he went on, stepping over to the window and drawing aside the curtain: "Look out and tell me what you see."

"I see Phillip street, and a cab at the corner, and a man over the way going into a pub after hours."

"What does he look like?"

"He looks like a beer fighter."

Sherlock smiled his slow smile of satisfaction.

"Watch that man," he said, "and tell me if he looks round as he goes into the bar."

"Yes, he does."

"Does he beckon with his hand, and is he joined by another man?"

"Yes, he is."

"I thought so. Moriarty, at every turn! That is no ordinary

---

[1] A reference to Moss Vale, a town in the Southern Highlands of New South Wales. Gov. Rawson's summer residence was in nearby Sutton Forest.
[2] James Moriarty was a barrister and Crown Prosecutor who also wrote several legal textbooks.

emergency. I would go myself, but—" and here he paused, lost in thought.

"Why not telegraph Sir Tarry, and see—"

"What, and have the telegram intercepted by Moriarty? Watson, you surprise me. Oblige me by pressing the bell."

A velvet-footed official came to the door.

"Are all arrangements made?" said Sherlock sharply.

"They are, sir."

"Have you rung up the press and told them at what time the detectives leave, and where they are going, and by whom they are wanted?"

"We have, sir."

"Have they been photographed and their descriptions circulated among the criminal classes?"

"They have, sir."

"Have they got a banner and masks for their faces and a bloodhound to follow the tracks?"

"They have, sir."

"Excellent, excellent," said Sherlock Holmes. "It is a great aid to detective work, Watson, to notify beforehand what you are going to do. It lowers the number of convictions and enables Neitenstein[1] to effect a saving of gaol expenditure. And now let us snatch a few hours' sleep. We can do nothing till the morning. Good night, Watson. Mind the step."

Next morning there was a great to-do. People were asking, "What had the Governor of South Carolina lost? Had the miscreants been arrested? Had Rozhestvensky's fleet[2] appeared on

---

[1] Frederick Neitenstein (1850-1921) was a prison reformer. In charge of New South Wales' prisons, he developed policies such as separating prisoners by classes and instituting physical drill and other programs to turn prisons into "moral hospitals." "Gaol expenditure" referred to his bureaucratic success in transferring the cost of housing lunatics in prison to another department, creating a great savings on paper.

[2] As admiral of the Imperial Russian Navy, Zinovy Rozhestvensky (1848-1909) led the Baltic squadron of 38 ships, including eight battleships, from St. Petersburg to Japan during the Russo-Japanese War, only to see them destroyed in the Battle of Tsushima.

the Upper Marrumbidgee and begun to shell the Barren Jack Reservoir?[1] Was a Russian emissary disguised as a commercial traveler trying to sell fire extinguishers to the burnt-out settlers? The public mind was all unrest, and all looked to the great detective to know what had been done.

Meanwhile, the detectives had started for the railway station with the utmost secrecy, accompanied by a German band, a banner, and a bloodhound. The time and place of their departure and the object of their visit were all chronicled in the society columns among the fashionable intelligence, and were read with interest by the criminal classes.

They followed up the blood-stained trail. "A Russian spy has passed along here," they said. But the desperado was found to be only an ordinary swagman, and the sleuth hounds of the law were puzzled.

"Strange!" they said, "that the criminals are not here to meet us after our departure was so extensively advertised." They returned as unobtrusively and secretly as they set out, and were met by four hundred people at the railway station, who cheered them heartily.

---

[1] A dam-created lake on the Murrumbidgee River in New South Wales. The name is a corruption of the Aboriginal name for the area, and is now called Burrinjuck. The Murrumbidgee is the second-longest river in Australia.

Public excitement ran higher than ever. The mysterious message—what was it about? Had the detectives arrested anyone?

It was then that the genius of our friend Holmes shone out more brightly; with more luster and luminosity than on any occasion in his history. He rigidly refused to give any information. "We have told the criminals what we are going to do," he said, "but it would never do to tell the public what the affair was all about. Enough for them to know that the criminals, whoever they were, were taken no unfair advantage of. Let it never be said that Sherlock Holmes descended to the low expedient of surprising a burglar. Any officer giving any information whatever will be sacked."

Later on in the day the Prime Minister, by one of those singular lapses of which even the greatest minds are capable, actually made public the details of the affair. There was nothing to make a fuss about, he said. There had been no crime committed, and he didn't see why the public should be kept in a state of unrest. He said that Sir Tarry Hawser had merely wanted two detectives to look after some unsalable bonds that the Carruthers Government[1] were trying to palm off on the British moneylend-

---

[1] Sir Joseph Carruthers (1857-1932) was premier of New South Wales (1904-1907). In Australia, the premier is appointed by the governor who is appointed by the monarch.

er; but the public would not believe this story at all.

"Why," they said, "should he wait until the middle of the night to remember about the bonds? No, there was a mystery in it, and Sherlock Holmes is the only man who can tell us."

When this was reported to Sherlock, he again smiled his deep, enigmatical smile.

"To the ordinary superficial observer, Watson," he said, "there was nothing in it. But the trained, deductive intellect discards all the theories of guarding bonds. The great mastermind of crime was at work in this."

"And what was it then that Sir Tarry Hawser wished the detectives to do? What did he wish them to guard?"

Sherlock Holmes looked round furtively and drew his questioner close to him.

"The family washing," he hissed. "He didn't like sending it down, considering the people that were about. Look out, Watson, and tell me what you see in the street."

"I see the same pub, and I think the same man going in to have a drink."

Sherlock Holmes gave his usual chuckle of triumph. "There you are, Watson," he said, "that proves that my suspicions were correct. Moriarty is yet at large."

A.B. "Banjo" Paterson

Sherlock Holmes' Daughter

H.H. Ballard

Without giving too much away, this story from the April issue of The Brown Book of Boston *contains a twist at the end that would probably delight today's readers of fanfiction.*

Harlan Hoge Ballard (1853-1934) was an educator in Lenox, Mass. He founded the Agassiz Association, named for naturalist Louis Agassiz, to encourage young people to study natural history. A learned man, he wrote several books on behalf of the association, as well as a translation of Virgil's Aeneid, *and two writing guides.*

While Ballard's appreciation of Sherlock was apparent, in another essay he concluded that learning was more rewarding than reading fiction: "Amateurs delight in effort regardless of the value of the thing achieved. Selfish pleasure in achieving kills interest, once the goal is reached. . . . Detective stories, once read, are forgotten. Sherlock Holmes cared nothing for his criminals after he caught them. But if efforts result in adding however slightly to the world's knowledge, or happiness, the pleasure of achievement becomes legitimate, and interest is lasting."

Would many equally learned Sherlockians agree?

It was our tenth anniversary. Some of us had not met since we stood in a row before good old Dr. Bancroft to receive our diplomas.

We had finished our coffee, pushed back our chairs, and lighted our cigars. We were still laughing at the story of Dr. Brown—"Billy" he used to be, and "Billy" he was again that night.

"Billy," then turned to a quiet banker who was sitting next to him, and who was known on Wall Street as Thomas Vanderpool, Esq., and cried, "Come on Van! It's your turn next! Gentlemen, we will now listen to the adventures of the banker."

Vanderpool had been the baby and the Beau Brummell[1] of

---

[1] A gentleman of Regency England (1778-1840) who was the arbiter of men's fashion. By favoring full-length trousers instead of knee breeches, knotted cravats, and shirts made from linen, he led the way toward the modern suit.

of the class, used to have a new pair of dark green kid gloves on every Sunday morning, and all that sort of thing, parted his hair in the middle, fond of the girls, but a good, clean fellow, though very quiet and a bit dull, and the last man in the world to have an adventure or tell it if he had.

So we all clattered our knives against our glasses, and shouted, "Van! Van! It's up to you, Vandy," until Tom was actually a bit fussed.

However, he got his cigar around to the other corner of his mouth, took off his gold glasses, and to the astonishment of every man present told the liveliest story of the evening.

"Fellows," said he, "as a rule in a banker's life there is not much doing. But as some of you may remember, I started in to be a surgeon, and possibly you may be interested to hear the remarkable experience which switched me off. It was in eighteen hundred ninety-four, no, ninety-three.

"I was on my way home from Greece. I had been working with the American Archaeological Society, and had just helped uncover the old Corinthian wall. We had embarked at Naples on one of the Lloyd steamers, *The Normannia*.[1] We took on a few passengers at Gibraltar, among whom I had noticed two ladies heavily veiled in black.

"About eight o'clock that evening I was lounging on the forward deck watching the moonlight and the water, when I heard a sort of feminine rustle, and was startled to hear my name pronounced with that hesitating accent which is a form of question. It was the younger of the two veiled women. I gathered in my pipe, and raised my hat and my eyebrows. 'Mr. Vanderpool of New York?' I bowed gravely and remarked quietly, 'but, if I may be pardoned the colloquialism, you have the advantage of me.' Ignoring my words, she went on more quickly: 'Your archeological work is interesting, of course, but

---

[1] There was a steamship by that name that was launched in 1890, but it was owned by Hamburg America, not Norddeutscher Lloyd. It was sold to the Spanish Navy in 1898 for use in the Spanish-American War, sold the next year for debt payment, and scrapped in 1906.

after all, Doctor, one regards that kind of thing rather as an avocation than as a permanent profession?'

"I was now nettled as well as perplexed. 'Madam,' I said, coolly, 'you appear to know enough of my personal affairs to be an acquaintance, but I fail to recognize your voice, and I must ask you to advise me whom I have the honor of addressing.'

"'Quite right,' she murmured, and threw back her heavy veil; then handed me a card on which were delicately written these words: Miss Elsie V. Holmes.

"Her face, even by moonlight, was not beautiful. Women would say there were beautiful things *in* it. Her forehead had fine curves amid a wealth of waving hair; her nose was aquiline, and her eyes—well, her eyes made you forget everything else, even the firm mouth and the too-dominant chin. They were dark and very large, but the thing I have never seen in any other human eye was a tiny sparkle of liquid fire in the center of the pupil.

"This was not often seen, usually she held her eyes half closed and dreamed out under the fringing veil of her long lashes; but when she opened them wide upon you in joy, or indignation, or love, the fire came.

"Before I recovered my self-possession the veil was again dropped.

"'Now, Dr. Vanderpool,' the words were low, almost pleading, 'I am going to ask of you a very great favor.'

"'First tell me,' I cried, 'how in Heaven's name you know me, and that I am a doctor?'

"'Not a physician, certainly,' she replied, 'a surgeon. I noticed you at your dinner; and from the way in which you held your knife it was evident that—but, after all, the important thing is that you *are* a surgeon, and that it is a surgeon I need, and quickly, come!' I and she moved toward the stairs leading down to the main cabin.

"I followed without hesitation. She passed swiftly down, and through the long dining-saloon, and entered the corridor into which the staterooms open.

"At the door of No. 17 she paused, drew a key from her bosom, and waited. 'Promise,' she then said in an earnest whisper, 'that you will guard with professional silence what you are about to see.' I bowed assent. The key clicked and I entered. I was struck by the size of the room. Instead of the ordinary cabinet, I found myself in an apartment as large as the drawing-room above, and evidently made so by removing partitions and throwing half a dozen staterooms into one.

"The luxury equalled the size of the room. Easy chairs of rich upholstery, a reading table strewn with books and papers, a curiously constructed wardrobe, a carved writing-desk, and strangest of all, a comfortable bed, set in an alcove at the farther end of the room and partly hidden by heavy curtains. Beyond this, a door slightly ajar gave a glimpse into a second room, smaller, but of extraordinary size and of equal richness of furnishing.

"Both rooms were brilliant with electric light. On the floor were signs of haste and confusion. A steamer trunk was open, and around it was a bewildering overflow of muslin, silk and lace, together with gleams of silver and cut-glass traveling gear. On a chair near the bed lay a black mourning dress, over which depended a heavy veil of crepe.

"'Your mother is ill?' I asked as I recovered from my first surprise. Miss Holmes darted a keen glance at me, then sweeping by, threw wide the curtains, and answered, 'It is my father.'"

"Certainly it was a man who lay there motionless: whether dead or alive I could not tell. My first impulse was to get away from this chamber of mystery and horror, but I was fascinated by the figure to whose side I had been so strangely brought. The hair was long, unkempt, and iron gray; the features strong and well cut; the hands—evidently the hands of a gentleman—lay idly by the side, the shapely fingers relaxed in the repose of—what? This question touched the nerve of my professional instinct. To find out what this stupor was, and if possible to relieve it, was my errand.

"In an instant my ear was pressed close over the heart. I heard no sound. 'Try this!' Something was pushed into my hand. It had an ear piece, like a telephone. It was, in fact a stethoscope; one of those tragic instruments which have whispered the story of life or death to many an anxious ear.

"I did not then stop to wonder how this young woman happened to have so curious an instrument at hand; but swiftly adjusting the larger opening over my patient's heart, I applied the other end to my ear, and listened while I held my breath.[1]

"During that fateful moment, I felt that the eyes of my fair companion were searching my face with an intensity of gaze like that with which a prisoner scans the faces of the jury when they return to give their verdict.

"Silence! Then a faint, almost imperceptible sound, as if a kitten were purring at a telephone a hundred miles away. It was enough. 'He lives!' I said, rather to myself than to the woman at my side. 'Thank Heaven!' she answered solemnly, and then I saw for the first time in her eyes that wonderful flash of fire. Then before I could move, or utter a word, Miss Holmes had emptied a vial of some dark green liquid down the throat of my insensible patient; and with the dexterity of a trained surgeon she thrust a glittering blade into his mouth.

"There was a red spurt of blood, followed by a sudden convulsion of the powerful frame; the eyes opened with a bewildered stare, a flush spread over the pallid features, and a deep drawn breath sounded in the stillness like a muffled groan.

"Miss Holmes seized my hand in her gratitude, and said, 'I thank you Dr. Vanderpool, that is all,—for the present.'

"I would have remained to await her father's more complete restoration, and to minister to the over-strained nerves of the daughter, but her decision was final.

"'Shall I not look in again during the evening?'

"'It will not be necessary, Doctor. This is by no means the first attack, though it has proved the severest. I know what to

---

[1] He was using a monaural stethoscope, a slender tube with a wide mouth at the top and a wider disk at the bottom that was placed over the heart.

do, as you have seen, but this time I dared not take the responsibility alone.'

"She busied herself at the bedside, and reluctantly I left her. I had the rest of the night in which to think it all over.

"This young woman had come aboard our ship accompanied only by a feeble old lady attired in mourning. I had never seen either of them before, yet the girl had sought me out. She had called me by my name, she knew my profession and something of my recent history. Though a stranger, and with absolutely no claim upon me, she had prevailed upon me to undertake in her behalf an unknown service. She had exacted a promise of secrecy before I knew what the secret was to be, and in place of the invalid mother whom I expected to attend, she had shown me a dying man whom she called her father.

"She had been afraid of nothing except that he might be dead. She had not dared to put the question to the stethoscope; but as soon as I had received from its lips the message of life, she had fearlessly administered one of the most powerful drugs known to the medical profession, and with her own hands performed a delicate and disagreeable operation in surgery; and this with as much composure as if she had been cutting a slice of bread.

"Withal she had shown wonderful womanly tenderness, and was even now performing the arduous duties of nurse; while to me she had shown a heart responsive to the slightest kindness, yet schooled to the most perfect self-possession.

"That flush of joy in her eyes! What had I to do with that? But the momentary pressure of her hand and the tone in which she had said, 'I thank you,' surely *there* was something on which my memory had a right to linger. At all events my thoughts were busy with her all that night.

"The next day was rough. The wind blew violently and scattered a blinding salt spray athwart the decks. By dinner time the steamer rolled so heavily that few passengers appeared. Miss Holmes, nevertheless, took her seat quietly at a distant table, and proceeded to satisfy a normal appetite without so much as a glance of recognition.

"With the dessert, however, an envelope, dainty, square, and plain, was brought with my coffee. It was addressed,

"THOMAS VANDERPOOL, M.D.
"Steamer Normannia"

"My first name too! I broke the seal. My eye caught the peculiar wrinkle and color of a Bank of England note. Money is a foe to sentiment. I quarreled with my fee. I felt the blood rise to my cheek, and put the envelope in my pocket unopened. After dinner, striding the tumbling deck, though nearly blinded by the rain, I read these words:

"DEAR DR. VANDERPOOL:—
"Kindly call again at No. 17 at eight o'clock this evening.
"E.V.H."

"The door of No. 17 opened before I could touch knuckle to it, and Miss Holmes welcomed me. An easy chair had been wheeled in front of a brisk open fire, guarded by a close and almost invisible network of brass. I afterwards learned that this open fire effect was produced by an arrangement of electric lights behind revolving spirals of flame-colored glass.

"A lurch of the ship seated me in the chair with little ceremony, and Miss Holmes, with a smile, seated herself not far away. I should not have known the room. It was reduced to half its length by the closing of previously unnoticed folding doors. The bed was no longer visible, disorder had been banished, and the open fire, a miracle on shipboard, threw a glamour into every corner.

"I spoke of this. 'Yes,' said Miss Holmes, 'an open fire is one of my father's hobbies, he always contrives to carry one with him.'

"'I trust your father is better.'

"'He is quite himself again, except that he is much exhausted.'

"'Shall I go to him?'

"'No, he needs nothing now so much as rest.'

"'But you summoned me.'

"'Not for my father,' Miss Holmes interrupted. 'This time I have called you on my own account. No, I am not at all ill,' she continued, in response to my glance of inquiry, 'but'—She hesitated, stopped, gave a little incoherent laugh, and burst into tears.

"It was as I had feared, a strong, nervous reaction after a day and night of deep anxiety. I could not restrain a glance of professional interest.

"'It is nothing,' she said, getting control of herself with an effort.

"'You need rest, Miss Holmes,' I said firmly, and I rose to my feet.

"'Yes,' she murmured wearily, 'Yes, I need rest, and Dr. Vanderpool, that is why I have sent for you.' All her austerity of manner was gone. She was trembling. She looked up to me appealingly.

"'But I am not a physician,' I replied.

"'I know' she began, 'It isn't that. It is—Dr. Vanderpool, won't you stay with me a little while?' The last words came involuntarily, as if forced from her in spite of her will.

"'If you will try a little bromo-caffeine,"¹ I suggested. 'I will see whether I can get some from the—'

"'No, no,' she answered impatiently, 'I don't need any drugs. I need a friend. Yes, I will speak out! I am surrounded by anxiety and peril, and I want you to save me!'

"'Me?'

"'Yes, Dr. Vanderpool,—you, for there is no one else.'

---

[1] An effervescent powder used to relieve headaches, indigestion, hangovers, and, according to one drug manufacturer, "with ladies the headache and backache of neurasthenia, hysteria, dysmenorrhoea and kindred disorders."

"I must have looked my astonishment, for she immediately replied to my unspoken thought. 'No, my brain is all right. I need your help. You won't refuse me, will you?'

"'I shall be only too glad to do anything in my power to bring you relief,' I protested; 'Will you tell me how?'

"'I will,' she replied slowly, and with a steady look into my eyes; 'You can take me away from my father.' With these words she threw a nervous glance in the direction of the folding doors.

"My fears were confirmed. This charming woman under the stress of anxiety and fatigue, was on the very edge of nervous prostration, possibly her brain was already affected by delusion. If so, I knew that the chances of recovery were few.

"I felt strangely drawn to the girl. A wave of compassion swept over my heart. I determined to do all in my power to save her. But from what? From anything and everything which might in any way harm or trouble her; from madness, if madness threatened her, from her father, if she rightly feared him; from herself, if—But, no, that thought was unworthy and absurd, and I banished it at once.

"Then, while I hesitated, turning these thoughts in my mind, Miss Holmes arose and came nearer to me. The electric lamps had been subdued on her father's account, and, in the fire-light, she was beautiful. Her weariness gave her an added grace. She swayed with the rolling of the ship and would have fallen, but I instinctively supported her with my arm. For an instant she clung to me, then quickly disengaging herself with a smile, conquered her faintness, and said quietly:—

"'Dr. Vanderpool, you are mistaken. I am not mad. Let me prove this to you first of all: What is the first conclusive symptom of insanity? It is morbid self-interest, an entire absorption in one's own feelings, thoughts, and troubles:—Am I right?' I nodded gravely. 'Very well—then let me remind you that I can think of others. Of my father's welfare I have not been careless.'

"'On the contrary—' I began.

"'No,' she interrupted, 'I have not overtaxed my strength. I have done my duty. But I have also found opportunity, Doctor, to have some regard for you. Having no claim upon you, I would not allow you to lose your rest last night. You have had troubles of your own;—perhaps perils.'

"I started. 'What do you know of me?' I demanded. She darted a keen glance at me, and asked demurely, 'Were you ever in Spain?'

"'It was at Gibraltar that I had the pleasure of seeing you first,' I replied.

"'Of course,' she laughed, 'how stupid I was.—And yet you are an American surgeon, traveling as a Grecian archaeologist! No matter; now I will tell you who I am, into what strange circumstances I am fallen, and how I am in possession of facts which it surprises you that I know. I am my father's only daughter. My home is in London. My father's marriage was, and has always remained, secret. Even his most intimate friend has never learned that my father has a daughter.' She stopped abruptly, and swiftly withdrew to a distance, adding in a louder, and more conventional tone;—'feeling really very much better and possibly may be able to see you.'

"Her quick ear had detected a sound which had quite escaped me; for as I looked up in astonishment, I saw standing at the opening fold of the door my patient of the evening before.

"Without the least embarrassment, Miss Holmes exclaimed, 'Speak of angels! I was just saying to Dr. Vanderpool that I hoped you might be able to meet him. Dr. Vanderpool, let me present you to my father.'

"He stood there tall and erect, his iron gray hair tossed back, a brier-wood pipe in his hand, regarding me through half-closed eyes and a halo of fragrant smoke.

"'I am glad of this opportunity of adding my thanks to these of my daughter,' he said, courteously extending his hand.

"Never had I felt such sense of power as the impress of his hand left upon me. As his slender fingers closed upon mine, and began slowly to contract, it seemed as if bone and cartilage must give way. Yet they instantly relaxed without giving the slightest pain. It was a hint of a fearful possibility. 'If that is his grip when he is sick, I don't care to try it when he is well,' I thought.

"In the presence of the father a sudden reserve came over the daughter. She seated herself at a distance and bent her head over some sort of needle work.

"'My daughter informs me,' continued Mr. Holmes, 'that she appealed to you yesterday in an impulsive manner, and she fears that you may have thought her rude. I see that she has summoned you again. For myself, this is quite unnecessary, and yet I am glad that you have come, for I am afraid that Elsie is over-doing on my account. Possibly she will take advice from a doctor and get some rest. We have both been under a severe strain, both mental and physical, for some days before we came on board. But I perceive,' he added, raising his hand to his head, 'that I am still in need of rest. If you can persuade Elsie to follow my example, we shall not need to detain you longer.' With these words, he bowed and disappeared behind the closing door.

"After a moment of silence, Elsie drew a long breath and exclaimed in a low voice: 'That was a narrow escape for us!'

"'What do you mean?'

"'Suppose he had heard what I was saying to you,' she answered, coming close to me again, and looking wistfully into my eyes.

"'What then?'

"'Your life would not have been worth that,' and she snapped her fingers. 'Excuse me a moment,' she added, and opening a small case, took from it a shining something, and followed her father.

"While, she was absent, I paced the room absorbed by the most perplexing thoughts. What business had I there? What right to receive the strange confidence of this strange girl? Who was I, to come between father and daughter? Then came back my first conviction. She was over-wrought, and, for the time, at least, irresponsible. At one moment I determined to go at once and forever away from this room, and to leave this mysterious couple to work out their own destiny. What affair was it of mine? But surely, to desert two invalids in need of care would be worse than unprofessional, it would be almost a crime. Did I persuade myself the more readily from a recollection of the appeal in Elsie's eyes? Did the remembrance of the pressure of her hand stiffen my professional conscience? At all events, I lingered; and as I lingered I felt a new sensation in her absence, a sensation of loneliness. While in this curious mood I found myself absently fingering the wooden case which she had left open upon the table. I put it down with a sudden sense of shame and horror. Shame at my own curiosity and meddling, and horror at the discovery that the case was one belonging to apparatus for the subcutaneous injection of morphine.

"Was this then the explanation of those dazzling eyes? Of that languid and tremulous pose? Of the strange things she had said? Or was it—

"'Not at all,' answered Miss Holmes quietly, as if I had spoken, while she took the box from my hand and replaced the hypodermic instrument, 'but Daddy really needed sleep, and now—*we shall not be interrupted!*'

"She had returned unobserved and again stood looking steadily at me, her face a little flushed and her eyes a little brighter than before. I could stand it no longer. Astonishment and indignation banished sympathy and sentiment.

"'Miss Holmes,' I answered gravely, 'as I see that you are quite capable of taking care of your father, and yourself, I will bid you good evening.'

"'Will you desert me then? O, very well, good evening Dr. Vanderpool.'

"Was she going to cry or laugh? I neither knew nor cared. Without another word or look, I passed swiftly to the door. It was locked.

"'Miss Holmes,' I cried indignantly, 'open this door at once.' She moved toward me, holding out her hand pleadingly.

"'Forgive me,' she murmured, 'but Doctor, how can I let you go until you have heard my story? You have had cruel thoughts of me, cruel and unjust. First you thought me mad, then weak and foolish, and now—heavens knows what wicked thoughts you entertain. In justice to myself I must explain. But, there—the door is open!—yet if you leave me'—With these words a great sob burst from her bosom, she sank upon the floor, and covered her face with her hands to hide the tears that came creeping out between her fingers.

"Once more my heart was moved to pity. I raised her tenderly and placed her in an easy-chair, flung myself into another, and said: 'I will not leave you.'

"'You couldn't, could you?' and she smiled through her tears.

"'No, I couldn't and I wouldn't.'

"She arose quietly and closed the door. Then, resuming her seat, she continued: 'Now listen, I am going to trust you with my life. My father is known as the greatest detective in the world. But all his supposed skill is due to me alone. On me he depends for every delicate inference. Has he ever gone into any difficult case without consulting me? After accepting a commission, does he not always go off alone for an hour or for a night on pretense of silent meditation? Does he not then return with calm assurance, and with a very sure solution? Why! Daddy never could have found out that you were a surgeon, or that you had been in Spain beyond Gibraltar. Daddy never sees! And yet how proud he is of his success and reputation! He could not live if it should become known that he depends upon a girl for his achievements. This is why he keeps me in seclusion. Who ever heard of Sherlock Holmes' daughter? I could not have spoken to you, if he had not fallen under the influence of that drug! You are the first man I have met in private since I was fifteen. Do you wonder that I seem strange? That my ways are unconventional, and direct and truthful? It is society that teaches women to lie. I have been debarred from society, therefore I tell the truth. The moment

I saw you, I was drawn toward you, I felt that here was the man who could save me from the life I loathe. My instinct rarely fails me, but to assure my judgment, I studied you, I concentrated upon you all the powers of observation and deduction with which I am cursed.'

"'With what result?' I queried.

"'With this result. I learned that you were sailing as Mr. Thomas Vanderpool, archaeologist, though actually a surgeon from New York.'

"'How did you learn that?'

"'One name is on the ship's register, the other on your luggage. Then I noticed that you have recently been a little embarrassed financially but that you have made unusual efforts to meet your liabilities, or rather those of a near friend. Your efforts have been partially successful, and during your absence the firm in which you are interested has got upon its feet again.

"'From a certain air of melancholy, I deduced a girl. Yet you are not in love. No man who is in love with one girl ever looks at another as you have looked at me. From all this I deduced that you must be bound to someone from whom you would be free. From the draft which you gave the purser, and which I observed on his desk when I paid our fare, I learned the name and address of your bankers. From them I learned of your business standing, and of the discovery of your firm, and got what clues I needed to your history. I also learned that the young woman to whom you were engaged—and who, by the way, was never worthy of you—has given you your freedom by marrying in your absence.'

"She spoke the truth, so far as I knew it, by whatever witchery or second-sight revealed. In my college days I had recklessly engaged to marry a desperate little flirt, who had accepted me, as I afterward learned, for the sake of my father's name and money. As my father's affairs had become involved her affections had cooled. We had parted with indifference on her part, with bitterness on mine.

"Yet I was bound in honor. To relieve my father's pressing

needs, I had accepted a position on the exploring staff of the Archaeological Institute at a good salary. And now our firm was again prospering, and I was free. My face showed my joy.

"Elsie looked me straight in the eyes without speaking. A radiant smile over-spread her features; she came closer to me, and laying her hand gently on mine, whispered: 'Do you still think that I am mad?'

"'You, are the most charmingly mad person in the world if you are,' I answered warmly.

"'I am not mad,' she continued. 'It is very simple. Look at this.' She held in her hand an instrument like a gold chronometer. Attached to it, however, in place of a chain, was a slender black cord. She showed me the back of it. It was concave like the receiver of a telephone.

"'This is Daddy's latest pet,' she said. 'I would not dare show it to any one else. No, don't interrupt! It is an improved Marconiphone. The older instruments are big and go off like pistols; this is small and nearly silent, and instead of dots and dashes, repeats the voice.'

"'A wireless telephone!' I exclaimed in surprise.[1]

"'Precisely:—now watch me.'

"She moved the pointer on the dial. 'That calls Gibraltar,' she said. She pressed the stem, or what would have been the stem in a watch, and placing her lips at the other side, said in her quiet tone, 'Give me 243-6. That is the central police station,' she explained.

"'Is this Sergeant Bateson? My friend Mr. Vanderpool wishes to speak with you.' Then she handed me the 'phone. Still thinking only to humor her delusion, I took the instrument.

---

[1] This is an example of imagination outpacing science. Alexander Graham Bell demonstrated the telephone in 1876. By 1900, a message could be sent using radio signals, and the next year Marconi sent a Morse-code signal across the Atlantic. There were hopes that a Marconiphone-like device like the one in the story was possible, and one was tested as early as 1907, but it would take years of research and development before it would be commercially available.

"'What shall I say to the Sergeant?' I asked with a smile.

"'Oh, anything—ask him if the anarchists have been captured yet.'

"I put my lips to the transmitter, feeling rather foolish, I confess, and said: 'Sergeant Bateson, have the anarchists been captured yet?'

"'Hold it to your ear, now, quick!' cried Elsie. I did so, and then indeed I was astounded, for I distinctly heard these words, in a gruff voice: 'Not yet, but presently, we hope.' Then came a buzzing sound, and communication was broken.

"'Did you hear anything?' Elsie asked breathlessly.

"'Yes,' I replied, 'I certainly got an answer.'

"'Very well,' said she, 'now you know how I talked with your bankers. I would call them up now, but, you see, it's about midnight in New York. Are you satisfied now?'

"'Yes, on that score,' I answered. 'Your mind is clear, and I am free at last.'

"'Then you will set me free, also?'

"'In what way?' For the second time I saw in her eyes that flash of purple fire, as she asked gently:

"'Are there, then, so many ways by which a young man can release a daughter from her father's control?'

"'You do not mean—,' I hesitated.

"'Well?'

"'That I marry you?'

"'After all, it is leap year,' she murmured, drawing close to my side.[1]

"I felt the intoxicating odor of her hair; I felt her eyes caressing mine; I felt the subtle warmth of her presence; and I am not St. Anthony.[2]

---

[1] Traditionally, women in Britain and Ireland could only propose marriage during leap years.
[2] Most likely a reference to Anthony the Great (c. 251-356), who was recognized as the first ascetic who went into the wilderness, specifically the Egyptian desert. The numerous supernatural temptations he underwent became a popular subject for artists and writers.

"My professional instinct came to my rescue. I realized that, after all, my first conclusion was correct, the terrible anxiety for her father had unhinged her reason. I must end the scene at once. I rose and said quietly, 'You have just given me my freedom. I will enjoy it for a little while.'

"'Then you refuse my love?' she demanded, springing to her feet.

"'It is too sudden,' I said.

"It was then that I saw in her eyes the red fire of anger. With one indignant sob she turned erect, then pointing to the door, exclaimed, 'Go! I neither dispute nor detain you! One day you will be sorry. You will remember Elsie Venner with tears. Well did my father name me for the heroine of the fatal snake-charm![1] I will go back to my lonely vigil by my father's side! I will return to my desolate lodgings, but never again will I lift a finger as my father's unknown, unthanked guardian angel. Go you back to your lancet and your spade,[2] and let my father catch his anarchists if he can,—and for me,—for me there are no more castles in Spain!'[3]

---

[1] She was named for the heroine in Oliver Wendell Holmes Sr.'s *Elsie Venner: A Romance of Destiny* (1861). Elsie was half-woman, half-snake after her mother was bitten by a rattlesnake while pregnant. Holmes called this one of his three "medicated novels," because the character's mental or health problem was diagnosed in the text. The novel also introduced the phrase "Boston Brahmin" to refer to the city's "harmless, inoffensive, untitled aristocracy."

[2] A lancet is a small, sharp-bladed tool used for surgery and dissection. The spade is a small-bladed tool used for digging and was a jibe at his archaeological work.

[3] The phrase, a variation of "to build castles in the air," originated in the medieval French poem *Roman de la Rose* (c. 1235). In this work of courtly literature about the acts of love, the God of Love tells the man yearning for a protected, private place to make love that:

> "Thou dreamiest thy beloved on
> Lies naked in thine arms, become
> Thy wife, and decks thy joyous home.
> And so shalt thou rejoice amain
> In building castles then in Spain,

"With these words, she uttered a terrible laugh and heedless of my relentless supplications, swiftly whirled the pointer on her golden dial, again called up the Police Station at Gibraltar, and pronounced the words, 'Granite—garnet!' Then brushing haughtily past me, as I stood distressed and bewildered, vanished down the corridor. I never saw her again.

"The next morning, before I was up, we passed an eastbound steamer, to which, as I was informed, two ladies in black had been transferred with bag and baggage. They were supposed to be mother and daughter.

"About three weeks after my return to New York, I received the following letter:

"London, Sept. 17, 1893.

"THOMAS VANDERPOOL, M. D.,
"New York, N.Y.
"Dear Sir:—

"Permit me to apologize for what under any but the most extraordinary circumstances would have been a cruel and criminal affront.

"Mr. Holmes and myself have for some months been engaged in a most interesting and at times perilous enterprise, undertaken in behalf of the young king of Spain. The life of a monarch and the integrity of an empire were at stake.

"The life of the king was threatened by anarchists. Intimations of the danger came to Mr. Holmes while he was at work

---

And find delight in joys unstable,
Built up of lies and foolish fable."

So for finding a private place with your lover, it's understandable that you'd imagine building a fortress, but why in Spain? There are several theories. Two of the most popular were that castles in the Moorish-occupied country were dazzling to French eyes. Another was that that building in a country other than your own was nearly impossible. The most likely explanation is simpler: the previous line's last word in the original *Roman de la Rose* ("compaigne") needed a word that rhymed in the next line ("Espaigne").

on another problem in London.

"In fact, the mistress of a notorious villain whose arrest Mr. Holmes had caused, used a sign while bidding goodbye to her lover, which was recognized as belonging to a group of Spanish anarchists whose headquarters are in Barcelona.

"Mr. Holmes traced them to their secret rendezvous, appeared among them in the guise of the absent prisoner, having taken care that the woman be detained in London, took part in their counsels, and learned the details of their plot. He then caused himself to be secretly enrolled among the royal bodyguard.

"At the moment when a bunch of grapes treacherously impregnated with a deadly poison was presented to the king, Mr. Holmes sprang forward with uplifted sword, swallowed the fatal fruit himself, raised the cry of 'Treason!' struck wildly at the terrified assassin and fell to the floor in pretended agony.

"Taking advantage of the uproar which immediately filled the palace, he made his way to the outskirts of the town, where I was waiting for him with the disguise in which you first observed us, and after narrowly escaping the vigilance of the enraged anarchists who were buzzing throughout lower Spain, succeeded in reaching the *Normannia*. The poison, whose effect had been delayed by our energetic movements, then did its work and but for my timely action, upheld by your kindly companionship, our labors would have had a sudden ending. Having prevented the assassination, our interest in the case was nearly over. It remained to follow and apprehend the leader of the anarchists whom Mr. Holmes had never seen, as he kept himself always in the background. We were informed that he had fled to New York which therefore became our own destination.

"Now, my dear Sir, to make a long story short, you bear a striking resemblance to this infamous and wily anarchist. Your outdoor labors in Greece have darkened your complexion to a Spanish hue; you had permitted your black hair to grow long;

and this desperate anarchist is an accomplished surgeon.

"Mr. Holmes felt sure that you were his man, but realized the difficulty of securing evidence sufficient to convict. He therefore laid a plan by which he hoped to entrap you. Knowing that the desperado of whom he was in pursuit was peculiarly susceptible to the allurements of the fairer sex, and withal a coward at heart, I was to impersonate the supposed daughter of the great detective, and, under pretense of great distress and symptoms of mental disturbance, enlist your sympathy and gain your affection and confidence.

"At the right moment I was to mention my father's name, and present him before you under circumstances which could not fail to elicit such evidences of alarm as would have been decisive against you.

"Had you manifested the least sign of fear or anxiety, you would have been arrested and conveyed to the dungeons of Madrid, where I fear you would have found more rope than justice.

"But for the second time in his life, Mr. Holmes was mistaken in his man. You were found to be not only the innocent archaeologist whom you professed to be, but also a gentleman of exceptional integrity and honor.

"'The matter of the supposed Marconiphone is easily explained. Mr. Holmes transformed an old watch case into a simple hand telephone, whose wire led to his own ear in the next apartment. Of your own history we really knew nothing other than such simple facts as Mr. Holmes deduced from certain indications needless to rehearse.

"'The real criminal has been apprehended and hanged.

"'Mr. Holmes begs you to accept with his apologies, to which I sincerely add my own, the enclosed draft on London for £1,000 as your fair share of the enormous fee which he has received from his Imperial Majesty.

"'Faithfully yours, *Watson*."

The Great Suit Case Mystery

Jacques Futrelle

Illustrated by Donnmar

Conan Doyle's reluctance to insert his creation into real-life crimes such as the Jack the Ripper case did not keep other writers from doing the same.

On Sept. 21, a suitcase containing a young woman's torso was pulled from the water near the Winthrop Yacht Club outside of Boston. Within a week, while police investigated, Hearst's Boston American tabloid splashed "The Great Suit Case Mystery" in four installments on its front page. Three weeks after Futrelle's story ran, a second suitcase was recovered containing the woman's arms and legs. The head was never found, but the rings she wore identified her as Susan Geary, a 21-year-old chorus girl.

As Futrelle's Holmes suspected, the girl died from a botched illegal abortion, and her body was cut up and dumped to protect the guilty. But at the time such matters could not be discussed in a newspaper.

The clinic's owner, called in the newspapers "Doctor" Jane Bishop, was never brought to trial; at her death in 1922, her obituary noted that she never spent a day in jail. Instead, police arrested Dr. Percy McLeod, an eminent Harvard-educated physician, who had been summoned in a last-minute attempt to save Geary's life. During his trial, several participants in the abortion tried to blame him for Geary's death, but the jury acquitted him. Only Bishop's underlings saw any jail time.

The case was so notorious that Mark Twain, interviewed in Seattle two months later, begged for a similar public outcry over Belgium's atrocities in the Congo.

Jacques Futrelle (1875-1912) was a reporter whose "Thinking Machine" stories featuring Professor Augustus S.F.X. Van Dusen was his attempt at an American rival to Holmes. The same year as "The Great Suit Case Mystery," he published in the Boston American his first Thinking Machine story, "The Problem of Cell 13." He quit newspapering the next year and wrote two novels and more than 50 Van Dusen stories. He died on the Titanic in 1912 after giving up his lifeboat seat to a woman. Sending his wife to safety, he remained on deck, last seen smoking a cigarette with John Jacob Astor IV.

"[With due apologies to Sir Arthur Conan Doyle, creator of the greatest detective in fiction]"

CHAPTER I

Sherlock Holmes sat cross-legged on his couch, like a Turk, with the folds of his familiar gown falling grotesquely about his lank figure as he smoked. The light in the room was dim and only the strong, keen face stood out clearly. Now he was enunciating a conviction, and when he spoke on such things as related to crime I was always interested. For certainly no man had been a greater student of his profession than had Holmes.

"There are only two reasons why some crimes are never solved," he was saying now. "One is the stupidity of the police, and the other is that on that rare occasion, once in a thousand years, when the brain of the criminal is equal or superior to the best brain that can be brought to bear against him. This latter rarely happens.

"It is an actual fact that the average criminal leaves a trail like a wagon road behind him," Holmes went on after a moment. "Why? Because he hasn't the mentality to cover his tracks completely; else in excitement growing out of a crime he leaves unprotected that one thing which, carefully considered, would inevitably lead to his detection. Therefore, the solution of a crime should be . . . in most cases it is . . . perfectly easy.

"Speaking generally, all crimes are committed under stress of what seems to be necessity. In dealing with crime one must always remember, too, that the mind of the criminal is abnormal always. A man whose brain is perfectly poised is never a criminal. He never faces that condition where he feels it necessary to kill another or to steal. If there ever comes a case, therefore, where an absolutely superior mind, perfectly poised, seeks to cover up a crime, it is in nearly all cases successful. These make the great mysteries."

For a time Sherlock Holmes sat silently smoking. I had heard him make similar statements before, and I had seen him time after time go over a path beaten bare by the police, and by his keen incisive reasoning and his great power of deduction and perception solve seemingly inexplicable riddles. Now I was thinking of that strange mystery of death here . . . the great Suit Case Puzzle.

Here it might be well to explain that Sherlock Holmes is now on a visit to the United States. I came over with him from London. We reached Boston on September 29, eight days after the dismembered body of a girl was found floating in a suit case near the Winthrop Yacht Club. Holmes had come here for a rest and when he rested he never read a newspaper. I had followed this tragic mystery with eagerness.

"Have you heard of the mystery here?" I asked now.

Mystery To Be Solved.

"No," he replied. "Tell me about it."

I told him what I knew from the public press, and he listened with that lack-lustre eye which means, in him, deep, concentrated thought. When I had finished the recital he paused to light his pipe; then:

"How long was the body in the water?"

"Four to six hours," I replied. "At half past five o'clock in the afternoon of September 21."

Holmes arose suddenly and paced back and forth across the room for a long time, thinking. Gradually his step grew quicker, and then I knew that that wonderful brain of his was busy. Finally, he stopped and turned on me, and there was an exultant tone in his voice:

"Watson, it looks good," he said. "It really looks worth while. Body in a suit case. Who owns it? How did it get in the water? Who is the girl? It looks good, Watson. I'm glad you called my attention to it."

Holmes rubbed his long, thin fingers together with a movement as nearly indicating enthusiasm as he ever showed. I reached over, picked up the hypodermic which lay on the table, replaced it in the case, and put the case in a drawer of the table. Holmes wouldn't need that now; for there was a mystery to be solved.

After a while Holmes slipped on his coat and went out. He returned shortly with an armful of newspapers, embracing every thing from the date of the murder. Then he read until eleven o'clock. At last he turned to me and I lay down my book.

"It's a pretty problem, Watson," he said. "Let me state the point to you briefly. Correct me if I make a mistake. A suit case, one of only five like it in the world, is found floating in the water. It is picked up. It contains the headless and limbless body of a girl. She is young. Probably beautiful. The body shows every indication of refinement. It had been in the water four to six hours; she had been dead not more than twenty-four hours. The dismemberment was the work of a skilled anatomist. No mark is left by which the body might ever be identified."

"Perhaps marks on her legs or arms which might give her identity were the cause of those limbs being removed?" I suggested.

"No," he said, somewhat shortly. "They were removed to make the disposition of the body more easy. There might have been marks on them, but it doesn't follow. The removal of the head served two purposes, one making it impossible to identify the torso; another to more easily dispose of it."

He paused, and his eyes narrowed to pin points.

"Let's see what we can get from the condition of the body," he mused. "Well cared for, well nurtured, velvety skin, pink and firm. Clearly that of a woman above the level. Wonderful skill in the dismemberment. The work of a skilled man, a man of unusual skill. Employed latest methods in removing limbs and head. We may assume, therefore, that he is now an old man, that he is a man of repute; that he was possibly of the same social level as the girl; might have known her" and his musings passed into inarticulate grunts.

"But the suit case?" I asked finally.

"I can't talk of that until I see it," he replied. "It has been positively identified by a pawnbroker and the original owner; and on the other hand by a shoemaker who says he repaired it. I dare say the shoemaker is right."

Two Men Concerned.

He sat for a long time thinking, and the mental process by which he adjusted minute details gleaned from the information at hand was almost perceptible in the workings of his keen, grave face.

"I think possibly from information now at hand," he said, "that there were two men concerned. Yes, I believe there were. One killed, the other dismembered the body and disposed of it, yes. Probably might have been a friend of the girl. Possibly a surgeon of high position dismembered the body and disposed of it. Yes, that seems to be clear," he mused.

"And then he ran away?" I suggested.

"No," said Holmes, almost sharply. "That would be the only dangerous thing he could do. He is now sitting at home probably, absolutely safe.

"Here, Watson, doesn't this appeal to you? A girl of high position errs, as others have done, seeks desperately to save her name, is mortally injured under the knife, is dying, a reputable man is sent for, a man of whose skill there is no question. She dies. So, then, to save her name, possibly because of friendship for the family, he conceives and executes the plan of disposing of the body. The actual slayer has little to do with it."

"But his high reputation?" I asked.

"Would only be preserved by his carefully disconnecting himself from the matter in every way by disposing of the body, for instance," said Holmes. "We must attribute to this man intelligence of the highest order, as well as ethics of the highest order. He committed no crime, therefore would not have made a mistake later. He made no mistake. He is bound to protect the other man through professional secrecy, then has desire to protect himself through his original desire to save the girl's name."

"You mean, then—"

"I mean that the solution of this mystery will hit high places," said Holmes. "We'll go out and do some work to-morrow, eh?"

CHAPTER II

Half a dozen times that night I was dimly aroused by the strange, weird music of Holmes' violin, his invariable stimulant to deep thought. For he didn't go to sleep; in fact, didn't go to bed. When I arose for breakfast he was sitting on the couch with closed eyes, and the bow of the violin was sweeping back and forth across the strings.

After breakfast we went to the State House, and under the magnifying glass Holmes minutely examined the suit case in which the mutilated torso had been found. Then he examined the single leather strap which had been around the suit case, and finally asked a few questions.

"What is the address of the shoemaker in Marlboro who said he did this work?" Holmes inquired.

A courteous police official told him.

"I believe Joseph Berkman, a pawnbroker, said he sold it on Tuesday before the finding of the body on Thursday?"

"Yes," said the official.

"The Marlboro man says he repaired the case on August 14 for a man who came in his place in an automobile with two ladies?" Holmes went on, reciting those things he had read.

"Yes," said the official again.

"And Berkman says at that time the suit case was in his store for sale?"

"That's right."

"Therefore," said Holmes, "if either of these is right, the other must be wrong?"

"That is apparent," said the official.

"Good day," said Holmes. "Thank you."

Then Sherlock Holmes did several things I didn't understand. For instance, he dropped into the Highway Commission's office in the Pemberton building and asked several questions about automobiles. Then he went to several advertising novelty houses, then finally had a look at the body, which was at the Harvard Medical School. I, too, examined it, being a physician and interested.

SHERLOCK HOLMES EXAMINING EXHIBITS IN SUIT CASE MYSTERY.

At the time he examined the body Holmes made no comment, but later, on the way out, he said:

Woman Of High Type.

"There's no question about it now. That woman is of the highest type. Now, Watson," and he rubbed his hands again, "we'll go solve this."

"How?" I asked, wonderingly.

"The key's in Marlboro," he said. "It is not a matter for conjecture, but what now seems to be an absolutely settled thing, that a man who puts as weird-looking a patch on a suit case as that one would know it again, and could account for every stitch in it. The man who owned the suit case would never have noticed carefully the work on the patch; neither would have the pawnbroker who bought it beyond seeing it was solid. But the man who put it there put his individuality into it; he would know his work again. Therefore, we must assure ourselves that he does know it."

Two hours later we were in Marlboro and in the little shop of the cobbler who had identified the suit case as one he had repaired. He reiterated his statement to us.

"Would you swear that was your work?" Holmes asked.

"I would," replied the cobbler.

"Have you the piece of leather from which you cut the patch?"

"Here it is," and the shoemaker produced a piece. "And here is the piece from which I made the handle loops," he added, as he produced another piece.

Then with the aid of a photograph he went over the patch stitch by stitch. Holmes was finally satisfied, and there was a look of triumph in his eyes when he turned on me. It was a look which said:

"We have solved the mystery."

Then Holmes made inquiries as to the appearance of the man and two women in the automobile. The cobbler remembered nothing of the women; the man was five feet two, weighed 170 pounds, perhaps, had a sandy moustache and small black eyes.

"Would you swear that this piece of leather is that from which you cut the patch?" asked Holmes.

"Yes," said the shoemaker, emphatically. "It was the only piece I had which would do for that, and I remember having cut it. I have bought no leather since at all."

In Dark Green Auto.

"And the automobile? What did it look like?"

"I only noticed that it was a small touring car shape, had no top and the body seemed to be of dark green. I couldn't see any more of it from my shop where I sat."

"This man said he was a Winthrop physician, had been in Worcester over Sunday, and was returning home?" asked Holmes. These were the reported statements of the cobbler in the press.

"Yes," said the cobbler. "That's what he did say, and nothing else."

We passed on. Five other persons in Marlboro confirmed the story of the automobile stopping at the cobbler shop, two saw the cobbler repairing the suit case, but did not notice it closely. One remembered that the automobile had yellow running gear, three that it had a dark green body.

"Now for the road," said Holmes.

We drove from Marlboro to Worcester, sixteen miles, in an open buggy, stopping at every house. Finally we found a girl who remembered the automobile; she had given a glass of water to one of the ladies.

"What did she look like?" asked Holmes.

"They wore masks," said the girl. "I couldn't see her face."

"And the man?"

She gave precisely the same description of him as the cobbler had given.

"And did you see a suit case?" Holmes asked, almost eagerly.

"Yes," said the girl. "It had the handle off. The man said he would stop somewhere and have it repaired."

"What was the color of the automobile?" Holmes went on, and now a strange note of triumph was in his voice.

"Dark green body, I think, and yellow wheels," said the girl.

From that point we drove rapidly to Worcester.

"I've got it, Watson. I've got it. I've got it," Holmes repeated several times to me. "It's a gasolene machine, ten horsepower, and if I only had the number we would have our man—at least the suit case owner."

In Worcester we made a tour of the garages of which there were five. Four times the books failed to show the automobile. In the fifth we got what we wanted.

"Sure I remember that car," said an employee. "A man and two women. The car stayed here over night, and I put five gallons of gasolene aboard."

Examined Suit Cases.

"Was there a suit case?" asked Holmes.

"Yes," said the automobile man. "The handle was off it."

Sherlock Holmes gripped my shoulder fiercely and the thin fingers sank deep into my flesh. I knew that grip; it meant victory.

"Do you happen to remember the number of that automobile?" he asked, and his voice was like dripping honey.

"Sure," said the automobile man. He consulted his ledger. "It was number ten thousand and blankety blank."[1]

Holmes looked at him a long time, then turned to me with an indrawn breath.

"Let's go to Boston, Watson," he said.

On the train he explained to me: "If there is one thing I don't know much about it is leather. I'll get a leather expert to examine this piece and compare it with the patch. If it is the same . . . well, we'll have the owner of the suit case just as soon as we can find the number at the Highway Commission."

Exultantly we sought out a leather expert, and he accompanied us to the State House. There again the suit case was brought out. The leather man looked from the leather Holmes had to the patch, then dampened the patch and examined it more closely. Finally he straightened up.

"Not the same at all," he said. "It's a difference like black and white."

Sherlock Holmes leaned forward suddenly and gripped the expert's shoulder.

"Not the same?" he gasped.

"No," said the expert. "One is grain leather; the other a

---

[1] Numbers omitted so that no one with that license plate would be accused inadvertently of murder.

sole leather split."[1]

Holmes looked at him amazed for a moment, then burst out laughing suddenly, as the fable he had constructed tumbled down. He laughed heartily for a moment.

"That was the time I was mistaken," he said to me. "Every man can be mistaken sometimes, even the cobbler out in Marlboro."

CHAPTER III

Next morning Sherlock Holmes was still amused at the wholly unexpected and somewhat startling elimination of the Marlboro cobbler's clue to the great suit case mystery. Over our breakfast he chuckled in dry appreciation of his own mistake.

"Whatever else comes up, the Marlboro end of the mystery is disposed of for all time," he said, as he lighted a cigarette. "Can you imagine the astonishment of the man who owned the suit case which was repaired in Marlboro if he should happen to learn how we ran down his automobile and how closely we followed his movements?"

"It would have been embarrassing for him," I said.

"Not necessarily," said Holmes. "His clearest alibi now is possession of the suit case which the cobbler repaired. If he had that, it couldn't have been found in the water. If he has disposed of it, it might be embarrassing, but can mean nothing. And right here is a little lesson in circumstantial evidence. For instance, a man has one of only five suit cases which are exactly alike; he has repairs made to it in the identical manner in which the suit case containing the torso was repaired; he is a doctor. Everything pointed to him, but that bit of leather, which eliminated him entirely. But suppose that leather had been the same?"

Sherlock Holmes finished his cigarette, then suddenly arose.

---

[1] Grain leather that has not been sanded or buffed to remove imperfections, resulting in a high-quality, durable leather. Split leather is created when the top-grain of the rawhide has been removed. The interior layers can be split to create suede, patent, and split-sole leather.

SHERLOCK HOLMES FINDS SUIT CASE CLUE.

"Now we'll go to work in earnest," he said.

Together we went out, and he directed our steps again toward an advertising novelty company which has offices in Franklin street, one of the places he had visited the day previously. I followed wonderingly.

"I am thinking of having some stickers made, about the size of a dollar, similar to the ones you showed me yesterday," Holmes said to a clerk. "Have you some samples?"

The clerk produced a score or more printed with chewing gum advertisements, in blank forms, with corn cures, with special brands of tobacco.

"I think this is the size I want," said Holmes, and he picked up one. Then he took from his pocket the outline of a sticker, round with raw edges, and compared this rough outline with the sample. "Yes, that's it," he said. "I should like to have a sample of all the stickers of this exact size that you have, those that are printed, I mean. I want to get a general idea of coloring and lettering."

He Smiled Enigmatically.

The clerk gave him thirty or more, and we went out with a last word from Holmes that he would decide in a couple of days. I was puzzled. I had seen Holmes do strange things before, but by the wildest stretch of imagination I could not connect the stickers he had with the case in hand.

"What are they for?" I asked finally.

Holmes smiled enigmatically, hailed a cab, and we were driven to Rowe's wharf. There we took a ferry to East Boston, thence went by the Narrow Gauge railroad to Winthrop. As we left the train there Holmes approached the station agent.

"Could you direct us to the Winthrop Yacht Club, please?" he asked.

"Shirley street, to your right," said the agent.

Holmes started away, then turned back as if by reason of an afterthought.

"Oh, by the way," he asked, "do you happen ever to have noticed a sticker like that on any baggage you have handled?"

The station agent looked thoughtfully at the circular bit of paper which Holmes produced.

"I believe I have," he said finally. "The other man here handles most of the baggage, however. He might remember."

"The express or baggage men don't use them, do they?" asked Holmes.

"Oh, no," said the agent.

"I was trying to find out if this method of labeling baggage is in general use," Holmes went on, easily. "It's really an excellent scheme. I'll see the other man after a while."

We passed on toward the Winthrop Yacht Club, Holmes intently studying the topography of the place as we went. By courtesy of an attendant of the club we were permitted to go out on the pier and from there Holmes scanned the waters, on past the narrow gauge road, past Washington street where the water was pouring through the sluiceway, and then out to sea.

"That's where the suit case was picked up," said the attendant, with a certain note of pride in his voice.

Holmes merely glanced at the spot indicated, remarked: "Beautiful view," and we went on again. From there we walked on down toward Shirley Point, pausing by the water's edge, once fifty feet below the club house, while Holmes threw an empty cigar box into the water, and we walked on. Half an hour later we returned. The cigar box had drifted along the edge of the water a hundred feet toward Shirley Point. Holmes noted it.

"Good," he exclaimed. "Now let's take a little trip on Lewis Lake."

We're Making Progress.

A boatman rowed us aimlessly about the edges of the lake, which is only a lake at high tide, then we started back toward the station.

"Land us at the sluiceway there," Holmes directed.

"Can't," said the boatman, tersely. "Tide's been going out for an hour and the suction would drag the boat so I couldn't land."

"Excellent," said Holmes, enigmatically. "Oh, by the way," he asked casually, "do you happen to know if there's a grating in the sluiceway?"

"I believe there was once," said the boatman, "but isn't there now, or if it is it has large holes in it. See here!"

He flung a small block of wood into the turmoil of the water at the sluiceway entrance. We crossed Washington street, and a moment later the block of wood was bobbling outside as it sped rapidly toward the trestle of the Narrow Gauge railroad.

"Beautiful!" exclaimed Holmes, as he rubbed his thin

hands delightedly. "We're making progress, Watson. We're making progress."

Then Holmes left me for a little while to cool my heels on the station platform while he talked to a baggageman who had appeared at the station: "that other man" referred to by the station agent, I presumed. Just what was said at that interview I didn't know then, but Holmes came out rubbing his thin hands briskly.

"Now, for Boston, Watson," he said cheerily.

We boarded a train at Rowe's Wharf then took an Elevated train to the Pleasant street station. There for an hour Holmes talked with various pawnbrokers. He confirmed Joseph Berkman's story of the sale of the suit case, and asked one question:[1]

"Did you see a sticker like this," and he showed the sticker which he had showed to the station master, "on the suit case? Or was there one like it when you sold it?"

"No," said Berkman. "There was nothing on it. I never use stickers of any kind."

"Good day," said Holmes, and we returned to our rooms.

"Well, what have you made of it?" I asked.

"I don't know yet," he replied. "Let me think."

He reached for his violin and I went to a matinee.

CHAPTER IV

When I returned to our rooms after the matinee, Sherlock Holmes was pacing back and forth savagely. He glared at me as I entered, and flung himself in a chair.

"How did you like 'The College Widow?'" he asked.[2]

---

[1] This is the actual name of the pawnshop owner, and his testimony reported in newspapers, about selling the suit case identified by a patch made to reinforce the handle was the first substantial clue in the case.

[2] A popular play from 1904 by playwright George Ade (1866-1944). The college widow was a woman who had a reputation for seducing willing students. Ade's play was filmed twice and parodied in the Marx Brothers' college comedy *Horse Feathers*.

"It's excellent," I replied. Then wonderingly: "But how did you know I'd been there?"

"Oh, never mind," he said shortly. "Say, can you conceive of any man who is fool enough to write his name and address on a suit case, then put the body of a woman in it and throw it in the water?"

"I certainly cannot," I replied. I was astounded. "What—"

"I don't know what, that's the matter," he responded sharply. "It is perfectly inconceivable—"

He stopped talking, sat thoughtful for a moment and went out.

I dined alone. At 8:30 Holmes had not returned, and went out to a vaudeville. At 11:30 he still had not appeared, and I went to bed. It was half-past 2 when I was aroused by the weird music of Holmes' violin. I turned over and the bed creaked.

"I know why now," Holmes called, and there was a note of exultation in his voice.

"Why what?" I asked, as I arose, pulled on a dressing gown and went into his room.

"Why a man wrote a name and address on a suit case, then put a woman's body in it and threw it into the water," he replied.

"Why?" I asked.

"It wasn't his own name and address," said Holmes. "Sit down a little while."

I sat down and looked at Holmes curiously. His thin face was white, almost haggard, and his keen eyes, in the dim light, appeared merely as two dark spots. His slim white hands caressed the violin, which he had ceased playing, and he spoke shortly. He was tired, exhausted by a mental effort.

"You've heard me say a hundred times, Watson," he said after a while, "that when you remove the impossible, whatever remains, however improbable, must be true?"[1]

---

[1] From *The Sign of the Four*: "When you have eliminated the impossible, whatever remains, however improbable, must be the truth."

"Yes," I replied.

"Well, here," he said, "you know I have said there were two men mixed up in this suit case mystery, one a physician whose practices are wholly illegal, and the other a surgeon of high reputation and social standing."

I remembered.

"Well, the physician, not the surgeon, is more of a fool than I thought he was. With all the care that the surgeon, who is guiltless absolutely of any crime in the matter, has shown in covering up his tracks so as to effectually protect his own name from a disgusting crime, the physician, the fool of low mentality, has laid it all bare. Now it only takes patience—but lots of it," he added, wearily.

I looked at him for a moment, amazed.

"I don't quite follow you," I said.

Holmes smiled, one of those smiles which by its very superiority had in the past aroused a feeling of resentment in me.

"Not quite following me seems to be a weakness of yours," said Holmes. "Let me make it clear: A physician made a mistake in the original operation and sent for this surgeon of high reputation to try to save the girl, possibly at the girl's request. The girl dies. The body is cut to pieces by the surgeon to dispose of the matter for all time, thus saving his name and that of the girl."

"You've said that before," I remarked.

"Yes," he went on, unheeding. "There is no question of that. Now the body was disposed of but before it was disposed of the physician, low of mind and foolishly cunning, wrote the name or initials of the surgeon of repute on a round sticker and pasted it on the suit case, the cover, left-hand upper corner."

"But how does that appear?" I asked.

"There was such a sticker on the suit case when it went into the water," Holmes declared. "A casual examination of the suit case showed the print of it—saw teeth and all. An examination under the glass showed it had only been recently removed, and it was removed clearly, not scraped off with a knife, but by long immersion in the water."

"Yes," I said. "Go on." I was beginning to understand.

"Now the man who originally owned the suit case tells me he never saw a sticker on it of any kind. The pawnbroker declares there was no sticker on it; he never uses them. Yet there was a sticker on the suit case when it went into the water. How did it get there? Obviously it must have been put there between the time it was brought up on Tuesday, and the time it went into the water on Thursday."

"That's perfectly clear," I said.

"Now no man is quite fool enough to put his own name or initials on a thing like that," Holmes went on, speaking with the positive tone of certain knowledge. "But a man who is silly enough to try to be cunning—the operating physician, for instance—is just about fool enough to put the name and initials of the surgeon on a sticker, paste that on the suit case and throw it overboard."

"To incriminate the surgeon in case the suit case should be found?" I put in eagerly.

Disposed Of At Night.

"Precisely," said Holmes. "This particular fool, however, forgot that water would take the sticker off. Therefore, when the sticker was lost, the name of a decent, respectable and reputable surgeon was saved from connection with the case. I'm glad it was lost."

Sherlock Holmes settled back on the couch and lighted his cigarette. I looked at him admiringly. This part of the mystery he had made clear by that startling gift of logic which he possessed. I reviewed it all as he stated it, and found no flaws, if the original estimate of the physician who first operated was correct.

"But how was the suit case thrown into the water at midday?" I asked, curiously.

"It wasn't thrown into the water at all," said Holmes.

"What?" I exclaimed. "How did it get there?"

"We will remove," said Holmes, "all consideration of the suit case having been thrown into the water from a train, boat, ferry, bridge, or otherwise. It was in the water when found, yes. But the man who conceived this thing would not have thrown the case into the water at mid-day while thousands might have seen."

"How can you reconcile the facts that experts agree the body was in the water only four to six hours, and it was found at 5:30 in the afternoon?" I asked. "That of necessity would have made the time of throwing it into the water about mid-day."

"Quite right," said Holmes. "The body was in the water only four or six, or possibly, probably eight hours altogether, in the water twice. The suit case, with the sticker attached, was thrown on the mud flats of Lewis Lake on the night preceding the finding at low tide. The surgeon whose mind planned it all reasoned that with the lungs left in the body it would float and be taken out by the tide, which was high about 4 o'clock on the morning of that day.

"Now this tide failed to remove the suit case," he went on, "and it was deposited somewhere in the marshes of Lewis Lake. The next tide, in the afternoon, which was higher, floated the suit case. It was caught in the swirl of the tide going out of the sluiceway, carried through and left near the yacht clubhouse."

"I see now," I put in eagerly. "And the cigar box you threw overboard—"

"Was to determine what direction anything would float there at one hour after high tide," said Holmes. "It demonstrated that the wind on that day of the finding of the body was not sufficient to have blown that suit case anywhere, because it was mostly under water. Therefore, it must have come from Lewis Lake. Coming from Lewis Lake, it must have been placed there, and the total time it was in the water was not more than eight hours."

"Do you think the scene of the murder was near Lewis Lake?" I asked.

"Yes, very near it," said Holmes.

"And I suppose you now know the name of the man who killed the girl?" I asked.

"I do know his name," said Holmes, quietly.

CHAPTER V

Sherlock Holmes leaned back on the couch, smiling genially, and locked his long fingers about his knees as he smoked. He was enjoying my amazement; and indeed it must have been something to afford him keen enjoyment at that particular moment.

"You know the name of the man who killed that girl?" I gasped. I couldn't quite believe that I had heard right.

"I do," he responded.

"Then get up from there and tell the police," I exclaimed. "Have him arrested immediately."

"He can't be arrested yet," said Holmes, with maddening calm.

"Why not?" I demanded. "Surely for a crime like that—"

"I don't know where he is," Holmes explained. He was smiling.

"Oh," I exclaimed. That hadn't occurred to me. "What's his name?"

"You are impatient, Watson," he said as he stretched his long legs and gaped slightly. "I haven't been to sleep for hours. I think I'll go to bed."

He slept until nearly noon and I waited impatiently for his next move. Just as he had reached that point where the pall of mystery which had veiled this tragic riddle was to be swept aside he had become strangely inactive. He lingered in the bath while I nervously turned the sheets of the newspapers, seeking that one thing which was not there, light on the puzzle. Then he dawdled over his breakfast, and, that over, he reached for his violin. I could contain myself no longer.

"Aren't you going to do anything else?" I demanded.

"Yes, after awhile," he said. "I thought we might go out and find the missing head, limbs—perhaps," and he smiled.

"Do you know where they are?" I asked anxiously.

"If I did I wouldn't go looking for them," said Holmes. "However, I have a few ideas."

It was fully 3 o'clock when I finally roused Holmes to action. Then he threw off the dressing gown and was preparing to go out when a step sounded in the hall, outside the door.

"It's a telegram for me," said Holmes, and he showed for the first time since rising a glint of animation.

Went To Rowe's Wharf.

I opened the door in answer to a knock, and a telegraph boy was there. He handed me an envelope.

"T'is for youse?" he asked.

The telegram was directed to Holmes. I passed it to him and signed the book. Holmes' lassitude disappeared in a flash; he was ready for work now.

"Good, good," he muttered several times.

We went out together and he led me straight to Atlantic avenue. We threaded our way from wharf to wharf there, through bustling crowds of hurrying work men. Finally we found the wharf Holmes was seeking. A big steamer was just tying up. We waited until the crowd had passed on its way.

"If you will wait for me here, Watson," said Holmes, "I should consider it a favor. I want to ask this purser a few questions; and he might not care to talk if two were present."

"Certainly," I responded, but I was chagrined.

Holmes was gone only half an hour or so, then we went to Rowe's Wharf. It was Winthrop again, I thought. But it wasn't. Instead Holmes left the train, me following, and together we went to the Saratoga street bridge.

"You know the police say the two suit cases with the body of the girl were thrown into the water here," Holmes remarked.

For half an hour we lingered there, looking from all sides

into the water. It was not a search for a second suit case—it was merely a general observation. Once, Holmes grew interested in a tiny spot he found and inspected it under his glass, but he arose disappointed.

From there we went on to Winthrop, alighting at the Winthrop Beach Station and went straight across to the beach on the ocean side. Holmes glanced around; there were a few persons in sight and none of these seemed to interest him. Still, this wasn't a search; I kicked over a half a dozen bundles of paper which had been washed up on the beach. They meant nothing except that a great many people at Winthrop eat short lobsters.[1]

Finally we sat down on the sand and Holmes lighted a cigarette and leaned back comfortably.

"Well," I asked. "Is this all?"

"I'm waiting for some one," he said.

There was a pause and he lazily watched the waves as they lapped at his feet.

"You know, Watson," he said finally, "there is good reason to believe that the head and limbs will never be found. While I have nothing which shows me clearly on this point, it seems the most natural thing to suppose that if they were thrown into the water they were thrown on this side—at night—and were swept out on the early morning tide."

Might Have Been Seen.

"Why on this side?" I asked, curiously.

"Well, if we admit that the suit case with the torso was put on the marshes of Lewis Lake, as appears logical to me at least," he said, "that seems a good reason why the second suit case, which might have contained the limbs, was not thrown there."

"I don't see—" I began.

"The mere act of taking one large bundle out on the

---

[1] Short meaning young lobsters. Catching them is illegal because it reduces the number of harvestable adult lobsters. When sold by street vendors and eateries, they would be served in newspapers.

marsh and leaving it would not attract particular attention from any one who happened to see," Holmes went on. "Lewis Lake marshes are a general dumping ground for Winthrop. Hundreds of persons throw bundles there—mostly short lobster shells," he said with a smile. "But the fact that a man took two bundles on the marsh and left them would attract attention, particularly when each bundle was very heavy."

"But at night?"

"There is a chance that some one would be near enough to see if a man tried to lose a bundle in the desert of Sahara," said Holmes. "It's a greater chance that he would be noticed if he left two. It would be part of the general scheme of the man who planned the disposition of the body not to attract attention. Therefore he may have thrown the second suit case or a sack with the limbs into the water on this side, and it is now far out to sea. The lungs floated the torso; this second bundle would have sunk, lacking that buoyancy."

"The head would have been heavy, yes," I remarked.

"Frankly I don't believe the head was thrown into the water at all," Holmes went on. 'I think, if the surgeon was of that high intellectuality which his every act indicated, that the head was destroyed in quicklime. That would have left no trace—save perhaps the teeth."[1]

The horror of the thought appalled me; yet the plausibility of it struck me forcibly. The head would be a certain means of identification if found; therefore it would naturally be destroyed by quicklime, where it would have been a difficult matter to dispose of the entire body that way.

After a while as we lay on the sand I noticed a man com-

---

[1] Quicklime is made from calcium oxide, a chemical compound that, when combined with water, creates heat. It was used to light theatres (where it was called limelight) before the invention of electrical lighting. However, it does not have the effect Holmes saw on the body. In his book *The Body Farm*, forensic anthropologist Dr. Bill Bass stated that "lime does reduce the odor of decomposition, but it also reduces the *rate* of decomposition. As a result, a lime-covered body may be less likely to get sniffed out, but it's more likely to linger."

ing along the beach toward us. He made as if to pass, but stopped when Holmes spoke.

"Did you find it?"

"Sure," said the stranger. "That's the place," and he jerked his head vaguely toward several cottages which stood a few blocks away.

"Ah," said Holmes. "I thought so. And the stickers?"

"Nothing doing," said the stranger.

"Thank you," said Holmes, and he handed out a bank note. "Second or third?"

"Third," replied the stranger enigmatically, and he passed on.

Holmes arose after a while, and I followed him as he strolled on along the beach.

"See that house there?" he asked finally, as he indicated with a nod of his head.

"Yes," I replied. "What about it?"

"That's where the girl was killed," he said.

CHAPTER VI

We strolled on along the beach, finally taking a train home. I had been informed by Holmes that he would that night return to Winthrop for a search of the house, which he assured me was vacant. Therefore, it was with a vast deal of impatience that I waited his pleasure.

It must have been 11 o'clock that night when we started. Winthrop was sleeping soundly when we arrived. We walked along for several blocks without encountering any one, and at last came to the house.

"Back door," said Holmes, and he went around.

The door was not locked, the house being vacant, and we entered without difficulty. It was pitch dark. Holmes lighted our way with a small electric flash tube,[1] which he carried.

---

[1] Actually a flashlight, invented by Conrad Hubert (1855-1928), a Russian inventor and businessman who changed his name from Akiba Horowitz after arriving in America. He founded the American Electrical Novelty and Manufacturing Co. and sold a flashlight promoted as "Ever Ready." In

Immediately, without examination of the lower floor, he proceeded to the second.

Then began one of those long, exhaustive, almost weirdly interesting searches which are part of the wonderful deductive system which Holmes employs in his work. It began in a closet upstairs. With the tiny bulb of light, Holmes went over every inch of paper, walls and flooring in the closet; he picked up several bits of paper, examined them minutely under his magnifying glass and then allowed them to flutter to the floor. With his glass, too, he went over the walls of the closet to the most remote corner.

"Anything?" I asked when he came out.

He shook his head and then began the same minute search of the room where we stood. First, the walls were gone over as high as he could reach, and around and around he went. Then the baseboards, then the flooring. There were innumerable scraps of paper and thick dust. But on his hands and knees, Holmes went over it all.

For half an hour he worked away without a word, and the scene became almost ghostly to me—nothing visible but the small round spot of light in the intense darkness, and occasionally a glimpse of Holmes' keen, hound-like face, with eyes drawn to a pinpoint, thin lips firmly set. When he concluded, he arose from the floor and shook his head; not one thing in that room had escaped his notice.

Another room was gone over in the same thorough manner and a third, completing the upstairs of the house. Every tiny thing, even to the smallest pieces of paper, were fully inspected. Finally, Holmes passed into the halls and down the stairs. For more than an hour, he hadn't uttered a word. As he concluded the examination of the last step of the stairs he turned to me.

"He's a clever man, Watson," he said almost admiringly.

1905, Hubert renamed his company American Ever Ready. Eventually, the Ever Ready name was applied to his batteries, now called Eveready, and the company is now called Energizer Holdings Inc.

"Clever, clever!"

Traces Of Quicklime.

Downstairs he began the same careful search.

"There is to my mind little chance of the actual crime having been committed downstairs," Holmes said as he began his work. "The window, you know. It is possible that any one might see in, or a chance caller might have heard or seen something."

"The house was occupied, then, at the time of the crime?" I asked.

"Surely," he said.

There were five rooms and a bath on the lower floor. The hall was soon finished. The parlor, the living room, the dining room and then another room which formed a part of the main part of the house were gone over. Then Holmes went to the bathroom. There was a thick layer of dust in the porcelain tub.

Where the search had been minute in the other rooms it was positively atomical here. Inch by inch, Holmes went over the floor, on his hands and knees, and over the walls in the same way. Then he turned to the porcelain tub. Around the water pipe he found a tiny sediment, scraped it up carefully, and examined it under his glass.

"Is it blood?" I asked.

"No," he replied, "not a trace, so far as I find."

He carefully went around the upper edges of the tub. Finally, he stopped with a little stifled exclamation, which I knew meant something. He subjected this to close scrutiny under his powerful glass, then took out a small microscope from his pocket and looked at it. The—whatever it was—on the knife was so tiny I could barely see it.

"It's quicklime," said Holmes finally. "A bare atom."

"Then the head was destroyed?" I gasped.

"Not necessarily," he said. "There is a chance that it was used as a disinfectant, or formed part of a disinfectant. It frequently is. However, it may mean something."

We went into the kitchen. First, the floors and walls were

gone over as in the other rooms, and then Holmes turned his attention to the range, which had been used for both coal and wood. Half buried in the ashes I saw two cigar stumps, thrown there since there had last been a fire in the stove, and a great deal of dust and ashes, but nothing else. That is, I could see nothing else.

Holmes removed these ashes in little handsful and they went under the glass. He straightened up with what seemed to be the butt of a cigarette in his hand. He looked at it eagerly under the glass, smelled it, then looked at it again.

"I've got it, Watson," he exclaimed, exultingly. "I've got it. And this, too." He held in his hand only the cigarette butt and a tiny piece of paper, torn, but I noticed it had saw edges.

Owner's Initials On It.

"What is it?" I asked wonderingly. "I don't see anything but a cigarette butt and a piece of paper."

"The cigarette butt has the initials of the owner on it," Holmes exclaimed. "It's a Turkish cigarette, very fine, of a special brand. The bit of paper is part of a sticker like this," and he produced one of the stickers.

"Well, what does it all mean?" I asked.

"Let's go to Boston," he replied, shortly.

It was 6 o'clock when we left the vacant house, and very light. We caught an early train in, and Holmes sought out a policeman. I was amazed when I saw him approach the guardian of the peace, thinking he was going to tell his story.

"Can you direct me to a drug store that's open now?" he asked instead.

The policeman did so, and we passed on. Inside, Holmes made a trivial purchase, then looked over the city directory, particularly the classification of trades and professions in the back. At last he concluded this task and motioned to me. We went out together.

"Well?" I asked.

"It's solved, Watson," he said. "Every thread of it has been run to its end. It's perfectly beautiful."

"Do you know the name of the victim?" I asked.

"I do," he said.

"And the name of the physician who performed the first operation?" I went on breathlessly.

"That, too," he declared. "I told you I knew that. It's perfectly beautiful, man! The prettiest crime—I mean, of course, in its features—I have ever had anything to do with."

CHAPTER VII

Deeply underlying the outward reserve of Sherlock Holmes, there is, I am pained to say, a love of the theatric. It is a part of the man; perhaps it arises from his profession. It exists and is dominant always in the recital of a story. For this reason, Holmes would tell me nothing then of what he had discovered, or even suggest to me the names of the victim, the surgeon, and the physician who, he declared, played principal parts in the tragedy. I had to wait in patience.

After we reached home, we slept for several hours, then Holmes arose and went out. Twice around the clock I didn't see him, but when he did come back late at night, he seemed tired and there was an indefinable trace of something else in his manner.

I knew it would be useless to ask questions, therefore I said nothing as he sat for an hour or more smoking and gazing out the window. His eyes were bright with a feverish brilliancy, and twice he reached for the hypodermic and the little tube of poison. Each time after he had thrust the keen needle far into the flesh of his arm he leaned back with a sigh.

Finally, he began to talk, and as he went on his voice ran from a low, thrilling tense note to the high excited voice of a man who seeks vainly to control himself. Then, he turned the light on that strange mystery which has proven impenetrable to the keenest police intelligence of the country.

"It has been a beautiful problem, Watson," he said. "And it has proven beyond all question the truth of my previous assertion that when a man of intelligence seeks to cover a crime he can do it successfully—if he is not a criminal."

"But I thought you had solved this?" I exclaimed.

"I have, but it was through the mistake of a fool who meddled and not because of any mistake of the man whose brain conceived the plan of disposing of the body of the girl," he said, and in his tone was an implied defense of the surgeon he had so frequently mentioned. "Yes, when a brain of power turns to crime the result is always extraordinary; it is only the stupid criminals who are caught. They write their name and address, one might say, on everything they touch."

He was silent for a little while, then suddenly with a sweep of his hand he indicated one end of the room.

Play A Little Tragedy.

"There's a stage," he exclaimed. "We will play a little tragedy. It is the old story of a woman who erred, but it is a wonderful one."

Again silence for a moment, and then he went on.

"There is now living in Boston a young surgeon whom we will call Dr. X. He is a graduate of the foremost school of surgery in this country, and for four years remained in Europe studying. His social position is high, he is well-to-do; he practices his profession for sheer love of something to do.

"Three years ago, he met and fell in love with a Miss W. She was the daughter also of rich parents, but two years ago her mother died. Her social position was, if anything, higher than that of the surgeon: but apparently she loved him, that is for a time. Then there came a break between them; it was possibly due to a remark made by another man, the son of a banker.

"At any rate the surgeon, grimly swallowing his grief at the loss of her love, applied himself to his profession, with the result that he achieved a high position. And still—I have this from his own lips—he loved the girl. It was an unobtrusive love, but none the less earnest.

"After a while he knew, vaguely, that the man who had been the cause of the break was himself paying court to Miss W. He said nothing, but continued at his work. He avoided them, so he rarely met the girl. In fact he rarely met anyone except professionally, for that social life which had once seemed so attractive to him when he and Miss W. were together had lost its charm. And for a year he didn't see Miss W.

"One day six months ago, he met her, and he learned she was engaged to be married to the son of the banker. He congratulated her, yet his love for her was as great as it had ever been. Three months later, he learned that sudden financial disaster had overtaken Miss W.'s family. Still, the marriage, he thought, and there again a fortune.

"Well, there wasn't any marriage, Watson. The son of the banker, a handsome, dashing man of that type which appeals to women too often—it's a pity—practically jilted Miss W. He was looking for power and control of funds which would make him a power. And meanwhile the girl trusting him, had erred—it was not an uncommon occurrence nor did it vary from that story which is told every day in other cases.

Grief Tore Her Heart.

"With no mother, with no one to trust and in fear of her father, the girl made that other mistake in a desperate attempt to save her own honor and the name she bore. She went to Winthrop, presumably as a visitor at a house there, and honor and grief were tearing out her heart. Perhaps suicide suggested itself.

"In Winthrop on Tuesday, September 19, there came that dreamless sleep under the knife. She awoke in good condition apparently, but through a blunder of the physician—whom we will call Dr. Nemo, and who was a fool as I said of inexcusable ignorance—there was poisoning. It was to be combatted. For a few hours the physician kept the secret, fearing for his own freedom should it become known.

"Then he told the girl; told her that death was approaching

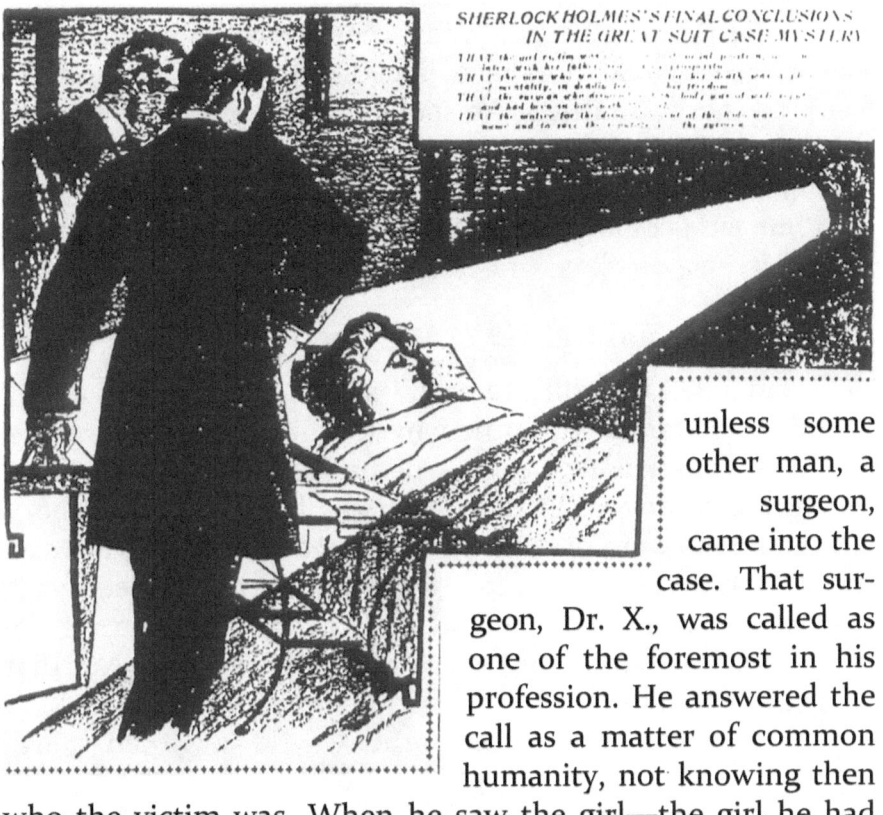

unless some other man, a surgeon, came into the case. That surgeon, Dr. X., was called as one of the foremost in his profession. He answered the call as a matter of common humanity, not knowing then who the victim was. When he saw the girl—the girl he had himself loved—there was the frenzied effort to save her. Not one thing was left undone, and if she could have been saved he would have saved her.

"Then, Watson, came one of the strange features of this strange case. Dr. X. operated; it was his knife that made that small wound on the right of the body; and a steady hand, steadied by a vision of the past, guided the knife. Of course, we know it was too late. The girl died. Two men, in the brilliant glare of their operating light, stood beside the body and wondered."

Sherlock Holmes paused, lighted another cigarette, and sat silent for a long time.

"But the dismemberment of the body?" I asked. "Why was that done?"

Holmes turned on me almost fiercely.

"Done?" he exclaimed. "Why, there were a dozen reasons. The surgeon could not have issued a death certificate. Dr. Nemo"—and he smiled as he spoke the name, a smile of derision—"could not issue one, therefore . . . " He waved his hands meaningly.

"But why couldn't a surgeon of reputation, Dr. X. for instance, issue a death certificate?" I insisted.

Saved Her Good Name.

"Had a death certificate been issued, the father and family would have wanted to know why the girl died," Holmes responded. "The law would have demanded to know why. The only thing to do was to dispose of the body. It saved, above all, the good name of the girl, even from her father; it saved the reputation of the surgeon, whose name, mentioned in the case in any connection, would have been ruin; it saved the physician, Dr. Nemo—and it saved the banker's son. Not that these last two deserved it."

"But surely there was some other way," I suggested. "Surely this—"

"Can you imagine the agony of a man of deep feeling, cutting to pieces the body of the woman he loved?" Holmes asked. "Wasn't it a strange position? Wasn't it one of the most dramatic things you have ever heard of?"

"I suppose so," I said, still unsatisfied, "but—"

"Why wasn't the body disposed of in some other way?" said Holmes. "It was impossible. There was only one way. The surgeon saw that way. He acted accordingly. Why, it was positively a great act of kindness. Some time, perhaps, that surgeon will be arrested, because of the stupidity of Dr. Nemo. But I hope that day will not come."

CHAPTER VIII

Together we sat silent for a long time. I saw Dr. X.'s motives now; it put the mystery in a different light. Punishment of Dr. Nemo meant punishment of Dr. X., therefore it was out of the question in Holmes's mind. We began to talk of the strange features of the case.

"You seemed to attach great significance to that sticker impression on the suit case," I said.

"It was through that that I solved the mystery," said Holmes. "That was the work of a fool—again Dr. Nemo. I reasoned this way: The sticker was not on the suit case when the man who sold it to Berkman had it; it was not on the suit case when Berkman sold it to—"

"To whom?" I asked quickly.

"To Dr. Nemo," said Holmes. "He's the man whom Berkman's description fits. As I was saying, that sticker was not on the suit case then. Therefore, it must have been placed on the suit case after it was purchased. It was on the case when it was thrown into the water. The water mercifully took it off."

"But you said it had the name or initials of the surgeon on it?"

"It did have. It wouldn't have been put on there for any other purpose. Dr. Nemo was not such a fool as to put his own name on it, but he was fool enough to put another man's name on it—the name of the surgeon. It was a sample of that particular brand of cunning which always opens a problem to public inspection. Mercifully the water washed the sticker off."

"But," I asked wonderingly, "how did you know from that sticker incident those things which came out later? For instance, the exact house?"

Written By Dr. Nemo.

"Readily found out. I merely asked a baggage man in Winthrop if he had ever seen baggage bearing a sticker of the size of that. He had frequently noticed it on a case of what seemed to be surgical instruments that same man carried. He had also noticed it on a trunk belonging to this same man. This man was a doctor; he remembered the name was Dr. Nemo. He told me so.

"That day when we were on the beach, he is the man who came to tell me where the house of this doctor was. He didn't know it and had to learn it. He did so and told me. Dr. Nemo moved from the house on the day of the girl's death. Then I searched the house."

"And there you found—" I began.

"The one thing which Dr. X. had left to betray himself: a cigarette butt. It had his initials on it; they are frequently that way. I applied these initials to surgeons shown by the directory. I found initials to correspond. I found the man whom I call Dr. X. He told me the story. He spoke entirely without reserve and made clear to me his motives in the matter. Since then I have verified his story as to the girl."

"But how did you happen to learn her name?" I insisted.

"Ah, that's luck!" said Holmes. "I received an anonymous letter which told me that. It bore the postmark, 'St. John, N.B.' It was written by Dr. Nemo," he added.

"For what purpose?" I was amazed.

"Because he is a fool," said Holmes. "He was frightened by the publicity which was aroused and, for some strange reason, wrote to give the name of the girl. He thought that identification might end the affair. The name was right."

Holmes talked on for an hour elucidating many points which had seemed wholly mysterious; of the disappearance of the head and limbs, which he declared would never be found; of his reasons for visiting the steamer and asking questions of the purser, which proved that Dr. Nemo had gone to St. John, and of a hundred other things.

But there were three questions in my mind—questions which hammered for an answer. These all related to the identity of the three principals in this strange tragedy. Holmes heard the questions and smiled slightly.

"It would seem no good for me to give you those names, Watson," he replied. "It's idle curiosity. Perhaps some day they may be known. I hope not."

"But will you give them to the police?" I asked.

"No," he said, finally. "I was interested in this case purely and simply as a problem. I shall sail for Liverpool tomorrow."

"And the mystery will never be solved?"

"Not publicly."

Holmes reached his slender hand for the hypodermic.

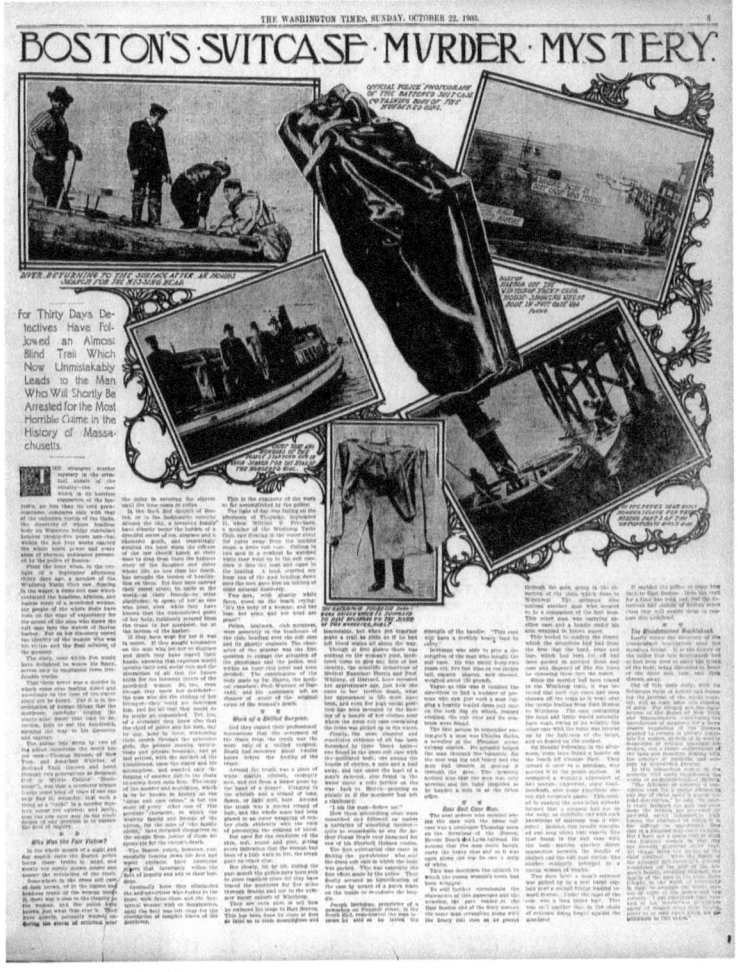

The Washington Times coverage, Oct. 22, 1905.

By a Hair

Jean Giraudoux

Translation by Kai-Ho Mah

An affair, a suspicious husband, a clue found in a strand of blonde hair: this thoroughly Parisian tale exhibits both wit and charm. Its author, Hippolyte Jean Giraudoux (1882-1944) was a novelist, dramatist, and playwright, probably most popularly known for The Madwoman of Chaillot, *which in 1969 was made into both a Broadway musical starring Angela Lansbury and a movie starring Katharine Hepburn.*

Giraudoux began his career as a journalist, and in 1908 became co-literary editor of the Paris newspaper Le Natin. *He wrote numerous short stories for the paper, including this one that appeared in Nov. 9, under the double pen name Jean Cordelier and Ch. Aivrard.*

"By a Hair" was translated by Kai-Ho Mah for the Baker Street Journal *and reprinted with their kind permission.*

I had just left the arms of Mrs. Sherlock Holmes when, as luck would have it, I happened on her husband.

"Well, good day!" said the eminent detective. "You'll have dinner with me? Haven't seen you for centuries!"

Some of my emotion showed on my face. Sherlock smiled shrewdly. "I see what's up," he said; "Monsieur is on his way to see a mistress."

If I said no, I'd seem secretive. If I said yes, I'd seem to be avoiding him. I replied, therefore, perhaps a little hastily, that the woman in question could quite well wait; that, if I didn't arrive at eight o'clock, it would be at nine; and that, moreover, if she didn't like it, I'd not go back at all.

Sherlock, by way of reply, put his hands on my shoulders, looked me in the eye and said: "Don't talk nonsense, dear fellow. I laid a trap for you. You're just coming from a rendezvous."

A shudder went through my body and came out through my hair, which stood on end. Luckily he added: "But that's enough joking. Let's go to the restaurant. Sorry we can't go to my place, but they're not expecting me. It's the maid's day off."

I thought I was saved. My friend was pondering over his soup, but I set him to musing about the case of a professional pickpocket and pimp. Suddenly, he kicked my ankle lightly.

"There's the proof." He took up the attack again. "The undeniable proof, the irrefutable proof," he explained, "that you've indeed come from a rendezvous: Your boots are only half buttoned up again.[1] Either you were caught in the act, an inadmissible hypothesis, for a woman's hand tied your necktie at leisure; or your mistress comes from a family that doesn't use a buttonhook, an English family, for example."

I affected a smile. "Every woman," I hinted, "has hairpins. A hairpin substitutes quite favourably for a buttonhook."

"Your mistress doesn't have any," he said nonchalantly. "Perhaps you don't know that certain English women have formed a league against hairpins. Besides, without going so far for an explanation, women who wear wigs don't use them. How well I know. My wife is one of them."

"Ah," I said.

Clearly, he was having a good time torturing me. Furthermore, the imbecile had seated me with my back to the window, and a draught was coming in which penetrated to my very marrow. I sneezed. In getting out my handkerchief, I pulled out and dropped a second one, edged with lace, a little bigger than a leaf and a little smaller than my hand. Sherlock put it on the table, and lost himself again in contemplation.

"It's a woman's handkerchief," he declared at last.

Then he smiled. "Simpleton," he said. "You let yourself be betrayed by a handkerchief. Since Iago and Othello, this sort of accessory belongs only in operettas. But I don't wish to be indiscreet. You'll allow me to examine it?"

---

[1] Men's shoes with buttons up the side were preferred for formal occasions. To fasten them, a buttonhook was inserted through the opening, hooked underneath the button, then drawn back, pulling the button through and closing the shoe.

"You may," I stammered like a fool. "It's clean."

I whistled under my breath to regain my composure. Then, since it was obvious that that was why I was whistling, I stopped. It was so quiet one could have heard a fly buzz, but the wretched creatures, intimidated, took care not to do so. My heart, beating full speed, roared amidst this silence like a motor. Sherlock drank a finger of claret, then a second finger, and then put down one of his own, the index, on the handkerchief.

"She's the wife of someone who is distrustful and who is shrewd," he said. "It has no initials."

In relief, I swallowed two large glasses of water. Sherlock sniffed the handkerchief and drew it delicately up to my nose. "What does it smell of?" he asked.

It smelled of "Congo" so frightfully that one could take it for squab, the gamy snipe aged for two weeks, that they served us. Indeed, it was the evening hunting season opened.

"What it smells of?" I murmured.

Fortunately, Sherlock doesn't listen to his interlocutors. He tosses out questions to which he is already formulating the answers. "To me," he reasoned, "it does not smell of anything. It is therefore a perfume to which I am accustomed—Congo, for example, my wife's perfume."

Those who have never been caught in a pile-driver or put through the rolling mill can never conceive what a vise was crushing my heart. I leaned over my plate and to find my appetite, in one of those silences which double the height of the column of air weighing down on our shoulders.

Sherlock continued to stare at me. "A hair," he said.

I leaned towards his plate. "It's not a hair," I said. "A bit of leek, no doubt."

Without answering, he got up, stretched out his hand towards me, and presented to me, between his thumb and index finger, after having plucked it from the collar of my overcoat, a golden hair, silky, pliant, in short, one of those hairs which are so becoming on the shoulder of the lover when the head of the mistress is still at one end.

"Then what's that?"

"That," I said in a tone that I wanted to seem indifferent, but which in spite of myself sounded provocative, "you said so yourself, is a hair!"

He placed it on the white tablecloth, took advantage of the opportunity afforded me by the draught and the reverie of my executioner to direct a sneeze in the direction of the hair, which rose up, undulating like a tail without, however—the blasted thing—falling off the table.

"Sneeze again," commanded Sherlock Holmes, who had obviously seen through my stratagem.

I thought it was a poor joke. "If you're so keen on my sneezing," I protested, "sneeze yourself."

He sneezed. The hair rose up, undulated—(as above).

"It's indeed a hair from a wig," he concluded. "The root clings."

The hair had fallen down again crosswise and separated us like a cadaver. It seemed to me still longer dead than living.

Sherlock emptied his glass and took hold of it as though it were a magnifying glass, the more abominable of him for doing so, despite my efforts to pour him a glass of chablis. "It's my wife's hair," he said.

I concealed my terror under the veil of amiable jesting. "Well, well," I bandied, "Madame Holmes is pretty. You flatter me."

He looked at me with an air of commiseration. "Poor friend," he said, "an Irish girl who has hung about all the pubs."

Death was better than uncertainty. I don't like to die slowly—especially in the presence of a stupid waiter who is listening to you while he serves you. I casually dismissed the intruder. "And you," I said, getting up and staring at Sherlock, "explain yourself."

That was taking the bull by the horns, but I'd have done even more.

My adversary, however, persisted in his deferential irony.

"In two words," he said. "You leave a rendezvous, you're ruffled at the sight of me; therefore it's to your interest that I not know the lady who lavishes her favours on you. Your boots are undone, therefore—you didn't re-button them. It's the day my maid goes away and leaves my wife alone. You pull out a handkerchief that belongs to my wife. I find on your shoulders a hair from her most beautiful wig. Therefore—"

I took a quick look around. Time passed in inverse ratio to the beating of my heart.

"Therefore," continued Sherlock, who was still staring at me with eyes of a boa about to swallow an ox, "therefore—draw your own conclusions."

I concluded by leaning back in my chair and caressing feverishly the grip of my revolver, an excellent twelve-shot Browning. What stupidity never to load it!

"Therefore," said Sherlock coldly, "confess it, my poor friend; I don't hold it against you. You are—the lover of my maid!"

"Waiter," I shouted. "Where the devil are you hiding? I've been calling you for an hour! Bring some champagne!"

Jean Giraudoux

Herlock's One Mistake

Henry A. Hering

This story appeared in A Souvenir, *a hardback book published by St. Paul's Church in Sketty, a village on Wales' south coast a few miles west of Swansea. In 1980, a limited edition of 27 copies was issued by Ferret Fantasy, Ltd., with some copies of* A Spectrum of Fantasy, *book collector George Locke's bibliography of science-fiction and fantasy literature from the 19th and early 20th centuries. Little is known of Henry Augustus Hering (1864-1945). He wrote short stories between 1896 and 1930 and is best known among fans of British supernatural fiction for the dozen stories in* The Burglars' Club *series.*

On turning over the notes I have kept of the many cases in which I was associated with the investigations of my late lamented friend Mr. Herlock Shomes, I am reminded that I have hitherto omitted to make public the only case in which he failed to display that marvellous deductive reasoning and quickness of perception which distinguished him, and which have, through the instrumentality of my poor pen, obtained for him a world-wide reputation. Perhaps the knowledge that in this case I was also at fault may have had something to do with my silence, but after long deliberation I have come to the conclusion that Shomes' reputation cannot possibly suffer from the recital of one single fault[1] in a career so long and extensive, and that I myself am fully able to bear any blame that may be attached to me; but that it was the cause of a display of temper towards myself, and the reason of a temporary estrangement with this remarkable man, will be for ever a source of sorrow to me.

My practice was not of the largest, even after my marriage, and on one particular morning, after making up the solitary bottle of medicine called for by my consultation hour

---

[1] The narrator apparently forgot the numerous mistakes Holmes made, beginning with underestimating Irene Adler in the first short story, "A Scandal in Bohemia."

and viewing my blank engagement slate, I told my wife not to expect me back before dinner as I was going to see Mr. Shomes.

"Better by far to attend to your practice, Jack," she said.

"Thank you, dear," I promptly replied, "my practice seems to be quite able to take care of itself;" and with this I left the house.

I found Shomes bending over a flask containing a pale green liquid which was boiling over a Bunsen burner.[1] He looked up as I entered, and an expression of annoyance crossed his face.

"You again, Spotson," he said curtly. Some men might have taken offence, but I know Shomes far too well for that.

"I again, as you say, my dear Herlock," I replied blithely. "What's your little game today? Dip the litmus[2] in, man."

Something had evidently annoyed him that morning, for he growled, "There's the sporting paper[3] over there, Spotson. For mercy's sake go to it."

I took up the paper, but had scarcely glanced at it when there was a rattle of a vehicle, which finally stopped before our door.

"Hearse . . . pair of horses . . . near one white star on forehead . . . far one had staggers[4] when a child . . . driver old

---

[1] A small device capable of burning gas from coal, methane, or petroleum for use in experiments. Designed by German chemist Robert Bunsen (1811-1899), the burner generated a hot flame with minimal brightness and no soot. The heat can be controlled with a valve that mixes the gas with air.

[2] A paper soaked with a dye derived from lichens and allowed to dry. When the paper is dipped into a liquid, it changes color showing whether the liquid is acidic or alkaline. As a result, the term "litmus test" is used outside of the lab as a metaphor for a guaranteed response to something (e.g., "the chairman wants a litmus test about who joins the party.")

[3] A newspaper that only covers sports. One popular sporting paper was *The Sporting Times*, a weekly particularly devoted to horse racing. It was known as "The Pink 'Un" for its pink newsprint.

[4] A disease found in farm animals caused by parasites or a metabolic disorder that creates an inability to stand or walk steadily.

horse-marine[1] . . . called for dipsomaniac[2] upstairs," said Shomes.

"Marvellous, marvellous!" I ejaculated, knowing it would please him. "Now, however do you know all that?"

"Simple enough," said Shomes, his face brightening up. "You can always tell a hearse by . . ."

There was a knock. The door opened, and a young man dressed in deep mourning[3] entered.

"The wrong place, sir," said Shomes. "Your grandfather died upstairs. Top landing, first door to the left."

"I beg your pardon," said the stranger with evident aston-

---

[1] The word has several meanings, some serious and some satirical. While horse marines existed in the U.S. Marine Corps in the later 19th century, the British Army had no official horse marine units, but some marine regiments were equipped with horses. In the Royal Navy, where marines were stationed aboard ships to fire on the enemy, lead raiding parties (and keep mutinous crews in line), the sailors used the term against anyone who had worse seamanship skills than the marines. In 1868, English music hall singer William Lingard's "Captin' Jinks of the Horse Marines" was a popular success about an unsuccessful soldier who sang:

The first day I went out to drill
The bugle sound made me quite ill,
At the Balance step my hat it fell,
And that wouldn't do for the Army

[2] An older term for alcoholic. It is still used today to describe someone who compulsively drinks. The word combines the Greek *dipso* for thirst, and *mania* for madness or frenzy.

[3] Mourning rites were still in place for the middle and upper classes during the Edwardian period, but moving slowly away from the heavy demands imposed during the Victorian age. For example, widows were permitted to wear dresses with black crepe trimming for the first six to eight months instead of the raven-like black crepe dresses for a year, and the heavy veiled bonnet could be dispensed for a lighter model after two months (men could get away with wearing anything black; even a black armband was acceptable). The widow was still forbidden from attending the funeral and burial, and could not receive visitors nor issue invitations for three months, and attending a ball or dance for the first year was a fatal social *faux pas*.

ishment. "Am I speaking to Mr. Herlock Shomes?"

"You are."

"I have called to see if you will assist me in a most important matter, Mr. Shomes. Are you at liberty?"

"Quite at your service," said Shomes, placing a chair for him "But why come in a hearse with two horses, near one white star on forehead, far one . . . ?"

I looked out of the window to verify his details. There was only a hansom[1] at the door. I told Shomes so, but he simply said:

"Spotson, for Heaven's sake let me go about my own business in my own way. I know perfectly well what is outside the door, and you will know even better in a minute if you won't be quiet. Excuse my friend's interruption," he continued to his visitor. "You were about to say your grandfather . . . ?"

"Not my grandfather, Mr. Shomes. It is about my uncle, or rather concerning his will that I have come."

"Proceed, sir," said Shomes, settling himself in his favourite attitude — body thrown back in the chair, eyes staring at the ceiling, legs crossed, elbows resting on the arms of the chair, and finger tips pressed one against the other.

"My name is Mortimer Banks," said the young man, "and I am a clerk in the city. My uncle, Edward Rawson, was a wealthy indigo merchant,[2] who died four weeks ago. It was an open secret, since confirmed by his will, that on his death his wealth was to be divided into five portions, one of which was bequeathed to me, and the other portions to four different persons. Each has only a life interest in the bequest so long as any of the others live. As each of the legatees dies, such interest becomes divisible in equal portions among the survivors,

---

[1] A two-wheel horse-drawn carriage that was fast and light. They were used as cabs in the cities. Name for its designer, York architect Joseph Hansom (1803-1882).

[2] A businessman who deals in the plant dye from India that ranges from deep, rich blue to violet. Indigo has been in use since 4000 B.C.E. in Peru and India.

the ultimate survivor coming into complete possession of the whole estate without reservation."

"A most interesting arrangement," said Shomes, "and one fraught with many possibilities. Go on, sir."

"The legatees were Richard Wade, a retired malster[1] living at Nailsworth in Gloucestershire; Mitchell Robinson, in business in Leicester; John Embsay, a Craven[2] farmer; a Miss Arabella Dabb, living in Leeds;[3] and myself."

Here Mr. Banks paused, and seemed to be labouring under considerable excitement.

"Proceed," said Shomes, "I am much interested."

"Well, Mr. Shomes, what do you think of this? Four weeks ago to-morrow, Wednesday, my uncle died. The following Wednesday, Richard Wade was found dead in bed, from heart disease according to the verdict of the jury. On the Wednesday after that, Mitchell Robinson committed suicide, apparently without any assignable reason. Embsay has been missing from home since last Wednesday; and according to yesterday's paper which I have here, he was found on Sunday tied up in a sack in the river Aire."[4]

Shomes leaned forward in his chair rubbing his hands together. "Go on, Mr. Banks. I am very much interested."

"That is all — so far," continued our visitor. "To-morrow is Wednesday again. It remains to be seen what will happen. Frankly I have come to you for advice, and even for your protection."

"You have done quite right, Mr. Banks," said Herlock, "and I will do the best I can for you. But before we go any further there is one little matter I should like us to be clear

---

[1] Someone who produces malt from barley used in the production of beer. *Gloucestershire* is a county in southwest England, on the border with Wales.
[2] A district in North Yorkshire about 235 miles north of London.
[3] A city in West Yorkshire.
[4] A major river in Yorkshire that passes through Leeds.

about. You have probably heard of me through the stories my friend Dr. Coyle — I mean Dr. Spotson[1] — is continually writing. In the main, they are correct, but he generally omits to mention that I expect some remuneration for my services. An idea has got afloat that I do my work for the pure love of the thing. This is not the case."

"Anything in reason I shall be prepared to pay."

"Let me see, three deaths and a possible fourth. I think a preliminary fee of twenty-five guineas should not be too much."[2]

"Certainly not;" saying which Mr. Banks pulled out a roll of notes and handed over the amount mentioned.

"Thank you," said Shomes carefully placing them in his pocket book. "Now we will proceed. The fifth legatee you say is a lady."

"Arabella Dabb, now living in Leeds, a former housekeeper of my uncle, whom at one time it seemed likely he would marry."

"Ah," said Herlock, "this is indeed interesting, and throws a glamour of romance over an otherwise commonplace tale of crime. What would the world be without the romance of love? Think how it spurs on youth to fame and fortune; how kings

---

[1] A joke referring to the belief that Conan Doyle did not write the stories, but acted as literary agent for Dr. Watson. Two years after this story appeared, Ronald Knox published "Studies in the Literature of Sherlock Holmes," one of the first papers that is part of "the game" played by fans as a way of explaining Conan Doyle's role in a world where Sherlock and Watson are real.

[2] A guinea is a coin worth one pound plus one shilling (or 21 shillings). The coin was originally made of gold from the Guinea region in West Africa hence its name. Its value fluctuated between 20 and 30 shillings until it was fixed in 1816. The coin was replaced by the pound that year, but guineas continued to circulate, and because of its aristocratic overtones (and hidden surcharge), a number of items were priced in guineas, such as professional fees, auctioned livestock and racehorses, art, bespoke tailoring and other luxuries. Twenty-five guineas (£26 and 5 shillings) would be worth in 2017 about £1,244 ($1,605).

have been content to lose their crowns for its sweet sake.[1] Even members of parliament have been known to forget the laws they helped to make at its behest."

Our visitor seemed considerably surprised at this sudden rhapsody, but I was only too well accustomed to that sort of thing happening at the most incongruous times. Shomes had sunk into a deep reverie. I went up to him and prodded him in the side. "Wake up, old man," I said. "Here's Mr. Banks waiting to tell you some more."

"Ah," said Shomes, with a start. "Sit down, Spotson. Mr. Banks, I am listening."

"I may add," continued Banks, "that during the existence of a previous will leaving all his money to his housekeeper, my uncle was once nearly poisoned by Arabella Dabb inadvertently putting arsenic in his soup instead of pepper."

"I am anxious to make the acquaintance of Miss Dabb," said Shomes. "She is, I think, the only one who will benefit by the death of the male legatees under your uncle's last will?"

"That is so. Here is the copy of the will."

"You are an extremely intelligent young man, Mr. Banks, and are making matters very easy for me. Have you the newspaper accounts of the other events?"

"No, but you can get them at any newspaper office. They appeared in the next day's issues."

"I will make a note of the dates. There. And Miss Dabb's address and your own? Thank you. Is there anything else you wish to say?"

---

[1] A poetical phrase that does not seem to be tied to any particular source. Although love is the object in several stories ("No sacrifice ever appeared to me great, that was made for its sweet sake"; *Ethel Churchill* by L.E. Landon), it has also been applied to subjects as varied as an old man adopting his grandson after his mother dies in childbirth ("Time leaves him fit for little but to take / The orphan in his arms and live for its sweet sake"; "Little Paul," by Rosa Vertner Jeffrey), and even the addiction of women's whist clubs ("in whist she lives, and moves, and has her being, and counts all things lost for its sweet sake"; "Women's Clubs," by Anna O. Goepp, *Household News*, October 1895).

"Nothing, except that it seems to me whatever you must do must be done quickly. My own life may be in peril to-morrow."

"That has occurred to me. I shall lose no time in the matter. Spotson, please look up the trains to Leeds. I hope to have an interesting interview with Miss Dabb to-day."

"Thank you, Mr. Shomes, thank you," said our visitor, warmly shaking hands. "I feel immensely relieved since I know you will take up the case. When may I expect to hear from you?"

"If you will call at this time to-morrow I shall be able to tell you something. Meanwhile one word of caution. Walk home in the middle of the road. Stay indoors till to-morrow; sleep as little as possible to-night, and it might be as well to have a watch dog in your room with you. Tip the officers on your beat, and finally be careful what you eat. Test all with litmus paper. Dr. Spotson will give you some and will tell you how to use it."

Five minutes later I showed Mr. Banks out.

On my return I found Shomes impatiently pacing the room.

"This is a great nuisance, Spotson," he said, "Banks interested me so much that I completely forgot I had important reasons for remaining in town."

"Could I not do your work at this end?"

"You might," said Shomes; and then he added ungraciously, "It's a mere matter of routine or I would not trust anyone but myself. Yes, I shall have to leave it to you as the other matter won't keep. I had better give you the facts of the case, so that you understand the importance of what I ask of you; but as long as I live it must be a secret. This is not for publication in your lifetime. I have your word?"

"Certainly, Shomes."

"A month ago I had a visit from a Foreign Office official. Our Government intends making a forward move in Egypt but does not wish to have European complications in consequence. A short time ago a secret Treaty was made between France and Russia, putting in black and white what move on our part would result in concerted action on theirs. Before our government takes an irrevocable step they wish to see what the result would be to their relations with France and Russia. I have been commissioned to get a copy of that Treaty."

I could not help showing the astonishment I felt, and Shomes resumed apologetically.

"At first I would have nothing to do with the matter, but they said Lord X. would take it as a personal favour, and it might be the means of averting a European war and so forth, and harped on the patriotic string until at last I agreed to do it. It has been a very simple matter so far as I am concerned. A half-hour's conversation on financial matters with a friend of mine, a high official in the French police, is all the trouble I have taken. The copy of the Treaty should reach me to-day[1] packed in a case of Zola's novels[2] which will be sent by a firm of French booksellers in Leicester Square. You must be here to receive it. Open the case to make sure the document is there, and wire me to the Leeds Post Office, so that I know all is well, but on no account lose sight of the document until I return. Don't leave this room. I shall not feel safe about it until I

---

[1] The word "today" was originally two words that over time was melded into one. People speaking Old English, an early form of the English language from roughly 650 to 1150, would say "to daege" to mean "on (the) day." Sometime during the 16th century, the word came to be written with the hyphen and would stay that way until the early 20th century. The same process happened with "tomorrow," which you will see written as "to-morrow" (in Old English they'd say "to morgenne" for "on (the) morrow").

[2] Emile Zola (1840-1902) was a popular French novelist and political activist. He was one of the first great naturalist writers, insisting on depicting all aspects of the lives of his characters no matter how unsavory. This included writing about a streetwalker's rise to high-class prostitute (*Nana*, 1880), and using graphically violent and sexually explicit scenes in *La Terre* (1887). As a result, most of his translated novels were banned in Great Britain, although his untranslated novels were allowed; being bilingual was presumably a defense against corruption.

have given it to the Foreign Office official who is to call at nine in the morning for it. You understand me perfectly, I hope."

"Quite so. If the document comes you may rely I shall be waiting here with it on your return."

Two minutes later Shomes had left the room to catch the mid-day train to Leeds.

With the help of a novel and a good lunch the time passed pleasantly enough. At three o'clock a small case arrived by messenger. I forced the lid open, and took out the volumes it contained. To my surprise, when I had withdrawn the last there was nothing below. A false bottom? I knocked the case apart. No, it was plain three-quarter inch wood, and there were only a few newspaper sheets of packing. Then the Treaty was not there after all! I took up the volumes. Ha! "*La Debacle. Edition de Luxe*"[1] was suspiciously light. I opened it. It was a mere case, and inside was the document so precious to our Government. I replaced it, put the case on a shelf next to the last volume of the *Strand Magazine*,[2] and placed the other volumes elsewhere. Then I scribbled a wire to Shomes couched in the enigmatical style he loved: "Frogs safe to hand. Tadpole included," and having thrown it out of the window to one of Shomes' street arabs for transmission, I resumed my book.

Barely an hour afterwards there was a knock at the door, and a stranger entered. He was irreproachably dressed in a

---

[1] A novel published in 1892 by Emile Zola about the defeat of France in the Franco-Prussian War of 1870. It is part of the Les Rougon-Macquart cycle of 20 novels about the lives of a fictional family during the Second French Empire (1852-1870). *La Terre*, mentioned in a previous footnote, is part of this cycle, although *La Debacle* is not as explicit in its content.

[2] The monthly magazine (1891-1950) that published Conan Doyle's Sherlock Holmes short stories. Named for the street where it was published, the magazine showcased work from many of Britain's great writers, including H.G. Welles, Agatha Christie, Dorothy L. Sayers, P.G. Wodehouse, and Edgar Wallace, as well as the "gentleman thief" Raffles stories by Doyle's relative Ernest William Hornung.

frock coat and striped trousers. His black tie was pinned by a large pearl, and his linen was of the whitest. He had a bunch of violets in his button-hole.

"Mr. Shomes?" said he enquiringly.

"Mr. Shomes is out at present," I replied. "My name is Spotson."

A look of great disappointment overspread his face.

"This is singularly unfortunate," he said. "I wished to see Mr. Shomes on a matter of the very highest importance. My name is Richards. I am from the Foreign Office."

"I think I know your business, Mr. Richards," I replied, "but Mr. Shomes does not expect you before to-morrow morning."

"That is so Mr. Spotson — Dr. Spotson, if I am not mistaken. We have all heard of you through your brilliant co-operation with Mr. Shomes in his work."

"I am quite content merely to be known as the chronicler of my friend's doings," I replied. "I am sorry I can be of no use to you Mr. Richards. Mr. Shomes will not be back till very late, and nothing can be done in this matter before the time arranged to-morrow."

"How very unfortunate," he replied. "To-morrow will be too late. Mr. Shomes has no doubt told you the details of the delicate matter he has at present on hand for us?"

"Yes, I know all."

"Then I need have no hesitation in saying that events in Egypt have come to a head rather sooner than we expected. This morning we received urgent wires from Cairo, and we have to send absolute and final instructions to-night in reply. A Cabinet Council has been hastily summoned for five o'clock to decide on the measures to be taken. It is of course of the highest consequence that our Ministers have full knowledge of the Franco-Russian Treaty before they come to a decision. Lord X. himself sent me here, hoping that Mr. Shomes would already be in possession of the Treaty."

"I regret to say I cannot let you have it. Mr. Shomes left

very distinct instructions on that point. He will give it you himself in the morning."

"Then I gather that you have it," said Mr. Richards with some excitement. "If so, Dr. Spotson, it would be scarcely less than criminal on your part to keep it back."

"I am not answerable to you for my actions, Mr. Richards," I replied sharply.

"Forgive me if I spoke hastily. I assure you I feel very deeply on the subject. I have just left Lord X., and if you knew the importance he attaches to the production of the Treaty you would understand my warmth. Your withholding it may cost the country thousands of lives and millions of treasure."

The man's earnestness impressed me with the gravity of the situation, and I felt the terrible responsibility that would rest with me did I act up to the letter of my instructions. Besides had not Shomes himself told me that patriotic motives and a desire to oblige Lord X. had induced him to meddle in the matter. Surely the same excuses held good for me.

I thought it over as well as I could, weighed the pros, and cons, of the situation, and finally decided it would, as Mr. Richards had said, be almost criminal on my part to let my country take a leap into the dark when I held the torch in my hand.

"Here is the document, Mr. Richards," I said at length. "I can only hope I shall have no reason to regret having given it to you."

"That you will never have, Dr. Spotson," said my visitor earnestly. "I thank you not only personally, but in the name of Lord X. and the Government."

I did not resume my novel for some time after he had gone. I had disregarded Shomes' explicit instructions, and unless he considered that events justified it I saw the end of my friendship with that truly remarkable man. However, the more I thought on the matter, the more was I convinced that I had acted as Shomes would have done under similar circumstances, and a comfortable dinner helped to restore my equanimity.

It was eleven o'clock before I was again disturbed, A hansom rattled up, and then I heard Shomes' quick footstep in the passage.

"Thank God!" he exclaimed as he saw me quietly reading before the fire, "I have had a scare to-day, Spotson, and no mistake. I was uncommonly glad to get your wire, uncommonly," and he grasped my hands.

I was surprised at this outburst on Shomes' part, for he was the most reserved and unemotional man I ever knew.

"Well, what about Miss Arabella Dabb? Have you any evidence against her? Is Banks safe for to-morrow?"

"I'm afraid Mr. Banks is very safe," said Shomes grimly, "but if I could meet him tonight he would hardly be so. It was all an infernal plant, a hoax, Spotson, to get me out of the way."

"What!" I ejaculated.

"Miss Dabb has kept a little tobacco-shop for twenty years and has never been out of Leeds in her life," continued Shomes. "She has never heard of this precious uncle of Mr. Banks; and no one else has either. The will was concocted yesterday by Mr. Banks, who dragged in the names of dead people taken from the newspapers. It was smart, very smart; I'll give Banks the credit for that. He took me in completely."

"But how could it benefit Banks?"

"Banks, Spotson! Banks stands for the French government who have got wind of this Treaty business. They found it out on Sunday, for I see from this evening's paper that my friend in the French police committed suicide yesterday morning. It was all a clever scheme on their part to get me away, so that they could search my rooms in my absence. Luckily you were here Spotson to baulk them. You've done me yeoman's service, and I beg you to forgive any little display of temper I may ever have shown at what I regarded as obtuseness on your part. I took the first train back from Leeds and have called on Lord X. on my way from King's Cross. I told him I would not be responsible for the safety of the Treaty overnight. The house may be blown up; anything may occur. The French Government will stick at nothing. A King's Messenger will be here any minute for it."

A cold shiver ran down my back at these words.

"But — but," I stammered, "Lord X. sent for it this afternoon."

Shomes bounded from his chair and stood glowering over me.

"What!" he yelled. "You did not let it go?"

"A Foreign Office man called to tell you that a special Cabinet Council had been hastily summoned for this afternoon, and that the production of the Treaty was a vital necessity. So I gave it to him from patriotic motives."

"And now Banks is on his way to Paris with it!" thundered Shomes, livid with passion. Then he absolutely lost control over himself. He flung open the door. "Out you go, you confounded bungler!" he blazed forth. "Never let me see you again. If you stay another minute I won't answer for the consequences."

I made for that door, and as I left it I distinctly felt his boot touch me. I left the house breathless and hatless. I had never seen Shomes in such a terrible rage. He was, as I have said, usually the most unemotional of men.

As I reached the street a carriage drove up, and a smart military-looking man got out. I have always been curious to know what Shomes said to that King's Messenger.

Such is a true account of Shomes' one mistake, and of the only serious hitch that occurred in my relations with him. At another time I will recount the singular train of events that led to our reconciliation, and cemented a friendship that only ended with the death of this remarkable man. For that Herlock Shomes really is dead, I am sure, is believed by all reasonable men, and I treat with scorn the suggestion that he is simply hiding from the too-pertinacious curiosity of his faithful friend and biographer.

The Adventure of the Lost Manuscripts

Edmund L. Pearson

Edmund L. Pearson (1880-1937) was a popular true-crime writer who was also a full-time librarian at the New York Public Library. He contributed essays on crime to magazines such as Vanity Fair, The New Yorker *and* Scribner's, *and published them in* Studies in Murder *(1924),* Murder at Smutty Nose and Other Murders *(1926), and* Instigation of the Devil *(1930). He also wrote about books, libraries, and librarians, and even successfully concocted a hoax pamphlet,* The Old Librarian's Almanack, *supposedly from 1773, that fooled newspapers into believing it was real.*

"The Adventure of the Lost Manuscripts" appeared in the Boston Evening Transcript *in two parts (June 28 and July 12). The introduction to part two was so entertaining that it had to be printed here. The story was reprinted by Aspen Press in 1974.*

The novel or story dealing with library work, we are told, has yet to be written. It will take a bold and resolute spirit to attempt it. One may, however, conjecture the manner in which certain writers would attack it.

The method of Sir Arthur Conan Doyle might be something like this:

THE ADVENTURE OF THE LOST MANUSCRIPTS

Part I

In early April of the year '92 Sherlock Holmes and I were sitting one afternoon in the old rooms on Baker Street. The rain was beating against the windows, and I was trying to while away the dismal hour with a light novel. Close attention to the pages was a trifle difficult, however, for Holmes had taken out his revolver and was engaged, in a manner at once nonchalant and absent-minded, in shooting the buttons off my waistcoat.

Already he had fired six shots, and only the top button remained. He then paused to reload the weapon, while I marvelled at the extraordinary marksmanship which he had displayed.

Suddenly there came a tap at the door, and Mrs. Hudson, the landlady, entered.

"A gentleman to see you, sir," she announced.

Holmes directed her to show the gentleman upstairs without delay, and then put his revolver in a table drawer.

"Let us hope it is a client, Watson," he said, "I am nearly dead of ennui. We will reserve the top button till a future occasion. Here he comes! How his feet shuffle on the stairs — his shoes are worn out; he is hard up: I think he must be —"

At this instant the bent figure of an elderly gentleman appeared in the doorway. Holmes greeted him.

"Good afternoon, sir, I am afraid you have left things at the library in considerable confusion."

The old gentleman sank into a chair and gazed in amusement at the great detective.

"This is astonishing, Mr. Holmes — how could you know that I am a librarian?"

Holmes closed his eyes and leaned back in his chair with an appearance of utter boredom.

"It is the merest child's play," he said; "on the under side of your coat sleeves are two streaks of reddish powder, such as come from nothing else in the world but an ancient book bound in sheepskin. You have a glistening patch on your right thumb, left there after affixing gummed labels to the backs of books. Moreover you wear thick spectacles, are somewhat stoop-shouldered, and have a general air of having to live on a salary about one-third as large as a white man[1] ought to get.

---

[1] Such comparisons were common for this era. Should they be eradicated because it makes us uncomfortable today? While that seems to be the trend in today's culture, I would argue against it. Reprinting racist material should never imply condoning it, and eradicating it keeps us from confronting our history and dealing with it. We read historical material in part to be entertained, but also to be educated. Retaining this material reminds us that no era is perfect, no people are perfect, and the words we create today will be judged by those who follow, and they may look back

Finally, here is your visiting card, which Mrs. Hudson, to whom you entrusted it, duly delivered into my hands. On its face I see the name of Professor Jabez Buchwirm, chief librarian of the Houndsditch Public Libraries. Putting all these facts together, trifling as they may be in themselves, and applying to them the method of deduction, I am irresistibly led to the conclusion that your profession is that of keeper of the books, or librarian. Am I right or am I wrong?"

"You are right," said Professor Buchwirm, "but I am astonished at the accuracy of your reasoning. Never have I seen anything like it. But that does not account for your correct inference that I left the library in a state of confusion. Affairs were indeed in a sad chaos. But how could you have known that? I left the library only four hours ago, having travelled hither in one of the swiftest omnibuses in London at a speed not less than two miles an hour, exclusive of stops."

"Again," said Holmes. smothering a yawn, "again, the matter is of extreme simplicity. Underneath your top coat I notice the black alpaca jacket which all librarians wear while at work. You removed your hat as you stood in the door and I observed the black silk skull cap which is the well-known badge of your profession.[1] Since you came out into the street wearing these indoor habiliments I conclude that you came away in a state of extreme agitation, and that your subordi-

---

and judge us as harshly as we might want to judge our predecessors. It is my personal and philosophical decision that, given a choice between suppression and free speech, I nearly always favor free speech.

[1] The origin of this unique clothing item has its roots in the religion of the middle ages. Medieval scholars were drawn from the clerical class, and they took with them their uniform of long gowns, which were useful in drafty and unheated buildings. They also wore hoods to cover their tonsured heads until they were replaced with the skull cap. Wearing the skull cap was retained into the early 20th century. In 1907, Pearson himself described the stereotype by asking "what is the badge by which one knows the librarian? Some will immediately answer 'a pair of spectacles, a black alpaca coat, silk skull-cap, straw cuffs and rubber heeled shoes.'" But change was coming. The profession was also becoming more female, rising rapidly in the U.S. from very few women in the 1850s to nearly 80% female by 1910.

nates were also excited or they would have told you about it. But come, Professor Buchwirm, you did not travel all the way to Baker Street to hear me discuss such minutiae. What is the cause of your agitation, and how can I help you?"

The professor passed his hand over his brow.

"I am afraid it is beyond your powers, Mr. Holmes, great as they are. Have you ever heard of the Sheraton MSS?"

"Not the private correspondence of the late Duke of Giggleswick?"

"The same. Excepting the Magna Carta[1] they are undoubtedly the most valuable documents in England."

"But surely they are in royal custody, or else in the British Museum?"

"You would think so, wouldn't you? Well, it might take too long, and incidentally bore the readers of this story too much if I should tell you how they came to be deposited in the Houndsditch Public Library, but deposited they were no later than last Saturday afternoon. And now they have disappeared."

"Disappeared?"

"Vanished utterly, Mr. Holmes. Imagine my distress! Those manuscripts are the private property of one of the most exalted personages in the realm — a person, Mr. Holmes, so exalted that I hope the printer, when he comes to put this in type, will use capital letters whenever he refers to Her. I cannot possibly mention Her name, except to hint that it begins with V, and to say that She frequently resides at Windsor."[2]

---

[1] A peace treaty signed in 1215 by King John (1166-1216) at Runnymeade that codified the legal arrangement between the king and his restive barons. Although neither side adhered to it and it had been nullified by the pope, it became an important political document, influencing how the English saw their history and how the colonists in North America created the American Constitution.

[2] The author is playing off the fact that several stories involved royal figures who couldn't be named, such as the disguised King of Bohemia in "A Scandal in Bohemia" and the woman (obviously Queen Victoria) who gave Holmes a emerald tie pin as a gift for solving the theft of the Bruce-Partington plans.

"Goodness gracious sakes alive!"

"I know you would be astonished, Mr. Holmes, I know —"

At this moment the door suddenly burst open, and two men entered the room. I recognized one of them as Inspector Gregson; the other was unknown to me.

"Well, Gregson!" said Holmes, "what can I do for you?"

"Good afternoon, Mr. Holmes," said Gregson, "still theorizing as usual? I think I can save you some trouble. This is my friend and colleague, Inspector Smith. And this gentleman, I take it, is Professor Buchwirm, who has lost the Sheraton MSS. It is too bad you did not come to the old shop, Professor, to Scotland Yard. You would have saved time. Luckily your assistant Mr. Noodle, sent for me, and I proceeded with my customary energy."

"Let us hear an account of your adventures, Gregson," said Holmes, reaching for the laudanum pitcher and swallowing a couple of quarts.[1]

"Yes, by all means," said the librarian, "I am all eagerness to hear what success attended your efforts."

"Well," remarked the inspector, seating himself besides his associate on the couch, "on getting Mr. Noodle's letter I took a cab for the library and instituted a search for the lost papers. Finding nothing, I asked all the members of the library staff what they knew about it. They knew nothing. One of them suggested that I look in the catalogue. I did so, but soon abandoned that method of search as too intricate even for an inspector from Scotland Yard. There are some things that are beyond the reach of mortal man. However, one of the library messengers remarked that a charwoman employed by the library had left the building only half an hour before the manuscripts were missed and instantly it occurred to my unerring intellect that she might know something about the

---

[1] Tincture of opium, typically 10 percent powdered opium by weight. Until the early 20th century, it was sold without a prescription. It was typically taken in drops; about 30 at one time (or .05 fluid ounces) was a standard adult dose for pain.

matter.[1] I sent the messenger to her lodgings with a note from me, and in less than an hour he returned with this slip of paper. My message to the woman said simply: 'Where are the Sheraton Mss?' and this is her reply."

He handed the professor a bit of paper. We all gathered about him and read these words: "Kat has got them."

"Marvellous!" ejaculated Professor Buchwirm, "I never thought of that cat. Doubtless you then had the cat searched?"

"I did," replied Gregson, "and —"

"Pardon me one instant, my dear fellow," said Sherlock Holmes languidly. "but even though the matter has not yet come to the notice of Scotland Yard, the ordinary spelling of the word 'cat' is with a 'c,' not a 'k.' The importance of the higher education in the detection of criminality is a matter on which I have already laid much emphasis, in fact, I have incorporated some of my views on the subject in a trifling monograph, which you may have seen, Professor."

"That may all be true, Mr. Holmes," replied the irritated inspector, "but how do you account for those facts? On the receipt of the charwoman's note, I asked to be led to the library cat, and I found her eating some papers, which I instantly rescued. I now have the honor, Professor, to return them to you."

So saying, Gregson drew some folded papers from an inner pocket and handed them to the librarian. That gentleman seized them with joyful cries, and, dashing across the room, grasped the inspector's hand.

"How can I ever thank you, my dear sir?" he exclaimed; "you have preserved my reputation, you —"

"Just one moment, if you please," said Holmes, who was now very nearly in a deep trance; "just one moment. If you will examine these papers through this powerful lens, you will be able to discern in large printed letters the words, 'The Daily Mail,' near the top. If you will continue the scrutiny with

---

[1] A similar situation occurred in "The Adventure of the Naval Treaty" (1893).

great care I think you will discover that these are not the Sheraton MSS., but a newspaper published here in London. You may be able to purchase a copy on the street, my dear Gregson, if you have the change with you, and are interested in the matter. The deciphering of manuscripts is an important part of the detective's work, professor, and I thought I could not be mistaken when I saw on those sheets an advertisement of Beecham's Pills[1] — a remedy not in use, I believe, in the year 1102, when the Sheraton MSS. were penned. Take the glass, professor, and see if you do not agree with me."

"It is indeed true," said the librarian, after a careful examination of the sheets, "but what shall I do now? The MSS. are still lost, I fear."

"I may be able to recover them," said Holmes, "unless, of course, you still prefer to leave the matter in the hands of the inspector."

"I think," said that officer, "we had better pursue independent lines of investigation. I am still retained by Mr. Noodle, and I shall return to the library."

With that the two inspectors left our apartments, and the librarian soon followed, after being assured by Holmes that he need not worry.

As soon as he had departed, Holmes roused himself from lethargy.

"Quick, Watson!" said he, "look over those morning papers and see how many German spies are registered at the principal hotels.[2] Ah, here it is — as I thought! Get your coat,

---

[1] A popular laxative invented by Thomas Beecham (1820-1907) and first marketed in 1842. The pills became the foundation of a pharmaceutical empire, and Beecham lives on as a brand name for cold and flu products. Two Beecham's ads featuring Holmes, "Sherlock Holmes and the Missing Box" and "The Last Letter from Sherlock Holmes," appear in the 1888-1899 volume.

[2] Many newspapers in this era, particularly in the smaller towns, regularly reported the arrivals of guests at the local hotels. Although Conan Doyle was unconcerned about German militarism at this time (see the 1911 essay for details), thriller readers were making best-sellers of "invasion literature" books such as *The Great War in England* (1897), *The Riddle of the*

and we will go out. No delay! You had best put your revolver in your pocket, Watson — this matter cuts very deep — very deep indeed! It is no exaggeration to say that the safety of the empire is at stake! Tell Mrs. Hudson to call a hansom, Watson, and be quick about it!"

Part II

Two or three of the most prominent librarians in the country, including Professor Oscar Gustafsen of Philander University, have written to the Transcript requesting the early publication of the rest of "The Adventure of the Lost Manuscripts," the story in which Sherlock Holmes attempts to solve a library mystery. Although it is now the custom to string out these stories through as many numbers as possible, an exception will be made in this case, and the second and final installment is given herewith. Following the humane method of the magazines, a synopsis is offered for the benefit of those who missed it:

SHERLOCK HOLMES *and Dr. Watson, sitting in their Baker Street chambers, receive a call from Jabez Buchwirm, librarian of the Houndsditch Public Libraries. The librarian reports the mysterious loss of the Sheraton Manuscripts — papers almost as valuable in their historical association as the original Magna Carta. The Sheraton Manuscripts are the personal property of the queen, but they have been deposited (for reasons understood only by the writers of detective romances) in Mr. Buchwirm's library. Before the great detective has time to express an opinion, his old antagonist, Inspector Gregson of Scotland Yard, butts in — or rather, we would say, intrudes upon the case, and announces that he has been retained by Mr. Noodle, the assistant librarian. He claims already to have recovered the lost manuscripts, and produces some papers on which the librarian seizes with glad cries.*

Holmes, however, by means of his superhuman powers and a magnifying glass, shows that he knows more about detective work

---

Sands (1903), *The Invasion of 1910* (1906), and *Spies of the Kaiser* (1909).

than Inspector Gregson (the pride of Scotland Yard) and more about manuscripts than Mr. Buchwirm, the learned librarian. After careful scrutiny he discovers that the papers brought in by Gregson are not the Sheraton Manuscripts (dating from the eleventh century) but a current copy of the Daily Mail. The inspector departs, baffled, but still on the job — or rather, it would be better to say, still intent upon his quest. The troubled librarian also departs (destination unmentioned) and then Holmes begins to display signs of energy. He calls for Watson to call for Mrs. Hudson (the faithful landlady) to call a cab. Then, bidding Watson to take his revolver with him, and remarking that the case "cuts very deep indeed" and that the safety of the empire is at stake, the two depart in search of the lost manuscripts.

They — or before we go on with what they do, we wish to pay a tribute of respect to the extraordinary and praiseworthy character of Mrs. Hudson, the landlady of Sherlock Holmes and Dr. Watson. That unusual woman permitted events of the most thrilling nature to transpire in her house — arrests, often with such violence as to resemble rough-and-tumble fights, faintings, attempted murders, and finally a total destruction of the entire edifice by fire.[1] Yet she never complained, never murmured, rose like the phoenix from the fire, and on the return of Sherlock Holmes from the alleged grave, was quite ready to creep forward and back across the room on her hands and knees and wiggle a wax bust of Holmes in such a manner as to tempt one of his would-be assassins to blaze away at it with a rifle.[2] Where can her like be found? Pinckney Street may be searched in vain for her prototype. All hail to Mrs. Hudson![3]

---

[1] Good heavens! In "The Final Problem," Holmes only says, "They set fire to our rooms last night. No great harm was done." Or did Pearson foresee the BBC *Sherlock* episode where that actually happened?
[2] As described in "The Adventure of The Empty House" (1903).
[3] Although set in London, Pearson inserted a reference to a street in Boston's Beacon Hill section. Now a historic district and expensive to live in, in the 19th century, Beacon Hill contained a mix of neighborhoods for the wealthy, workers, immigrants, and African-Americans. Many homes served as boarding houses, hence the source of Holmes' compliment. Today, a two-story home at

Now, having offered this little garland of roses to the landlady, let us get back to the great detective and the good Dr. Watson, for a really ridiculous amount of time has already been wasted while that hansom was being called, and unless something is done pretty soon the thieves will get away with the Sheraton Manuscripts, take them to America and sell them to Mr. J.P. Morgan.[1]

Here we have Holmes and Watson, then, in a cab, just turning the corner of Baker and Regent streets (and if they haven't a corner, we don't care at all).[2] They are both irreproachably clad in frock coats and top hats — just the most convenient costume in the world for tracking criminals in, and if it were not for the lean, eager face of the great detective you would not guess in what desperate business he is engaged.

His lean, eager face is tilted languidly back at this moment, however; his eyes are closed, and he is dreamily humming some little thing by Grieg or Dvorak, or somebody else to make the reader of this believe that the writer is familiar with the best music. At last he stops humming — just as the hansom passes Liberty's[3] — opens his eyes, and addresses Dr. Watson. Now, we are off at last.

"My dear Watson, did you notice anything peculiar about the cab-driver before we got in this cab?"

"Yes," I replied. "I observed him closely."

"And what did you notice, may I ask?"

---

1 Pinckney Street built in the 1790s was offered for sale at $1.2 million, which at 991 square feet works out to a whopping $1,211 per square foot.

[1] The Gilded Age's greatest financier and banker, Morgan (1837-1913) made a fortune acquiring and merging companies including what became General Electric, U.S. Steel, International Harvester, and AT&T. During the Panic of 1907, he single-handedly arranged deals with the U.S. government and major New York banks to halt the crisis that threatened to bankrupt thousands of account holders. Morgan was also a major collector of books, prints, paintings, and other art objects, and a benefactor of museums, colleges, and trade schools.

[2] They don't meet at a corner, but run parallel about a half-mile apart.

[3] A luxury department store on Great Marlborough Street in London's West End. Named for Arthur Lasenby Liberty (1843-1917), who founded the store in 1875.

"Well, he wore a derby hat, and had a rather red nose."

[Note by the Editor: "Englishmen don't wear derby hats; they wear bowlers."]

[That is all right — how do you know that this cabman is an Englishman? Perhaps he is an American.[1] Some mystery here — but wait a little.]

"Very keen of you, Watson," replied Holmes, "very keen indeed, but as most of the London cabbies wear hats, and all of them have red noses, these facts are not by themselves sufficiently remarkable for purposes of detection. You are improving, Watson, you are undoubtedly improving, but did you chance to observe that this cabby had a rifle under one arm, a belt of cartridges around his waist, the unmistakable bulge of an automatic pistol under his breast pocket, and a bowie knife[2] in his teeth? Did you also chance to see the light Gatling gun which he had in front of him, on the roof of the cab?"

I was forced to confess that these details had escaped me.

"Well, well," Holmes returned, "all trifles, no doubt, but the trifles may sometimes prove of transcendent importance. You remember that it seemed a trifle to Gregson when I noticed that the Duchess of Porchester's pet cockatoo had suffered a slight loss of appetite. Yet from that observation I deduced the facts which led to the arrest of Reginald St. George and the clearing up of the Blisworth glass-eating conspiracy."

"I remember it perfectly," said I, "but what do you deduce from the heavily armed condition of this cab-driver?"

"He apprehends some danger," said Holmes, "but I shall be able to speak with greater confidence after we get to the library. I hope the building will not be closed! You notice that

---

[1] The hard felt hat with the rounded crown is called a derby in the U.S. and a bowler in the U.K. This exemplifies the phrase, attributed to George Bernard Shaw but not confirmed, that "England and America are two countries divided by a common language."

[2] A long knife with a crossguard at the handle, and wide blade that narrowed to a swooping "clip" point. Made for Jim Bowie (c. 1796-1836), a Texas revolutionary figure who died at the battle of the Alamo.

200 | The Best Sherlock Holmes Parodies and Pastiches

I did not take the librarian with us?"

"I did, and supposed you had some good reason for it."

"Quite so. There is not room for three in a hansom, and he did not look as if he could pay for a four-wheeler. I certainly did not care to do so. But, hullo! Hullo! This must be Gregson at work! Dear, dear, what a time they are having!"

Our cab had stopped suddenly just as we turned into Trafalgar Square. *[Query by the Editor: "What? On the way to Houndsditch?"]* [1]

[You leave me alone, will you?]

The entire square was filled with constabulary and soldiers. Five or six hundred members of the police force, armed now with revolvers, surrounded the Nelson Monument. Farther along, and drawn up so as to encircle one of the hotels and extend far down the Strand, were two brigades of soldiers. Skirmishers who were deployed poured a steady fire at a small building, while from the vicinity of the National Gallery three or four siege guns dropped explosive shells into the same building. The troops were in command of Lord Kitchener, and Winston Churchill had charge of the police.

[Note by the Editor: "Isn't this an anachronism? Kitchener wasn't a peer in 1892, the date of your story."]

[Read my essay on "The Value of the Anachronism in Literature."][2]

---

[1] A square in central London in the City of Westminster, named for the battle of Trafalgar (1805), a naval victory during the Napoleonic War. At its center is Nelson's Column, a monument to Admiral Horatio Nelson, who led the British forces and died during the battle.

While we're here, let me add that Houndsditch is a road in the eastern part of London, about three miles east of Trafalgar Square. As the name implies, it was the site of a ditch that was part of Londinium's wall since Roman times, and became a longtime dumping site for refuse, especially dead dogs.

[2] At least he has Trafalgar Square, the Strand, and the National Gallery correctly situated, otherwise ... Herbert *Kitchener* (1850-1916) was the army commander who played key roles in the Sudan invasion, the Second Boer War, and the first half of World War I. He drowned in the sinking of the *HMS Hampshire*. Winston Churchill (1874-1965) would later serve as prime

"Ah!" said Holmes, rubbing his hands briskly, "our friend Gregson seems to have turned out the forces in good shape. I suppose he thinks he has caught the men who stole the Sheraton Manuscripts at last. Here he is now!"

The inspector was indeed approaching our cab.

"Ah, Mr. Sherlock Holmes, it's you is it? Glad to see you, Dr. Watson! But you are a little too late — we've got the rascals treed without your assistance."

"They are in there, are they?" I asked, pointing to the house, in which at that moment four lyddite shells[1] exploded simultaneously.

"There they are," he answered, "or, rather, I should say, there he is. Yes, sir, Mose the Muffin Man, the most dangerous criminal who ever came out of Russia, is in that building at this moment, with the Sheraton Manuscripts in his pockets. But we will have him yet, even if we have to send to the Colonies for help!"

"But do you think," Holmes inquired, "that your force is sufficient? There may be bloodshed with such a desperate man at bay, unless you overpower him."

---

minister during World War II and 1951-1955, but at this time had been an army officer and war correspondent who had seen action in British India, the Anglo-Sudan War and the Second Boer War (where he had been captured but escaped in a way that brought him notice at home). He had served in parliament and several government posts, but at this time as Home Secretary he played a role in the siege of London's Sidney Street in January 1911. The police had surrounded a house where two Latvian anarchists wanted for murder were hiding. A firefight ensued, and the outgunned police called on the army for help. After six hours, fire broke out inside the building, one of the anarchists was shot as he looked out a window, and police let the house burn down, killing the other suspect. Churchill was at the scene, and some believe that he had taken command. He insisted that he didn't, except to reaffirm the police decision to "let the house burn down rather than spend good British lives in rescuing those ferocious rascals."

[1] An explosive made with picric acid, a chemical compound derived from sources such as natural resin, indigo, and animal horn. It was the first high explosive that could withstand the shock of being fired by conventional artillery. In Britain, it was manufactured in Lydd and hence called Lyddite.

"Four dreadnoughts are coming up the river," said Gregson, "and a strong body of suffragettes[1] are ordered to make a flank attack from Northumberland Street. Hark! They are going to charge! Isn't it a magnificent sight?"

It was indeed superb. Three regiments advanced at that moment and took the house at the point of the bayonet. They burst open the front door, dashed in — and brought out a crippled man in an invalid's wheelchair!

"Well, I'll be blowed!" said Gregson. "Who can that be?"

"It looks, my dear inspector," said Holmes, quietly, "very much like that crippled beggar who sells matches in Baker Street. Surely you do not mean to claim that he is your Russian criminal!"

"There's some mistake here!" said the infuriated Gregson, now baffled for the second time within an hour.

"I fear there is," returned my friend, "and Watson, if you will be good enough to tell our driver to proceed, we will continue on our way to the library. Very pretty display of soldiers, though, Gregson, very pretty indeed! How well those Highlanders march! Goodbye, Gregson, and if you capture any more criminals this afternoon, do let me hear of it. I should enjoy seeing the Colonials arrive."

For half an hour our hansom traversed the London streets. Holmes sat in a reverie, while I noted the regions we passed through, and thought of the many curious and tragic incidents connected with them which Holmes had investigated with me as his companion. There was the house in Upper Brixton[2] *[Editor: "Oh, Lord!"]*, the house in Upper Brixton connected with the singular case of General Poindexter and the Serpent Wor-

---

[1] In Britain, the suffragist movement under Emmeline Pankhurst (1858-1928) had turned to arson, vandalism, and bombings in their attempt to get women the vote. In America, several states had already allowed women to vote, and more would do so in coming years.

[2] A neighborhood across the river Thames opposite central London. No wonder the editor gave up arguing.

shippers. There was the villa in St. John's Wood¹ in which the pretender to the throne of Bulgaria met his sudden and mysterious death. There was the low, squalid alley not far from St. Paul's *[Editor: "Was this a seeing-London tour?"]*, the low, squalid alley, I say, in which Holmes lived for two weeks in the winter of '89 while he was investigating the peculiar circumstances connected with the disappearance of the beautiful Mrs. Lydford and the poisoning of the Brazilian envoy.

While I was musing over these bizarre and terrible cases, our cab stopped and Holmes jumped out.

"Here we are at the library," he said. "Follow me, Watson, and we will be at the bottom of this mystery before long, I think."

We hurried into the building and Holmes accosted the first attendant we saw.

"I wish to speak to Mr. Buchwirm, the librarian," he said.

"Your ticket?" inquired the official.

"My what?"

"Your ticket, countersigned by two householders of London — you are not permitted to use the library without it."²

"Do you know who I am? I do not want to use the library. My name is Sherlock Holmes, and I wish to see Mr. Buchwirm instantly."

The attendant cowered.

"Oh, yes, sir! Thank you, sir! Right this way, sir! Yes, sir! Thank you, sir!"

Holmes cuffed the man slightly, and he went away murmuring:

"Yes, sir! Thank you, sir!"

"There is no time for fooling," exclaimed Holmes abrupt-

---

¹ We're north of the river again, in the wealthiest part of London.
² Before the establishment of public libraries, there were private libraries which used residency requirements or a fee to enter. One of them, the London Library, is still in operation at 14 St. James's Square, and requires, according to its website, "an independent referee who could confirm your name and address if requested."

ly. "This is the librarian's room, I think. Come on, Watson!"

He opened the door. I followed him into a small apartment. Mr. Buchwirm, whom we had seen last at the rooms in Baker Street, sat at a desk in the center of the room. He hurriedly put some papers into his pocket as we entered.

"Ah, Mr. Holmes. I trust you have found the Sheraton Manuscripts by this time?"

"Yes, Mr. Librarian, I'm glad to say that I have!"

"Indeed! Then pray let me have them as soon as possible."

"Certainly, Mr. Buchwirm. I am delighted to do so. Ah, allow me —"

And Holmes leaned over and deftly removed from the librarian's inner pocket the papers which he had concealed there.

"Here, my dear Mr. Buchwirm, are the lost papers!"

The librarian sat down again and chuckled slightly.

"No, Mr. Holmes, if you will again apply your magnifying glass and your well-known powers of deduction you will see that what you have there is a copy of The Strand Magazine — a periodical published here in London, price sixpence — American edition, with a far more hideous cover, fifteen cents. That is not the Sheraton Manuscripts at all — in fact, my dear Mr. Holmes — there ain't no such thing!"

"What!" shouted Holmes.

"Fact, I do assure you, Sherlock, my boy."

"Then who the deuce are you? Oh, I have it."

And Holmes with a sudden swift movement tore off the man's false beard.

Great Heavens! We both sprang backward in astonishment, for there sitting at the librarian's desk was no other than —

[Editor: "Let's stop it here and make 'em wait till next month. The Strand Magazine would do it."]

[Never will I be guilty of such conduct!]

No, the man at the librarian's desk was no other than the great arch-enemy of Sherlock Holmes, the Napoleon of Crime, Professor Moriarty himself!!!

[To the printer: Plenty of exclamation points here.]

"But this is impossible," screamed Holmes. "You are dead! I threw you over the Matterhorn myself, with my own hand, or else it was the Katzenjammer Falls,[1] or something awfully steep and deadly! You cannot be alive!"

"That is all right," returned Professor Moriarty, blandly. "You are just as dead yourself, my dear Sherlock. I threw you over the same place at the same time you killed me, but I can't remember the name of it any more than you. So it's a case of hoss and hoss, as the Americans say."[2]

"But what are you doing here in this librarian's disguise?"

"Simple enough! I had to adopt some disguise under which to carry on my vast criminal operations. Who so free of suspicion as the librarian? Does not everyone consider him a harmless old duffer? Is he not everywhere thought a nice, doddering old party? So here I am, Sherlock, president and chairman of the board of directors of the Crime Trust, Ltd., and quite ready to furnish you with arson and murder, mysterious disappearances, counterfeiting, blackmail, highway robbery, and all branches of crime, single or assorted, penny plain or tuppence colored.[3] Get out your magnifying glass, my boy, and let me show you some of our newest varieties!"

---

[1] Sherlockians know, of course, it was the Reichenbach Falls in Switzerland. Holmes confused the scene of their struggle with the Matterhorn, a beautiful pyramidal peak and one of the highest mountains in the Alps, and "The Katzenjammer Kids," a popular U.S. comic strip that began in 1897. A *katzenjammer*, by the way, is a real word. It's German for "cat's wail" and describes a state of bewilderment or depression.

[2] An extremely rare idiom that meant that two things are equal. Probably inspired by horse racing. It was popular enough during the late 19th century to inspire a musical farce with that title, but rarely appears in slang dictionaries.

[3] A phrase originated by Robert Louis Stevenson (1850-1894). During the 19th century, toy theatres were a popular toy. Children would cut characters, props, and scenery from preprinted sheets of paper that were sold in two styles: uncolored for a penny, and hand-colored for two pennies. The catch-phrase implied that you could get the basic model for cheap, but the luxury model would cost you more.

The Adventures of Shamrock Jolnes

O. Henry

One reason short-story writer William Sydney Porter (1862-1910) wrote frequently about crime was that he experienced it personally. He had served time in Ohio after being convicted of embezzling from his father-in-law's bank, although it's suspected that he took the fall to protect the owner. In prison, he was a model inmate. A licensed pharmacist, he was made night drug clerk and given a room in the hospital wing. When not treating inmates, he listened to their stories and worked on his stories. There is even one theory that his pen name was inspired by where he served: the OHio penitENtiaRY.

This story appeared in the New York Sunday World Magazine *of Feb. 7, 1904, and in between covers in* Sixes and Sevens *(1911).*

I am so fortunate as to count Shamrock Jolnes, the great New York detective, among my muster of friends. Jolnes is what is called the "inside man" of the city detective force. He is an expert in the use of the typewriter, and it is his duty, whenever there is a "murder mystery" to be solved, to sit at a desk telephone at headquarters and take down the message of "cranks" who 'phone in their confessions to having committed the crime.

But on certain "off" days when confessions are coming in slowly and three or four newspapers have run to earth as many different guilty persons, Jolnes will knock about the town with me, exhibiting, to my great delight and instruction, his marvellous powers of observation and deduction.

The other day I dropped in at Headquarters and found the great detective gazing thoughtfully at a string that was tied tightly around his little finger.

"Good morning, Whatsup," he said, without turning his head. "I'm glad to notice that you've had your house fitted up with electric lights at last."

"Will you please tell me," I said, in surprise, "how you knew that? I am sure that I never mentioned the fact to any one, and the wiring was a rush order not completed until this morning."

"Nothing easier," said Jolnes, genially. "As you came in I caught the odor of the cigar you are smoking. I know an expensive cigar; and I know that not more than three men in New York can afford to smoke cigars and pay gas bills too at the present time.[1] That was an easy one. But I am working just just now on a little problem of my own."

"Why have you that string on your finger?" I asked.

"That's the problem," said Jolnes. "My wife tied that on this morning to remind me of something I was to send up to the house. Sit down, Whatsup, and excuse me for a few moments."

The distinguished detective went to a wall telephone and stood with the receiver to his ear for probably ten minutes.

"Were you listening to a confession?" I asked, when he had returned to his chair.

"Perhaps," said Jolnes, with a smile, "it might be called something of the sort. To be frank with you, Whatsup, I've cut out the dope. I've been increasing the quantity for so long that morphine doesn't have much effect on me any more. I've got to have something more powerful. That telephone I just went to is connected with a room in the Waldorf where there's an author's reading in progress.[2] Now, to get at the so-

---

[1] At the beginning of the 20th century, natural gas rose in popularity as a fuel source, and companies began building pipelines to ship it across state lines. Depending on the location, and the presence of state regulations, prices ranged from 40 cents to $1.30 per 1,000 cubic feet.
[2] The Waldorf-Astoria hotel was a popular site for author events. It was there that in 1900, the Nineteenth Century Club debated the question, "Is Cheap Literature Cheapening Literature?" Professor H. Thurston Peck, editor of *Bookman* magazine, favored high prices for books. It kept cheap fiction out of the marketplace, he argued, because it forced readers to think before buying an expensive book: "The man of many books was a rarity. The man of a few books is a rarity to-day. The man of many books is a nuisance." Publisher S.S. McClure disagreed. Cheap literature brought the standard and classical works into every home, fostering the taste for inexpensive literature instead of cheapening the quality. He also said that

lution of this string."

After five minutes of silent pondering, Jolnes looked at me with a smile and nodded his head.

"Wonderful man!" I exclaimed; "already?"

"It is quite simple," he said, holding up his finger. "You see that knot? That is to prevent my forgetting. It is, therefore, a forget-me-knot. A forget-me-not is a flower. It was a sack of flour that I was to send home!"

"Beautiful!" I could not help crying out in admiration.

"Suppose we go out for a ramble," suggested Jolnes.

"There is only one case of importance on hand now. Old man McCarty, one hundred and four years old, died from eating too many bananas. The evidence points so strongly to the Mafia that the police have surrounded the Second Avenue Katzenjammer Gambrinus[1] Club No. 2, and the capture of the assassin is only the matter of a few hours. The detective force has not yet been called on for assistance."

Jolnes and I went out and up the street toward the corner where we were to catch a surface car.[2]

---

critics were not needed, because readers were so discriminating that a publisher could not sell a poor book.

[1] *Katzenjammer:* A reference to "The Katzenjammer Kids," a popular U.S. comic strip that began in 1897. *Katzenjammer* is German for "cat's wail" and describes a state of bewilderment or depression. *Gambrinus:* Also spelled Cambrinus, a mythical folk hero in European culture credited with inventing beer. He is depicted as a Falstaffian-sized man, with a large belly and a full beard. Stories about him have been traced back to several regions of France and Germany, but his popularity rose in 1868 with the story "Cambrinus, Roi de la Biere" in *Tales of a Beer Drinker* by French folklorist Charles Deulin (1827-1877). Cambrinus is an apprentice glassblower who sells his soul to Beelzebub to win the heart of his master's daughter. He becomes renowned as a musician and becomes the first mortal to brew beer. Gambrinus lives for more than a century, and thwarts Beelzebub by dying and turning into a beer barrel. Deulin later published *Tales of King Cambrinus* (1874), making him to beer brewing what the Brothers Grimm was to fairy tales. Numerous beer brands have appropriated Gambrinus for their purposes, and a statue of the king stands in Milwaukee.

[2] A streetcar, to distinguish it from a subway or an elevated train.

Halfway up the block we met Rheingelder, an acquaintance of ours, who held a City Hall position.

"Good morning, Rheingelder," said Jolnes, halting. "Nice breakfast that was you had this morning."

Always on the lookout for the detective's remarkable feats of deduction, I saw Jolnes's eyes flash for an instant upon a long yellow splash on the shirt bosom and a smaller one upon the chin of Rheingelder — both undoubtedly made by the yolk of an egg.

"Oh, dot is some of your defectiveness," said Rheingelder, shaking all over with a smile. "Vell, I bet you trinks and cigars all around dot you cannot tell vot I haf eaten for breakfast."

"Done," said Jolnes. "Sausage, pumpernickel, and coffee."

Rheingelder admitted the correctness of the surmise and paid the bet. When we had proceeded on our way I said to Jolnes:

"I thought you looked at the egg spilled on his chin and shirt front."

"I did," said Jolnes. "That is where I began my deduction. Rheingelder is a very economical, saving man. Yesterday, eggs dropped in the market to twenty-eight cents per dozen. To-day, they are quoted at forty-two. Rheingelder ate eggs yesterday, and to-day he went back to his usual fare. A little thing like this isn't anything, Whatsup; it belongs to the primary arithmetic class."

When we boarded the street car we found the seats all occupied — principally by ladies. Jolnes and I stood on the rear platform.

About the middle of the car there sat an elderly man with a short, gray beard, who looked to be the typical, well-dressed New Yorker. At successive corners, other ladies climbed aboard, and soon three or four of them were standing over the man, clinging to straps and glaring meaningly at the man who occupied the coveted seat. But he resolutely retained his place.

"We New Yorkers," I remarked to Jolnes, "have about lost

our manners, as far as the exercise of them in public goes."

"Perhaps so," said Jolnes, lightly; "but the man you evidently refer to happens to be a very chivalrous and courteous gentleman from Old Virginia. He is spending a few days in New York with his wife and two daughters, and he leaves for the South to-night."

"You know him, then?" I said, in amazement.

"I never saw him before we stepped on the car," declared the detective, smilingly.

"By the gold tooth of the Witch of Endor!"[1] I cried, "if you can construe all that from his appearance you are dealing in nothing else than black art."

"The habit of observation — nothing more," said Jolnes. "If the old gentleman gets off the car before we do, I think I can demonstrate to you the accuracy of my deduction."

Three blocks farther along, the gentleman rose to leave the car. Jolnes addressed him at the door:

"Pardon me, sir, but are you not Colonel Hunter, of Norfolk, Virginia?"

"No, suh," was the extremely courteous answer. "My name, suh, is Ellison — Major Cornfield R. Ellison, from Fairfax County, in the same state. I know a good many people, suh, in Norfolk — the Goodriches, the Tollivers, and the Crabtrees, suh, but I never had the pleasure of meeting yo' friend, Colonel Hunter. I am happy to say, suh, that I am going back to Virginia to-night, after having spent a week in yo' city with my wife and three daughters. I shall be in Norfolk in about ten days, and if you will give me yo' name, suh, I will

---

[1] A figure from the Bible who appears in the first book of Samuel. Israel's King Saul had banished all of the necromancers and magicians from his kingdom, but when the Philistines threaten to invade, he turned to prophets and dreams to seek a solution. When that fails, he goes in disguise to the Canaanite city of Endor to find the witch. She calls up the spirit of Samuel, the prophet who had appointed Saul the first king of Israel. He criticizes the king for failing to obey God, and predicts that he'll be destroyed along with his army in battle the next day. Samuel's prediction comes true, and the king commits suicide.

take pleasure in looking up Colonel Hunter and telling him that you inquired after him, suh."

"Thank you," said Jolnes; "tell him that Reynolds sent his regards, if you will be so kind."

I glanced at the great New York detective and saw that a look of intense chagrin had come upon his clear-cut features. Failure in the slightest point always galled Shamrock Jolnes.

"Did you say your three daughters?" he asked of the Virginia gentleman.

"Yes, suh, my three daughters, all as fine girls as there are in Fairfax County," was the answer.

With that Major Ellison stopped the car and began to descend the step.

Shamrock Jolnes clutched his arm.

"One moment, sir," he begged, in an urbane voice in which I alone detected the anxiety — "am I not right in believing that one of the young ladies is an adopted daughter?"

"You are, suh," admitted the major, from the ground, "but how the devil you knew it, suh, is mo' than I can tell."

"And mo' than I can tell, too," I said, as the car went on.

Jolnes was restored to his calm, observant serenity by having wrested victory from his apparent failure; so after we got off the car he invited me into a cafe promising to reveal the process of his latest wonderful feat.

"In the first place," he began after we were comfortably seated, "I knew the gentleman was no New Yorker because he was flushed and uneasy and restless on account of the ladies that were standing, although he did not rise and give them his seat. I decided from his appearance that he was a Southerner rather than a Westerner.

"Next, I began to figure out his reason for not relinquishing his seat to a lady when he evidently felt strongly, but not overpoweringly, impelled to do so. I very quickly decided upon that. I noticed that one of his eyes had received a severe jab in one corner, which was red and inflamed, and that all over his face were tiny round marks about the size of the end of an uncut lead pencil. Also upon both of his patent-leather shoes were a number of deep imprints shaped like ovals cut off square at one end.

"Now, there is only one district in New York City where a man is bound to receive scars and wounds and indentations of that sort — and that is along the sidewalks of Twenty-third Street and a portion of Sixth Avenue south of there. I knew from the imprints of tramping French heels[1] on his feet and the marks of countless jabs in the face from umbrellas and parasols carried by women in the shopping district that he had been in conflict with the amazonian troops. And as he was a man of intelligent appearance, I knew he would not have braved such dangers unless he had been dragged thither by his own women folk. Therefore, when he got on the car his anger at the treatment he had received was sufficient to make him keep his seat in spite of his traditions of Southern chivalry."

"That is all very well," I said, "but why did you insist upon daughters — and especially two daughters? Why couldn't a wife alone have taken him shopping?"

"There had to be daughters," said Jolnes, calmly. "If he had only a wife, and she near his own age, he could have bluffed her into going alone. If he had a young wife she would prefer to go alone. So there you are."

"I'll admit that," I said; "but, now, why two daughters? And how; in the name of all the prophets, did you guess that one was adopted when he told you he had three?"

"Don't say guess," said Jolnes, with a touch of pride in his air; "there is no such word in the lexicon of ratiocination. In Major Ellison's buttonhole there was a carnation and a rosebud backed by a geranium leaf. No woman ever combined a carnation and a rosebud into a boutonnière. Close your eyes,

---

[1] A style of women's shoe in which the heels are curved well forward of their base and the back and breast line also have a pronounced curve. This could only be created by hand, so this style disappeared in the 1920s as machines took over the production process. Also called a Louis heel, after King Louis XIV (1638-1715), who wore them as high as 5 inches.

Whatsup, and give the logic of your imagination a chance. Can not you see the lovely Adele fastening the carnation to the lapel so that papa may be gay upon the street? And then the romping Edith May dancing up with sisterly jealousy to add her rosebud to the adornment?"

"And then," I cried, beginning to feel enthusiasm, "when he declared that he had three daughters —"

"I could see," said Jolnes, "one in the background who added no flower; and I knew that she must be —"

"Adopted!" I broke in. "I give you every credit; but how did you know he was leaving for the South to-night?"

"In his breast pocket," said the great detective, "something large and oval made a protuberance. Good liquor is scarce on trains, and it is a long journey from New York to Fairfax County."

"Again, I must bow to you," I said. "And tell me this, so that my last shred of doubt will be cleared away; why did you decide that he was from Virginia?"

"It was very faint, I admit," answered Shamrock Jolnes, "but no trained observer could have failed to detect the odor of mint in the car."[1]

O. Henry

---

[1] A reference to the mint julep, the mixture of bourbon, powdered sugar, water, and mint, that originated in Virginia.

Maddened by Mystery:
or, The Defective Detective

Stephen Leacock

This is one of the most popular and reprinted Sherlockian parodies, and deservedly so. Drawn from Leacock's collection Nonsense Novels, *it was the only parody E.C. Bentley chose for* The Second Century of Detective Stories *(1938) and appeared in both Ellery Queen's* The Misadventures of Sherlock Holmes *(1944), and the equally excellent* Mini Mysteries *(1969), where I first encountered it as a lad. Stephen Leacock (1869-1944) was a popular Canadian teacher, writer, and humorist. Since 1947, the Stephen Leacock Award is given annually for the best humor book by a Canadian writer.*

The great detective sat in his office. He wore a long green gown and half a dozen secret badges pinned to the outside of it.

Three or four pairs of false whiskers hung on a whisker-stand beside him.

Goggles, blue spectacles, and motor glasses lay within easy reach.

He could completely disguise himself at a second's notice.

Half a bucket of cocaine and a dipper stood on a chair at his elbow. His face was absolutely impenetrable.

A pile of cryptograms lay on the desk. The Great Detective hastily tore them open one after the other, solved them, and threw them down the cryptogram-chute at his side.

There was a rap at the door.

The Great Detective hurriedly wrapped himself in a pink domino,[1] adjusted a pair of false black whiskers and cried,

"Come in."

His secretary entered. "Ha," said the detective, "it is you."

He laid aside his disguise.

---

[1] A small, rounded mask that covers the eyes and the space between them. It is derived from the Latin *dominus* for "lord" or "master," combined with the Latin *masca* for "nightmare" or "specter."

"Sir," said the young man in intense excitement, "a mystery has been committed!"

"Ha!" said the Great Detective, his eye kindling, "is it such as to completely baffle the police of the entire continent?"

"They are so completely baffled with it," said the secretary, "that they are lying collapsed in heaps; many of them have committed suicide."

"So," said the detective, "and is the mystery one that is absolutely unparalleled in the whole recorded annals of the London police?"

"It is."

"And I suppose," said the detective, "that it involves names which you would scarcely dare to breathe, at least without first using some kind of atomizer or throat-gargle."

"Exactly."

"And it is connected, I presume, with the highest diplomatic consequences, so that if we fail to solve it England will be at war with the whole world in sixteen minutes?"

His secretary, still quivering with excitement, again answered yes.

"And finally," said the Great Detective, "I presume that it was committed in broad daylight, in some such place as the entrance of the Bank of England, or in the cloak-room of the House of Commons, and under the very eyes of the police?"

"Those," said the secretary, "are the very conditions of the mystery."

"Good," said the Great Detective, "now wrap yourself in this disguise, put on these brown whiskers and tell me what it is."

The secretary wrapped himself in a blue domino with lace insertions, then, bending over, he whispered in the ear of the Great Detective:

"The Prince of Wurttemberg has been kidnapped."

The Great Detective bounded from his chair as if he had been kicked from below.

A prince stolen! Evidently a Bourbon![1] The scion of one of the oldest families in Europe kidnapped. Here was a mystery indeed worthy of his analytical brain.

His mind began to move like lightning.

"Stop!" he said, "how do you know this?"

The secretary handed him a telegram. It was from the Prefect of Police of Paris. It read: "The Prince of Wurttemberg stolen. Probably forwarded to London. Must have him here for the opening day of Exhibition. 1,000 pounds reward."

So! The Prince had been kidnapped out of Paris at the very time when his appearance at the International Exposition would have been a political event of the first magnitude.

With the Great Detective, to think was to act, and to act was to think. Frequently he could do both together.

"Wire to Paris for a description of the Prince."

The secretary bowed and left.

At the same moment there was a slight scratching at the door.

A visitor entered. He crawled stealthily on his hands and knees. A hearthrug thrown over his head and shoulders disguised his identity.

He crawled to the middle of the room.

Then he rose.

Great Heaven!

It was the Prime Minister of England.

"You!" said the detective.

"Me," said the Prime Minister.

---

[1] When it comes to bloodlines and accomplishments, this royal family makes the Windsors look like the *nouveau riche*. The Bourbons started by ruling Bourbonnais, a small province in central France, between 913 and 1327. They established a toehold on royalty in 1272 when one of their daughters married Louis IX's younger son. They scraped by as a cadet branch of the royal family until Henry IV ascended in 1589, and ruled France until the revolution in 1792. The family made a brief comeback after Napoleon's fall in 1814, then came back again the next year and hung on until the 1830 revolution. Another cadet branch of the Bourbons ruled for another 18 years (1830-1848) until it was time to call it a day.

"You have come in regard the kidnapping of the Prince of Wurttemberg?"

The Prime Minister started.

"How do you know?" he said.

The Great Detective smiled his inscrutable smile.

"Yes," said the Prime Minister. "I will use no concealment. I am interested, deeply interested. Find the Prince of Wurttemberg, get him safe back to Paris, and I will add £500 to the reward already offered. But listen," he said impressively as he left the room, "see to it that no attempt is made to alter the marking of the prince, or to clip his tail."

So! To clip the Prince's tail! The brain of the Great Detective reeled. So! a gang of miscreants had conspired to—but no! the thing was not possible.

There was another rap at the door.

A second visitor was seen. He wormed his way in, lying almost prone upon his stomach, and wriggling across the floor. He was enveloped in a long purple cloak. He stood up and peeped over the top of it.

Great Heaven!

It was the Archbishop of Canterbury!

"Your Grace!" exclaimed the detective in amazement—"pray do not stand, I beg you. Sit down, lie down, anything rather than stand."

The Archbishop took off his mitre[1] and laid it wearily on the whisker-stand.

"You are here in regard to the Prince of Wurttemberg."

The Archbishop started and crossed himself. Was the man a magician?

"Yes," he said, "much depends on getting him back. But I have only come to say this: my sister is desirous of seeing you. She is coming here. She has been extremely indiscreet and her fortune hangs upon the Prince. Get him back to Paris or I fear she will be ruined."

---

[1] The traditional ceremonial headgear, consisting of a cap with a front and back flap pointed at the top and sewn partway up the sides.

The Archbishop regained his mitre, uncrossed himself, wrapped his cloak about him, and crawled stealthily out on his hands and knees, purring like a cat.

The face of the Great Detective showed the most profound sympathy. It ran up and down in furrows. "So," he muttered, "the sister of the Archbishop, the Countess of Dashleigh!" Accustomed as he was to the life of the aristocracy, even the Great Detective felt that there was here intrigue of more than customary complexity.

There was a loud rapping at the door.

There entered the Countess of Dashleigh. She was all in furs.

She was the most beautiful woman in England. She strode imperiously into the room. She seized a chair imperiously and seated herself on it, imperial side up.

She took off her tiara of diamonds and put it on the tiara-holder beside her and uncoiled her boa of pearls and put it on the pearl-stand.

"You have come," said the Great Detective, "about the Prince of Wurttemberg."

"Wretched little pup!" said the Countess of Dashleigh in disgust.

So! A further complication! Far from being in love with the Prince, the Countess denounced the Bourbon as a pup!

"You are interested in him, I believe."

"Interested!" said the Countess. "I should rather say so. Why, I bred him!"

"You which?" gasped the Great Detective, his usually impassive features suffused with a carmine blush.

"I bred him," said the Countess, "and I've got £10,000 upon his chances, so no wonder I want him back in Paris. Only listen," she said, "if they've got hold of the Prince and cut his tail or spoiled the markings of his stomach it would be far better to have him quietly put out of the way here."

The Great Detective reeled and leaned up against the side of the room. So! The cold-blooded admission of the beautiful woman for the moment took away his breath! Herself the mother of the young Bourbon, misallied with one of the greatest families of Europe, staking her fortune on a Royalist plot, and yet with so instinctive a knowledge of European politics as to know that any removal of the hereditary birthmarks of the Prince would forfeit for him the sympathy of the French populace.

The Countess resumed her tiara.

She left.

The secretary re-entered.

"I have three telegrams from Paris," he said. "They are completely baffling."

He handed over the first telegram.

It read:

"The Prince of Wurttemberg has a long, wet snout, broad ears, very long body, and short hind legs."

The Great Detective looked puzzled.

He read the second telegram.

"The Prince of Wurttemberg is easily recognized by his deep bark."

And then the third.

"The Prince of Wurttemberg can be recognized by a patch of white hair across the centre of his back."

The two men looked at one another. The mystery was maddening, impenetrable.

The Great Detective spoke.

"Give me my domino," he said. "These clues must be followed up," then pausing, while his quick brain analysed and summed up the evidence before him—"a young man," he muttered, "evidently young since described as a 'pup,' with a long, wet snout (ha! addicted obviously to drinking), a streak of white hair across his back (a first sign of the results of his abandoned life)—yes, yes," he continued, "with this clue I shall find him easily."

The Great Detective rose.

He wrapped himself in a long black cloak with white

whiskers and blue spectacles attached.

Completely disguised, he issued forth.

He began the search.

For four days he visited every corner of London.

He entered every saloon in the city. In each of them he drank a glass of rum. In some of them he assumed the disguise of a sailor. In others he entered as a solider. Into others he penetrated as a clergyman. His disguise was perfect. Nobody paid any attention to him as long as he had the price of a drink.

The search proved fruitless.

Two young men were arrested under suspicion of being the Prince, only to be released.

The identification was incomplete in each case.

One had a long wet snout but no hair on his back.

The other had hair on his back but couldn't bark.

Neither of them was the young Bourbon.

The Great Detective continued his search.

He stopped at nothing.

Secretly, after nightfall, he visited the home of the Prime Minister. He examined it from top to bottom. He measured all the doors and windows. He took up the flooring. He inspected the plumbing. He examined the furniture. He found nothing.

With equal secrecy he penetrated into the palace of the Archbishop. He examined it from top to bottom. Disguised as a choir-boy he took part in the offices of the church. He found nothing.

Still undismayed, the Great Detective made his way into the home of the Countess of Dashleigh. Disguised as a housemaid, he entered the service of the Countess.

Then at last a clue came which gave him a solution to the mystery.

On the wall of the Countess's boudoir was a large framed engraving.

It was a portrait.

Under it was a printed legend:

THE PRINCE OF WURTTEMBERG

The portrait was that of a Dachshund.

The long body, the broad ears, the unclipped tail, the short hind legs—all was there.

In a fraction of a second the lightning mind of the Great Detective had penetrated the whole mystery.

THE PRINCE WAS A DOG!!!!

Hastily throwing a domino over his housemaid's dress, he rushed to the street. He summoned a passing hansom, and in a few moments was at his house.

"I have it," he gasped to his secretary. "The mystery is solved. I have pieced it together. By sheer analysis I have reasoned it out. Listen—hind legs, hair on back, wet snout, pup—eh, what? does that suggest nothing to you?"

"Nothing," said the secretary; "it seems perfectly hopeless."

The Great Detective, now recovered from his excitement, smiled faintly.

"It means simply this, my dear fellow. The Prince of Wurttemberg is a dog, a prize Dachshund. The Countess of Dashleigh bred him, and he is worth some £25,000 in addition to the prize of £10,000 offered at the Paris dog show. Can you wonder that—"

At that moment the Great Detective was interrupted by the scream of a woman.

"Great Heaven!"

The Countess of Dashleigh dashed into the room.

Her face was wild.

Her tiara was in disorder.

Her pearls were dripping all over the place.

She wrung her hands and moaned.

"They have cut his tail," she gasped, "and taken all the hair off his back. What can I do? I am undone!!"

"Madam," said the Great Detective, calm as bronze, "do yourself up. I can save you yet."

"You!"

"Me!"

"How?"

"Listen. This is how. The Prince was to have been shown at Paris."

The Countess nodded.

"Your fortune was staked on him."

The Countess nodded again.

"The dog was stolen, carried to London, his tail cut and his marks disfigured."

Amazed at the quiet penetration of the Great Detective, the Countess kept on nodding and nodding.

"And you are ruined?"

"I am," she gasped, and sank to the floor in a heap of pearls.

"Madame," said the Great Detective, "all is not lost."

He straightened himself up to his full height. A look of inflinchable unflexibility flickered over his features.

The honour of England, the fortune of the most beautiful woman in England was at stake.

"I will do it," he murmured.

"Rise dear lady," he continued. "Fear nothing. I WILL IMPERSONATE THE DOG!!!"

That night the Great Detective might have been seen on the deck of the Calais packet boat with his secretary. He was on his hands and knees in a long black cloak, and his secretary had him on a short chain.

He barked at the waves exultingly and licked the secretary's hand.

"What a beautiful dog," said the passengers.

The disguise was absolutely complete.

The Great Detective had been coated over with mucilage[1]

---

[1] A general term for the gluey substance produced by many plants, including aloe vera, flax, and okra, and some microorganisms. One form it takes

to which dog hairs had been applied. The markings on his back were perfect. His tail, adjusted with an automatic coupler,[1] moved up and down responsive to every thought. His deep eyes were full of intelligence.

Next day he was exhibited in the Dachshund class at the International show.

He won all hearts.

"Quel beau chien!"[2] cried the French people.

"Ach! was ein Dog!"[3] cried the Spanish.

The Great Detective took the first prize.

The fortune of the Countess was saved.

Unfortunately, as the Great Detective had neglected to pay the dog tax, he was caught and destroyed by the dog-catchers. But that is, of course, quite outside of the present narrative, and is only mentioned as an odd fact in conclusion.

Stephen Leacock

---

comes from the root of the marshmallow plant and was used to make the traditional version of that sweet treat. Mucilage was sold as glue used for labels, envelopes, and postage stamps.
[1] A device at the end of railway cars that, when pushed together, automatically linked them without needing a worker to help.
[2] What a beautiful dog!
[3] Oh! What a dog!

The Adventure of the Lost Baby

Carolyn Wells

Illustrations by H.C. Townsend

Carolyn Wells (1869-1942) was a prolific author and poet, producing more than 170 titles over four decades, including 75 mystery and detective stories. It is a measure of our appreciation of her that we included six of her stories in the 223B Casebook series.

This tale is from her International Society of Infallible Detectives series, a supergroup of literature's greatest sleuths that anticipated by decades superhero groups such as the Avengers and the Justice League. They consist of Holmes and Watson; C. Auguste Dupin by Edgar Allan Poe; Arsene Lupin by Maurice Leblanc; Monsieur Lecoq by Émile Gaboriau; Raffles by E.W. Hornung; Luther Trant by Edwin Balmer and William MacHarg; and Professor Augustus S.F.X. Van Dusen, a.k.a. "The Thinking Machine" by Jacques Futrelle. This story was found in the Washington Evening Star Sunday Magazine *of Feb. 21, 1913. Nothing is known of artist H.C. Townsend.

The members of the International Society of Infallible Detectives were assembled in their rooms on Faker street. It was a very rainy day, and they were hoping against hope that a case worthy of their individual and concerted intellects might be brought to them. At last, as a last resort, Arsène Lupin said in despair to the president:

"Do look out of the window, Holmes! Most always when you look out you see a case approaching."

With his somewhat hackneyed, bored shrug, Sherlock Holmes removed his pipe from his finely chiseled countenance and placed it carefully in an embroidered pipe rack given him by a grateful client, who was light complected and an Episcopalian, and whose missing pearls he had once found. Sauntering to the window, he looked saturninely out into a landscape of perpendicular wetness.

"It's all right," he said drearily. "She's coming. A middle-aged lady, not poor, but somewhat parsimonious, an ant

"It's all right," said Holmes. "She's coming."

suffragist, and a reader of *The Ladies' Own Ledger*.[1] She has lost an article of great value."

But Holmes spoke slowly, and Watson had time only to breathe the first syllable of his trite and classical response, when the lady was ushered into the room.

"Good afternoon, Gentlemen," she said, sinking into a chair offered her by the blithe Watson.

President Holmes gazed at her, as if reading and translating her secret soul.

Lupin, Dupin, Lecoq, and Vidocq, who had risen, made right-angular French bows, hands at hearts. The Thinking Machine kept his seat and gazed at her from his querulous blue eyes, his chin resting on his folded hands, which in turn rested on his knobbed walking stick, which in turn rested, of course, on the floor.

---

[1] A fictional magazine for women that suggests *Godey's Lady's Book* or *Ladies Home Journal*.

Luther Trant fidgeted a little, and Raffles smiled like the handsome dog that he was.

"I deduce it is raining," said Holmes, looking sternly at his visitor.

"You knew that before," observed Lupin, with a Gallic leer.

"But I ignored that," declared Holmes, "and I deduced it entirely from the lady's umbrella and rubbers."

"Marvelous, Holmes, marvelous!" exclaimed Watson, thrilled to the uttermost fiber of his appreciation.

"You have lost something, Madam," said Holmes, shaking his saturnine forefinger at her.

"Good land, Sir! how did you know that? Was it in the papers?"

"No. But I'm sure you're not mixed up in a murder case, and there's no other crime except robbery; so I know it's theft. The article you lost is —"

"Oh, Holmes," exclaimed the Thinking Machine querulously, "let the lady herself tell what she has lost! She knows more about it than you do."

"I am not sure of that," returned Holmes dubiously, a grim smile lighting up his dark face; "but go on, Madam, tell us what you do know, or think you know, of the case."

"Well, Sir, you see I am a widow."

"I deduced you were a widow," put in Holmes, "as soon as I saw your wedding ring and your black crepe veil."

"Marvelous, Holmes, marvelous!" observed Watson a trifle mechanically.

"You also deduced that she read *The Ladies' Own Ledger*," said Vidocq. "Can you prove that?"

Languidly Holmes lifted his weary forefinger and pointed to the jabot[1] at the lady's throat. Too true, it was made of a Turkish washcloth, deftly plaited into shape, and worked in cute little designs with red marking cotton. It had been de-

---

[1] A fabric necklace, made from lace or cambric, that fell from the throat. It was usually either pinned around the throat or attached to a neckband or collar. Jabot is the French word for a bird's crop, or a portion of its throat.

scribed in that very month's paper, and they all knew it.

"And how did you know she was ant suffrage?" asked the Thinking Machine.

"So many dinky frills on her petticoat, which I saw flippering about as she crossed the street."

"And that she was parsim —"

But Lecoq's rude speech was stayed by Raffles, who clapped his hands over the speaker's mouth.

"Oh, fiddle strings!" cried Holmes. "If she had on such extravagant lingerie, she could afford a taxi, and as she didn't have one she — she was — walking for her health," he concluded, as the lady stared straight at him.

"My name is Mrs. Plummer," she began, "Mrs. Ezra J. Plummer. But I suppose, Sir, you would have known that too, if I hadn't told you."

"Of course," responded Holmes carelessly. "Go on."

"Well, I've lived alone ever since Ezra died, nineteen years come next June, and I've kept my house and home just as it always was. I ain't great for changing my furniture with every whip-around of the fashion. The plush chairs in my parlor are just as good now as the day we bought 'em; two of 'em red and three green and the sofa red. Black ebony frames, they have, picked out with gilt, and a neater parlor suit ain't to be found."

"Charming set of furniture," said Raffles politely.

"Tasty idea that, of red and green alternating. And you've lost those chairs, Madam?"

"No, Sir, burglars don't take chairs. What I've lost is a work of art, the chief ornament of my parlor, my choicest possession. A treasure, indeed!" Mrs. Plummer broke down completely and began to cry.

The four French gentlemen, being of sympathetic and emotional dispositions, wept also. The Thinking Machine wriggled uneasily in his chair.

President Holmes gazed out of the window with neatly folded arms. "A work of art!" he hissed. "Ha, a parallel case to the *Mona Lisa!*¹ What was it, Madam, a picture, a statue?"

"Ah, how clever you are!" she exclaimed. "You've almost hit it. Try again!"

"A statuette, an antique, a curio, a bronze?" the eager detectives suggested one after another.

"No!" exclaimed Mrs. Plummer. "You'll never guess! It was a Rogers Group."

"Rogers Group! What is that?" asked Lecoq, for the fame of the Great Grouper had never penetrated his benighted land.

"Oh, Sir," exclaimed Mrs. Plummer, "it was one of his choicest designs! It was *Weighing the Baby,* and — oh, if you could see the old doctor peering through his glasses, and the nurse with her clasped hands, and the infant — ah, the infant! — gone!"²

Again she broke down and wept as women will when babies are concerned. And the four Frenchmen sympathetically and copiously followed her lead.

"Ah, a kidnapping case!" exclaimed Luther Trant; while the Thinking Machine inquired tensely:

"How much did the baby weigh?"

But President Holmes interrupted. "Proceed, Madam, to give us the details of the robbery."

"Well, Sirs, it was this way. I went out to the Sewing Society this afternoon, and of course I locked the house all up as usual. The Rogers Group was in the parlor, on a marble-topped table with a scarf of garnet plush. Sirs, every parlor

---

¹ See "The Adventure of the *Mona Lisa*" in the 1910-1914 book.
² American sculptor John Rogers (1829-1904) was the Norman Rockwell of his time. He produced sculptures of charming scenes that were mass-produced in cast plaster. Typical sculptures showed a magician pulling a rabbit from a hat before a child and his father, two men playing checkers on a barrel in a general store, a scene between John Alden and Priscilla Mullens from the legend of the courtship of Miles Standish, and Abe Lincoln with Gen. U.S. Grant and Secretary of War Edwin Stanton.

But Wells was mistaken in her description of "Weighing the Baby." It showed a merchant using his large scale for the task, watched by the contented mother and a little boy. One was sold at auction in 2011 for $300.

window was protected by safety catches, and the front door was tightly locked; indeed, all the windows and doors were securely fastened."

"In a word, that parlor was hermetically sealed!" declared Luther Trant sententiously.

"Ha! Hermetically sealed!" cried Rouletabille. That is all a case needs to make it interesting!"[1]

"I left at two o'clock," went on Mrs. Plummer dramatically, "left at two, and when I returned at four that Rogers Group was gone! Not a vestige of it remained. Gone was the baby and the doctor. Gone the scales and the nurse — gone!"

"Gone! Gone!" echoed Dupin, wringing his hands. He was often overwhelmed by excessive sympathy, as were the other French gentlemen.

"And the house hermetically sealed!" pondered Rouletabille exultantly. "There is no problem so delightful as that! Do you remember in *The Yellow Room*[2] there —"

"Are there any clues?" asked President Holmes, deliberately cutting short Roly-Poly's reminiscences.

"I don't know, Sir," replied the lady. "I've heard you mustn't touch a body until the Coroner comes; so I supposed it was the same with robbery. So I locked up the house again and hurried over."

"Quite right," returned the saturnine Holmes approvingly. "I'll go there at once. Come, Watson."

Though seemingly ignored, the others grabbed their hats and all burst out of the door at once, in true detective eagerness to be first on the scene.

The rain had stopped, so the party stepped briskly along

---

[1] Joseph Rouletabille is a new character, so let's take a moment to describe him as the reporter and amateur detective created by Gaston Leroux (1868-1927), best known for writing the novel *The Phantom of the Opera* (1910). Rouletabille (pronounced "Rou-let-a-bill") starred in seven novels between 1908 and 1923, and two sequels by Nore Brunel in 1947.

[2] Joseph Rouletabille first appeared as the reporter and amateur detective in *The Mystery of the Yellow Room* by Gaston Leroux (1908). It is one of the first locked-room mysteries and is still worth reading today.

the still-wet pavements; and then, solemnly unlocking her front door, Mrs. Plummer ushered in the ten men.

"The room! Which is the room?" asked Rouletabille hoarsely; for here was a case in which his very soul delighted.

"Here!" and Mrs. Plummer dramatically threw open the parlor door.

Too true, the bay window where for nineteen years the Rogers Group had proudly stood, was empty. Gone indeed the priceless work of art! Gone the kind old doctor, the proud nurse, and the avoirdupois[1] baby!

"Ha! Footprints!" muttered President Holmes, and in a trice he was down on his knees with magnifying glass, compass, and T-square. But the magnifying glass was not needed, for the footprints were of goodly size. Carefully, Holmes laid a diagram to scale, and with the help of some of the others a paper pattern was cut exactly like the footprints and a duplicate given to each member of the club. From these they were to trace the criminal.

"And we can do it!" said Vidocq assuredly.

"Well," said Mrs. Plummer, as if the words were forced from her by a lashing conscience, "those footprints are mine. When I came in, it was some muddy."

"Why did you not tell us in the first place?" demanded Trant.

"Well, you see, I had on my old shoes, and they always were too big for me, anyway."

"Fine example of the eternal feminine!"[2] commented

---

[1] The system of weights based on ounces, based on the Old French *aveir de peis* or "goods of weight." The word can also be used in a humorous fashion to mean heaviness, as in this sentence from *The Bancroft Strategy* (2010) by Robert Ludlum: "The Yemeni eased his avoirdupois upon the leather chair at his desk."

[2] The idea that women are defined by an essence that is uniquely theirs, usually tied into ideas of feminine values vs. masculine values, fertility, the purity of the virgin and sanctity of the mother. Feminists such as Simone De Beauvoir (1908-1986) argue that these values are creations of the patriarchy and everyone has the right to define their own existence.

The next few moments brought startling results.

Trant. "But stay! The miscreant must have left. I will photograph this plush chenille cover and these plush chairs in hope of getting his thumbprint."

But the next few moments brought startling results. Dozens of fingerprints were found on the dusty surfaces of brackets and mantel. Then Raffles found a tuft of feathers, doubtless from a lady's boa. The Thinking Machine found a handkerchief marked "G", Dupin found an old letter, Vidocq an eyeglass case, and Lecoq a glove. Raffles found a gray barrette, and Holmes picked up a market list.

"Now, Gentlemen," said the president, "you each have your separate clues. Go your ways, make your deductions, and meet tomorrow at our rooms, where I will show you the robber."

The Infallible Detectives went their ways, secretly incensed at Holmes' arrogance.

The next day at three o'clock they all trooped back to the rooms of their association, and each brought with him a lady, a citizen of the town.

"Ha!" exclaimed Holmes. "The villain seems to be plural."

"And feminine," added the Thinking Machine, looking askance at the buxom dame he had captured.

"First we must take all their pictures," declared Holmes.

"We expected that," said Mrs. Green, who had been identified by the G on her handkerchief and was spokeswoman for the party. "We put on our best clothes on purpose. Shall we be in a group or single?"

The ladies fluttered about in pleasant anticipation of being photographed. The performance over, the detectives questioned their captives, whom they had easily identified by the various clues. Each one declared that she had been in Mrs. Plummer's parlor between two and four o'clock the afternoon previous.

"Then," said Holmes, "do you confess that you purloined Mrs. Plummer's Rogers Group?"

"We do!" exclaimed the ladies in a chorus.

"You admit that you took it with felonious intent, in other words you stole it?"

"We did," declared the ladies unanimously. "And you can't put us in jail for it, because we can prove that we were in the right."

"Prove it," said President Holmes.

"I am the president," began Mrs. Green, "and these ladies are members of our Village Improvement Society.[1] In the interests of our work we are often obliged to remove —"

"Ah, yes," exclaimed Holmes, "I quite understand — quite — quite! Not another word, I beg of you, my dear Madam! All is understood. You ladies are excused, and Mrs. Plummer has no case, no case at all. Good afternoon, Ladies."

"Ah, yes, but stay one moment." said Rouletabille. his eager eyes agog with intense interest. "Please, please, may I ask the solution of the only question that interested me in this case? How did you get into that hermetically sealed house?"

Mrs. Green looked at him pityingly. "Sir," she said, "I took the key out from under the mat, and afterward replaced it."

---

[1] A group dedicated to improving a village's infrastructure, such as promoting the use of sidewalks, shade trees, parks, and the elimination of roadside dumps and other unsightliness. Well-run groups can make substantial changes to the look of an area, at the risk of turning into power-mad martinets who will fine a homeowner for flying a flag or planting a vegetable garden.

Water, Water Everywhere and Not a Drop For Tea

Anonymous

When World War I broke out in 1914, the German Empire herded British civilians into internment camps. Many of them were housed at a horse racetrack outside Berlin. Facing the prospect of a long stay, the internees made the best of their situation. They turned the stables into barracks, built wooden sidewalks to traverse the mud and named them for streets in England, set up businesses, including tailors, cafes, and even a casino, and figured out ways to pass the time. One enterprising inmate launched a private postal system with mailboxes and stamps called the Ruhleben Express Delivery — the R.X.D. in the story. There was even a newspaper and a magazine, In Ruhleben Camp, *from which this story was taken.*

"Come in," cried a familiar voice in answer to my knock on the heavy sliding door of the box stall. I discovered Sholmes reclining in a deck chair wringing some lost chords out of the soul of a concertina.

"My dear Whyson, I am delighted to see you," he said, motioning me to an easy margarine box. "You will find the tobacco in that clog on the shelf."

"But," I began.

"Oh, that is quite all right," said Sholmes, picking up an empty box and suspending it by a nail over the peep-hole in the door. "You will observe, my dear Whyson, that should anyone try to look through that hole he would simply see the inside of the empty box."

"Marvellously simple," said I, "and quite worthy of you, my dear Sholmes!"

"And now, Whyson," said Sholmes, when we had settled ourselves comfortably with our pipes. "Where have you been hiding yourself, I have seen nothing of you lately?"

"I have been rather busy the last few days," I replied. "This morning, for instance, I went early to the Canteen for a hard-boiled egg. But after waiting some hours in the line, the man next but one in front of me got the last. I next went to the Parcels Office and after waiting a few more hours nearly succeeded in getting a parcel. That is to say all of the contents of the thing addressed to me were confiscated with the exception of two glass jars of jam and those were broken."

"Most annoying," said Sholmes.

"Yes, one is kept constantly busy here doing nothing," I replied. "This afternoon I waited a further two hours trying to get a ticket for Wagner's *Gotterdammerung*[1] and all I could manage was a seat on the top of one of the stoves."

"That is very hard," said Sholmes.

"And very cold," I added.

"But now my dear Whyson I have just been presented with a very pretty problem, something that will interest you. Of course, I have a lot of other things on hand, the affair of the missing lion's head, the disappearance of the balance sheet from the boiler-house, the mystery of the bucket from barrack eight, the fraud of the gilt watch-chain and the like. But as you know, my dear Whyson, I do not regard the problems that come my way from the point of view of the pecuniary profit that may accrue therefrom but solely as a specialist in mystery." I could see that Sholmes had been presented with a problem after his own heart for seldom have I seen him as near excitement as he was on this occasion.

"Well, tell me all about it, Sholmes," I cried, "and it will really seem like old times."

"Here you are," he replied and handed me an R.X.D. card from the Captains' Office.[2]

---

[1] Translated as "Twilight of the Gods," it is the last of four operas in the *Der Ring des Nibelungen (The Ring of the Nibelung)* cycle by Richard Wagner (1813-1883). It takes four nights and 15 hours to perform the Ring Cycle—*Gotterdammerung* takes five hours by itself, not counting intermissions—but when you're in a prison camp, time is the one thing you have plenty of.

[2] Each barrack had a captain in charge who wore a white armband bearing his title and barrack number. From their office, they were responsible for

It ran as follows: "Dear Mr. Sholmes, we find ourselves in a frightful difficulty and would be indescribably grateful if you would come to our aid. Every night a number of men from various barracks steal from their beds and disappear until morning, in many cases not returning for the count at six thirty. This is, as you will readily recognise, a very serious matter, and we trust that you will not deny us your assistance. P.S. Please do not mention this to anyone outside the Captains' Office as it would never do for the Camp to think that there was any problem, however difficult that we are not capable of solving without any outside help whatever."

Sholmes smiled somewhat sarcastically as he saw me reading the post-script. "Rather like the appeals we used to get in the old days from Scotland Yard only not so well put, eh, Whyson?"

"Well, have you any ideas?" I enquired, knowing full well by the way he stroked his chin that my inimitable friend had already formed some theory which would lead to a speedy solution of the Captains' woe.

"Yes, we have some ideas on the matter, and we will put them to the test to-night when I shall be glad of your company and maybe of your assistance, Whyson. Meet me by the flagstaff at ten-thirty, will you. By the way, don't bring your service revolver as it might go off and so land us in trouble—that is, to say, in barrack eleven."[1]

At ten-thirty, I stole along to the appointed meeting place where I found my friend awaiting me. Thanks to my previous experiences of a like nature, I had taken the precaution to put

---

keeping records, maintaining discipline, and working with the commandant. They were considerably unpopular with the prisoners, in part because they refused to release information about the money, particularly from the inmates' families, that passed through their hands.

[1] The camp's cells consisted of two horse stalls, each subdivided into two cells, and furnished with a wooden plank for a bed. Prisoners could be sent there for one to three days at any guard's discretion for violating the camp's rules, such as smoking in the barracks, burning naked candles, shirking the compulsory weekly bath, or insolence.

my dark trousers over my pyjamas so that we should not be conspicuous, and Sholmes nodded approval when he noted this evidence of my having benefited from his lessons. "But, my dear Watson, why cover up your white trousers and leave your white jacket to give us away? Still, it won't matter for this little trip. Now, come along and do walk lightly so as not to wake them."

This, I thought, was a little exaggerated, believing that he referred to the people sleeping in the barracks.

Noiselessly, we crept down Bond Street[1] and we were just opposite the Lobster's stores when Sholmes gripped my arm.

"See them?" he whispered hoarsely.

Sure enough, I saw several figures leaning against the boiler-house.

"What are they making?" I asked, for like many others in this camp, I am in the throes of Otto-Sauer[2] and this has a prejudicial effect on one's English at times.

"Sleeping," replied Sholmes simply. Then, after a pause, "Well, we'd better be going back to barracks."

"But what about these people? Are these the missing men? What are you going to do about it?" And I put the querries in a heap.

"My dear Whyson," drawled my friend, "Like the dramatic societies, I think my best course now is one of masterly inactivity. It is up to the captains now, as our friend Millington[3] would say."

---

[1] Wooden sidewalks were built to limit the mud and debris stirred up by the inmates, and they quickly acquired nicknames. Like its London counterpart, Bond Street was where many inmates set up their shops and businesses.

[2] A language-learning method created by Thomas Gaspey, Emil Otto, and Carl Marquard Sauer that emphasized using conversations to reinforce memorizing the words.

[3] "Masterly inactivity" was coined by Sir James Mackintosh (1765-1832), a Scottish politician who observed that the House of Commons, which "faithful to their system, remained in a wise and masterly inactivity." Millington was probably a civilian internee. The camp magazine mentions a D. Millington who was returned to England in March 1916.

"But my dear Sholmes, it is all so absurdly simple. How did it occur to you that these men were to be found there?"

"Observation, my dear Whyson, only observation. Tell me how do you spend most of your time here?"

"Why, in lining-up, of course."

"Just so. And about what do you swear most?"

"Why, about lining-up, of course."

"Just so. And do you sleep well when you have been to the Casino?"

"Why, no, of course not."

"Just so. Well, there you are."

"Where?"

"Well, come now, my dear Whyson, you have been privileged to study my methods all these years. Surely it is quite obvious to you. Let us look at the facts. Firstly, all the men who disappear are casino-schein holders.[1] Secondly, they are quite normal during the day but do this mysterious vanishing act at night. Trouble in the night, my dear Whyson, is usually attributable to stomache trouble. Then, the fact that these men's subconsciousnesses must by this time be saturated with the idea of lining-up. There you are, my dear Whyson."

And my extraordinary friend hastened away towards his box and his beloved concertina.

Postage stamps from Ruhleben intern camp.

---

[1] One enterprising inmate founded a combination casino and restaurant. Monthly tickets ("scheins") were sold allowing the holder to spend up to two 1-hour shifts a day, and a sentry was posted at the door to control admission.

The Mystery of the Leaping Fish

Tod Browning and Anita Loos

The 223B Casebook series is supposed to reprint stories, but we'll make an exception for this one. It probably holds the record as the weirdest Holmes parody ever: a silent film starring leading man Douglas Fairbanks (1883-1939), co-written by Tod Browning (1880-1962), the future creator of the cult classic Freaks (1932), and Anita Loos (1889-1981), later to write Gentlemen Prefer Blondes. On top of that, it contains as much drug humor as a Cheech and Chong movie.

Coming out the same year as William Gillette's Sherlock Holmes, The Mystery of the Leaping Fish stars Fairbanks as private detective Coke Ennyday, who investigates a dope-smuggling millionaire who wants to marry by force the beautiful girl who rents floats at the beach. Fairbanks downs drugs with abandon, wears outrageous disguises, dances like a fool, battles villainous Chinamen, and gets the girl, but not before she rescues herself. There's even an epilogue that makes fun of the movie business. The recap below, with the title cards, gives just a hint of the strangeness. Fortunately, the movie is freely available online.

"Home of the world's greatest scientific detective, Coke Ennyday."

"Coke Ennyday took no chances on admitting a visitor without consulting his scientific periscope."

"You must consent to marry Fishy Joe within the week."

"Have no fear. Coke Ennyday the scientific detective will protect you."

"Japs on the leaping fish! Get the cans! At last a clue!"

"Smuggling! The secret is mine!"

"Coke Ennyday is on our trail!"

"Opium!"

"In Chinatown, the laundry where the gang does its dirty works."

"Girl, you are in my power."

[Not for long—*Editor*]

244 | The Best Sherlock Holmes Parodies and Pastiches

[The end—*Editor*] "But not the end of this story ..."

[Epilogue: Douglas Fairbanks reads to a studio boss the *Leaping Fish* script he wrote.—*Editor*]

"No, Douglas, you had better give up scenario writing and stick to acting."

[The very end—*Editor*]

Narpoo Rum

Anonymous

The Belgium town of Ypres on the border with France was the scene of some of the worse fighting of the war. Five major battles were fought around it, and so many British soldiers died there that during peacetime it became a pilgrimage site for veterans and families.

In early 1916, soldiers from the 12th Battalion, Sherwood Forest, came across an abandoned printing press, and a sergeant with printing experience refurbished it. Thus was born The Wipers Times, *a trench journal named for the British soldiers' attempts to pronounce Ypres. Like many journals, it was put together largely through improvisation and interrupted by fighting. It also underwent numerous name changes as the Foresters moved from place to place. Against the odds, the* Times *survived, and grew so popular that it was adopted by the British Expeditionary Force and renamed itself* The B.E.F. Times.

The Wipers Times ran several Sherlock parodies, but "Narpoo Rum" was one of the few that told a complete story. Because they were produced by untrained soldier-editors and printed under challenging conditions, there were numerous misspellings and inconsistencies. To make it easier to read, this version has been edited lightly and the dialog broken into paragraphs. As for the title, narpoo—pronounced "nah poo"— was an attempt by British soldiers to say the French phrase "il n'y a plus" (ill-knee-a-ploo) meaning "there's none left" or "no good."

Dramatis Personae:

Cloridy Lyme[1]—A Sanitary Inspector.
Madeline Carol—A French Girl.
Intha Pink—A Pioneer.
General Bertram Rudolph de Rogerum—The Earl of Loose.
Lord Reginald de Knellthorpe—His Son.
Q. Wemm—A Storekeeper.
L. Plumernapple—A Soldier.
Herlock Shomes—The Great Detective.

---

[1] Chloride of lime was a powdered mix of lime and calcium chloride. It was used as a disinfectant in the trenches and in a solution to wash the gas off anything that the gas had touched, including skin and guns.

Dr. Hotsam—His Admirer

Chapter 1.

"My dear Hotsam, nothing of the kind I assure you," said Shomes, in his comfortable dug out in Quality Street.[1] "My methods are based on deduction. For instance, you hear someone coming up the stairs. Well, that is all the untrained ear can hear, but I know it's a soldier with many ribbons, an Irish accent and a friend named Reggie. How do I know? My dear fellow—"

At that moment the door opened, and General Bertram Rudolph de Rogerum entered. Casting himself in a chair he demanded a cocktail.

"Well, my dear general," said Shomes, placing his finger tips together, "how can I help you?"

"What! you know me?" gasped the general.

"Oh yes!" said Shomes, as he tilted his vermoral sprayer[2] and squirted a quart into his left arm.

"Well," said the general, "I have come about a very mysterious affair. Three nights running the Brigade rum ration has disappeared."

"Good heavens!" ejaculated Hotsam.

"Aha!" said Shomes, "this promises to be a most interesting case." With that he picked up his violin, and proceeded to play dreamily. "Now I am ready, general, tell me all about it."

"Well," said the general, "as you know, my men mostly dislike rum, so that when it comes up I have it put in one of the outhouses. Three mornings ago, when my son, a priceless lad, if I may say so, and above suspicion, went to look at it, he found it had disappeared. This has happened on both the following nights, and so I thought you might be able to help us."

---

[1] A reference to the romantic comedy play written by J.M. Barrie (1901). The play proved so popular that when its stars, Seymour Hicks and his wife, Elialine Terriss, moved to Surrey, their street was renamed "Quality Street." Hicks also co-wrote the Sherlockian parody play *Under the Clock* (1893).

[2] A handheld tank with a pump and hose, used to treat trenches and dugouts contaminated by chlorine gas.

"Have you no clue at all?" snapped the great detective.

"Only that Wemm's store seems to be more popular with the soldiers than formerly," said the general.

"Leave the matter in my hands, general, I will find your rum," said the detective. With that, the general went off jauntily, whistling "Another Little Drink Wouldn't Do Us Any Harm."[1]

Immediately he had gone Shomes sprang up. "Now Hotsam, we must to work!" Hastily throwing off his smoking jacket, he donned a tin-hat, mackintosh and gum boots, and disappeared into the night.

Meanwhile in the lovely French evening, Plumernapple was paying court to Madeline Carot, the pretty daughter at the local estaminet.[2]

"Well, it's only 'arf past eight," he murmured, "and there ain't no perlice corprel about."

"No compris,"[3] she gurgled, as she made to shut the door. Picking up his A frame,[4] he sadly made his way along the road.

At Wemm's store a very merry party was in progress, and Hotsam, taking the air, strolled across there. Pushing open the door, he saw Q. Wemm entertaining many friends from among the neighbouring troops. He was immediately made welcome, and a mug of hot liquid was thrust into his hand.

Casting his eyes round, they fell on a heap of jars in the corner. "The Rum!" he gasped.

Chapter 2.

It was Xmas. The sturdy figure of General Bertram Rudolph

---

[1] A song from *The Bing Boys are Here*, a popular revue that year in London's West End. Subtitled "A Picture of London Life," it follows the adventures of two boys from Binghamton in the big city. It was light, inconsequential fare and the perfect antidote for war-weary civilians and soldiers home on leave.

[2] The French word for a small café that sells alcoholic drinks.

[3] French for "I don't understand."

[4] A type of trench built by linking wooden frames that looked like an upside-down "A" only with a flat top. Boards connected the legs of the frames to hold back the earthen walls, and a boardwalk was built atop the crosspiece.

de Rogerum was plodding along the snow-covered road jauntily whistling a Xmas carol. Every now and then a frown crossed his handsome face as he thought of the missing rum ration, and how the evidence seemed to point to none other than his son, Lord Reginald de Knellthorpe. Had Reggie in a reckless moment stolen the rum? Heaving a deep sigh he fell into a crump hole[1] which had been hidden under the white mantle of winter.

Meanwhile what was happening at Wemm's store? At Hotsam's exclamation "The Rum" a guilty look spread over Wemm's face, and his assistant guiltily stole through the door. Hotsam sprang in front of the jars. "Open one," he thundered. Shakingly Wemm compiled, and poured out a glass of the liquid. Hotsam examined this and found it to be solution for vermoral sprayers. With a nod to Wemm he went out. On returning to his dug out he found Lord Reginald de Knellthorpe in possession of the armchair shooting rats.

"Hullo, old boy," said Knellthorpe, "what about papa's rum?"

"Look here Reggie," said Hotsam, "Do you know anything about it? Shomes is on the track and you might be able to help him." Reggie paled.

"Shomes," he gasped, picking up his helmet and gas mask, "Shomes! Good heavens, then all is lost." Staggering to the door he disappeared into the night.

Mixing himself a drink Hotsam sat down and began to go over the evidence. Suddenly the door opened, and the Earl of Loose entered.

"Good evening, General," said Hotsam.

"General be dammed," snapped Shomes' voice, "Has Reginald de Knellthorpe been here?"

"Just this minute gone," said Hotsam.

Dashing to the door Shomes rapidly disappeared, followed by Hotsam. Suddenly two shots rang out and Shomes dropped in the snow, crying "Follow him, follow him." Hotsam dashed madly in pursuit, and didn't stop till he fell down the shaft at

---

[1] A crater caused by an exploding shell. *Crump* is an Old English word meaning a hard blow or hit.

the Old Fosse.[1]

Picking himself up, Shomes returned to his dug-out and bound up his wrist where the shot had struck him. Baring his forearm he injected a gallon out of his vermoral sprayer and picked up his violin.

Down in the village Madeline Carot sat at the door of her old mother's estaminet. Her face brightened as she saw the sturdy figure of Intha Pink coming up the road.

"Oh Intha," she exclaimed, "I thought you were never coming to see me. Where have you been?"

Hurriedly glancing up and down the road Pink slipped into the estaminet and closed the door. "Rum!" he gasped.

Madeline got him a glass of rum which he swallowed at a gulp. "Has Shomes been here?" he demanded. "Yes," she replied, "He was here this morning, and had a glass of rum."

"Then we are lost!" shouted Intha, and disappeared through the door.

Hotsam, meanwhile arrived at the bottom of the shaft. Taking his flash lamp from his pocket he proceeded to examine his position. The first thing his light fell on was a pile of jars stacked in a corner. "The rum!" he gasped.

Chapter 3.

It was raining. Shomes, who had business of a pressing nature that night, shuddered as he pulled aside the gas curtain of his dug-out, and looked up and down the trench.

Dropping the curtain hastily he injected a good dose from his vermoral sprayer, and disguised himself as a sergeant. He then swallowed half-a-pint of rum and went out into the night, to proceed on an urgent and secret mission to the "Culvert Arms" at Hooge.[2] Making his way along the duckboards to the waiting aeroplane he jumped aboard and disappeared into the darkness.

---

[1] Probably a local landmark, as fosse means a long narrow trench. From the Latin *fossa* for ditch.

[2] A small village about four miles east of Ypres. Three years of fighting destroyed the village, which has since been rebuilt.

Meanwhile, the Earl of Loose was in a very troubled state of mind about his son. In addition to the mysterious disappearance of the rum Reggie had been playing fast and loose with the pretty dark-eyed daughter at the neighbouring chateau. So much so indeed that the poor old Earl was considering the advantages of sending Master Reginald back to school. Professor Spot had just recently opened a finishing school for young gentlemen in the neighbourhood.

He had just made up his mind to send Reginald for a course when his eye fell on the young scapegoat ambling along smoking a cigarette, and without his gas helmet. Choking back an expletive the General hurried after him, and was only just in time to see him disappear into the corner estaminet where Madeline dispensed beer daily.

The general stealthily approached, and looking through the back window saw Reginald with the girl in his arms. On the ground was a stack of rum jars at which Reggie was pointing while saying something to the girl. At this sight the General clutched at his collar and swooned.

Hotsam, who on examination had found all the jars at the bottom of the Old Fosse to be empty and of a condemned pattern, gathered himself together and proceeding by the old workings soon found himself by the corner estaminet.

Hearing laughter and voices he made his way to the back and fell over the unconscious form of General Bertram Rudolph de Rogerum, the Earl of Loose.

Picking himself up he looked in at the window.

"The Rum!" he gasped.

Chapter 4.

The Clue of the Torn Letter

Skilfully landing his plane in the Square of the ancient town of Ypres, Shomes resolved to dine at the Hotel des Ramparts before proceeding up the Menin Road to the Culvert Arms. Having partaken of an excellent dinner, Shomes once more donned his tin-hat, raincoat and gum boots thigh,[1] and proceeded by way of the Menin Gate up the Menin Road. As he walked, the fearful events of his last great adventure in that district flashed through his mind with painful distinctness. He was roused from his reverie by the weary whirr of a five-nine,[2] and realized with a start that he had reached his destination. Looking around with a dawning sense of horror he saw that the Culvert Arms was no more. Shomes amazed, perplexed, but by no means non-plussed hastily injected a double dose from his vermoral sprayer, and sought for a clue. Down in the deep and muddy ditch where once the ancient hostelry had stood, he passed a few battered stones, and in the dark and sluggish waters found an envelope, muddy and torn, and readable as far as:—

    TOR

        IMES

            TERS (P

Shomes spoke no word, but a close observer would have noted that his face, seen in the white glare of the Very Lights[3] had a look of grim and purposeful satisfaction.

Chapter 5.

About the same time as Shomes was making his important

---

[1] Rubber boots issued to keep the feet dry and free of trench foot, in which feet exposed to cold and damp conditions turn black and the skin dies.

[2] A German howitzer that fired a shell with a diameter of 5.9 inches. Mounted on a two-wheel carriage, it could be moved close to the front line to fire a devastating barrage.

[3] Signal flares fired from a specially made pistol. Named for its U.S. inventor, Edward Very (1847-1910). Sentries used them at night to light up the battlefield. The horror of being caught in the open under one was expressed in a trench song sung to "When Irish Eyes Are Smiling":

    When Very lights are shining,
    Sure they're like the morning light
    And when the guns begin to thunder
    You can hear the angels shite.

discovery at the ruined Culvert Arms, Hotsam was endeavouring to revive the fainting Earl and at the same time to keep a vigilant watch through the estaminet window. The General at length recovered consciousness, and joined Hotsam at the window. A strange sight met their eyes. Lord Reginald de Knellthorpe stood with his back to the window supporting the fair Madeline, who appeared to be weeping bitterly. Muttering with impotent rage the old Earl thrust open the door, and followed by Hotsom, entered the room. Lord Reggie turned an amazed and tear-wet face towards them, and simultaneously the Earl and Hotsam burst into tears. Hotsam with alacrity put on his gas helmet, corked up the open rum jar, and opened the window. The General drying his tears, furiously asked his weeping son the reason of his presence there.

"Well, you see, father," said Lord Reggie, "Madeline" (he tenderly wiped the eyes of the beautiful girl) "told me that she had seen some rum jars in here, and, thinking that they might contain the rum that I am suspected of stealing, I came here to examine them, they appear to contain tear gas."[1]

The Earl, with a new burst of tears, joined the hands of Reggie and Madeline, and Hotsam feeling that his presence was no longer required, strode out into the night, leaving the Earl and the young lovers smiling through their tears.

Chapter 6.

The End of Shomes?

Hotsam, very fatigued, at length reached the comfortable Quality Street dug-out, where he found a signaller, who handed him one of the dreaded pink forms. He resignedly took the wire and read:

"Meet me at YPRES at once AAA Obtain bus from GEN. BERTRAM RUDOLPH de ROGERUM AAA Urgent Sick AAA"

Hotsam sighed, and after much trouble obtained the bus,

---

[1] Rum is British slang for strange or suspect, making them very rum jars indeed.

254 | The Best Sherlock Holmes Parodies and Pastiches

and eventually reached Ypres. In the Square he found Shomes, seated in his plane. "Come, Hotsam," he cried, "jump in, there is no time to be lost, they shall not escape us this time." Hotsam obeyed, and Shomes, having started up the motor, jumped in, and they were off. After some hours in the air, Hotsam shouted, "Where are we going, Shomes?" He could not catch the answer, so was silent. Suddenly a flash! a crash! and two men and an Archied aeroplane[1] were falling though the night.

Chapter 7.

At Last?

Intha sat in a large shell-hole in the grounds of Elvarston Castle.[2] He was not happy. He had been knocked down by a G.S. wagon,[3] machine-gunned on the road, whizz-banged[4] in the trench, and, finally, had taken his "A" frame to the wrong dump. As he rested he thought of many things. He thought of war, he thought of snow, he thought of rum. Why had he had no rum for some days now? Because some scoundrel had stolen the Brigade supply. Suddenly a great resolve grew in the soul of the Pioneer;[5] we would find the missing liquid! Fired by enthusiasm, he arose, and, casting away his now useless "A" frame, made his way as quickly to the Estaminet of Madeline

---

[1] Anti-aircraft fire, inspired by a popular London show in which a girl sang "Not now, Archie" whenever her boyfriend tried to kiss her. Pilots began saying that when their planes came under fire, so an archied plane had been "kissed" by the gunners on the ground.
[2] A stately home in Derbyshire, north-central England. Actually a manor home, it was built in 1633 and extended several times.
[3] General Services wagon. These horse-drawn wagons were used to transport supplies to the front line.
[4] Seasoned soldiers quickly learned to identify shells by size, effects, or sounds. Whizz-bangs were fired by high-velocity guns that came in before you had time to take cover. The word was also used to described hastily written official postcards.
[5] A soldier trained in engineering and construction. They were tasked to build field fortifications, bridges, roads, and camps. Pioneer came from the Old French *pionnier* which meant "foot soldier."

Carot. After some protest, Madeline quietly admitted him.

"I'm a bloomin' policeman now," he said, "and don't you bloomin' well forget it. I saw a staff-officer leave 'ere at eight-fifteen, wot yer goin' ter do aba'ht it?"

"You no tell," said Madeline, "and I give you beer."

"Narpoo!"

"I give you some rum."

"The RUM!" thought Intha.

Chapter 8.

What Cloridy Lyme Saw

Cloridy Lyme straightened his aching back with a groan and gazed around the stricken streets of Bapaume[1] in the cold grey light of dawn with every appearance of profound distaste.

"When I joined this here mob I 'ad visions of bayonets; and spearin' bits o' paper and orange peel on a pointed stick," mused he. Gazing upwards at the lowering sky, he saw a strange sight. A sausage was drifting by, scarcely clearing the roofs of the ruined houses. Two men hung precariously in the rigging, and a trail rope dragged over the ground. As he watched, the rope caught in a tree stump, and the two men, hastily sliding down it, inquired of the astonished sanitary inspector their whereabouts. On hearing that they were in Bapaume, Shomes (for it was none other than he) said calmly, "just as I thought, my dear Hotsam, my deductions are sometimes at fault but very rarely I think." Glancing sharply at the pointed stick held by Cloridy Lime, he suddenly seized it, and tore from the end a piece of paper which, after perusing, he handed to Hotsam, saying, "Just as I told you my dear fellow."

---

[1] A district in northern France near the Belgian border, about 66 miles south of Ypres. During the Somme offensive earlier in 1916, more than 57,000 British soldiers were killed or wounded attempting to recapture Bapaume, the highest one-day casualty rate in the army's history. By the time this issue was printed, the British had recaptured Bapaume three weeks before.

Hotsam took the paper and read,

>   EDI
>   WIPERS T
>   SHERWOOD FORES

Chapter 9.

Back at Quality Street

"But my dear Hotsam, the whole thing is so absurdly simple," said Shomes curling his long wiry body up in his comfortable bunk.

"What! You really have solved the problem of the missing rum?"

"There never was a problem, and the rum was never stolen."

"For heavens sake explain, Shomes, I really cannot follow your abstruce[1] reasoning."

"You surely remember my good fellow, that at the time the rum was supposed to have been stolen, it was almost impossible to buy whisky in this country."

"Yes I remember it very well indeed, but what has that to do with the question?"

"My good Hotsam, cannot you follow me now?"

"I really cannot, Shomes."

"You met the Earl and his staff many times during those trying days, did you not?"

"Yes, I saw them nearly every day."

"Did they strike you as men who had suddenly become total abstainers?"

"No, I cannot say they did."

"Well, just think a little, my dear Hotsam. Whisky was unobtainable then, what did they— Pass the whisky and put on the gramophone my good fellow. I think we are entitled to a tot."

---

[1] Difficult to follow, obscure.

The Looking-Glass

Anonymous

One would not expect Holmes to possess the knowledge to offer make-up advice to women. Yet here we have him in the "Page for Women" section of the Sydney Morning Herald *of July 18, 1917, discussing with Watson the problems the fairer sex encounter preparing for the day. Note that the anonymous author knew enough of the canon to recall Sherlock's deductions about the position of Watson's shaving mirror in "The Boscome Valley Mystery."*

Sherlock Holmes, and his friend Dr. Watson, were sitting at a table in one of our popular tearooms, into which streams of women of all ages, were pouring, for it was 4 o'clock, the hour sacred to afternoon tea.

Seeing the accustomed look of profound absorption on the great detective's face, Watson waited, for he knew that an illuminating flash would presently be vouchsafed him, throwing a strong searchlight on the follies and fancies of the womenkind of to-day.

"I perceive, Watson," said Holmes at length, "that the architecture of the average dwelling-house of Sydney is sadly defective."

Marvelling at his friend's perspicacity, the doctor waited for more wisdom, which presently came.

"The lady who has just passed us," the critic went on, "wearing a black velvet hat, with a big cerise rose[1] in front, has made up the left side of her face much redder than the right. From this I deduce that she dresses in a badly lighted room, and that her dressing table is so placed that the light comes on her right. Consequently, she puts on more rouge than is necessary on the left cheek, which is in shadow. But in 'plein air,'[2] as

---

[1] A deep reddish color, such as that found on a cherry (which is what the word means in French).
[2] French for "open air," it refers to the act of painting outdoors in the available natural light. This is in contrast to studio painting, where a sub-

the French call it, the effect, as you see, is not good. The cerise patch on her left cheek does not even match the rose in her hat. Now, if the architect who built her house had known his business, he would have planned the dressing room so that the looking-glass must either stand in a bay window, which is the best position of all, or else that the light should fall over the left shoulder of the occupant of the room when she stands at her looking-glass. The dark bedroom is responsible for many bad complexions.

"Women are accused of being vain, Watson, but it is their extreme diffidence and nervousness that cause them to try and mend their appearance. They look in the glass and see that they are, to use their own word, 'frights,' and without any scientific knowledge, or even much skill or taste, they set to work to whiten and raddle[1] their faces in a light that a futurist artist[2] would consider confusing.

"No painter would lay brush to inanimate canvas in a bad light. His conceit or vanity would not allow him to work in unfavourable conditions. Yet a women apparently thinks that any old colour applied in any reckless way is better than her own, while her hair she really prefers to be of an unearthly hue.

"Take my tip, the true ideal of the complexion-menders is the pantomime dame,[3] Mrs. Ali Baba, or Widow Twankey—they are the beauties. They can revel in Watteau[4] brocades

---

ject may be artificially posed and lit.

[1] Reddish. A red pigment made from ochre, an earthy pigment containing clay and ferric oxide.

[2] A member of an artistic and social movement that was launched in Italy in the early 20th century with the intention of breaking with the past. The idea spread to include music, literature, painting, politics, and architecture.

[3] Pantomimes are family friendly musical comedies staged during the Christmas holidays, based on popular stories such as "Aladdin" and "Ali Baba." Widow Twankey and Mrs. Ali Baba are the mothers of the heroes.

[4] Jean-Antoine Watteau (1684-1721) was a French painter whose name was attached to fabrics and styles that appeared in his paintings. A brocade is a

with short skirts and in impossible heels, with dinky handbags, and the latest hats with brightest trimming, in copper hair, contrasting with turquoise-blue frocks; in pinkest cheeks, glowing on each side above a 'cupid's bow' of vermillion paint.

"But the dame, gaudy as she is, knows better than to consult 'her' looking-glass in any light but the very latest electrics. 'Her' artistic conscience would never allow her to make up in semi-darkness.

"Observe this girl," the sage went on "with the dead white face, so thickly floured that the natural sheen of the skin is quite covered as with a coat of whitewash, and with her lips a thin red line of blood.

"Is it pretty, that effect? No, it is not pretty, but it is supposed to be the sign of the 'vampire woman." A course of moving pictures would bring her to that.

"To my trained mind, Watson, it presents only the conclusion that the white lady and others like her have minds absolutely uninformed on the subject of the laws of reflection and refraction. They do not know that no looking-glass, not even the best and most carefully made mirror, placed in good light, reflects truly. No woman's complexion is really as bad as the looking-glass makes it out to be. If you doubt it, look at my face in that mirror opposite, and then at me.

"Yes, I thought you'd say so. I'm a much better-looking chap than my counterfeit presentment.

"But come, we have moralised enough to-day," and pressing the button, Sherlock Holmes and Dr. Watson took the lift and ascended into spiritland.

---

richly decorated fabric made of silk and sometimes gold and silver threads.
[1] A movie trope popularized at the time by actresses such as Theda Bara (1885-1955) who portrayed women as dark and mysterious creatures who lure men to their destruction.

When the Spirits Rapped
A Nasty Incident in the Career of Sherlog Combes
Anonymous

While Conan Doyle never used Sherlock to promote his Spiritualist beliefs, there were those who used the detective as a way of taking the movement down a peg. The events at a typical séance described below were exaggerated for comic purposes, but not by much.

This was published in the March 29, 1919, issue of London Opinion, a magazine that targeted a male readership with its mix of serious and satirical articles. It ran for 50 years, and was most famous for creating the "Lord Kitchener Needs You" recruitment poster that appeared on its cover. It was quickly adopted by James Montgomery Flagg, who substituted Uncle Sam for the renowned general.

Sherlog Combes sat in his study, wrapped in thought and a Jaeger dressing-gown.[1]

He was conscious that he was growing old. "In my younger days," he mused, "I should never have bought that purse from that race-course swindler for half-a-crown and expected to find the three half-crowns[2] in it. But with regard to the three-card trick in the train coming back, I really had bad luck in losing my tenner. I thought the manipulator was doing the

---

[1] Clothing consisting of animal fibers such as wool. Dr. Gustav Jaeger (1832-1917) theorized that humans would be healthier if they wore natural animal fibers next to the skin. This created a demand for wool-jersey long johns, which in England was fulfilled by "Dr. Jaeger's Sanitary Woollen System Co. Ltd.," founded in 1884 by businessman Lewis Tomalin, who acquired the rights from the doctor. Jaeger is still in business and known for its classic "twinset and pearls" image and natural-fiber clothing.

[2] A "short-con" popular at race courses along with the three-card Monte game described below. From the back of his wagon, a hustler would attract a crowd by offering to sell a small leather purse at an distinctly low price. He would then sweeten the deal by placing a coin in the purse. The hustler would palm the coin and replace it with a brass slug. Amazingly, these purses sold well.

trick so clumsily that he was exposing which was the lady.¹ But I was wrong.

"However," he ran on in his reverie, "when Dr. Potson calls on me again—and I suppose he will, although he has left me severely alone of late—I shall have something startling to tell him of my discoveries about the spirit world."

Here the ancient sleuth picked up his weekly copy of The Styx,² a journal devoted to spirits (the medium brand, not the strong), and his eye caught the following announcement:

"SPIRITS! SPIRITS! SPIRITS! — PROFESSOR TRIXTER (the World's Most Famous Medium) will hold a séance at 3.0 sharp. How would you like to talk to Julius Caesar? Admission. One shilling."

Two hours later he was being carried rapidly in a luxurious sixty horse-power automobile (the property of the General Omnibus Company), and soon afterwards reached the flat in Bloomsbury where the séance was to take place.

The flat had the appearance of having been selected in a great hurry. It was unfurnished and dirty. A large room on an upper floor had been prepared for the ceremony by the simple expedient of darkening the window, and improvising seats out of soap boxes and planks.

Sherlog Combes was admitted by a hefty individual whose appearance alone would have quenched the ardour of a less enthusiastic investigator. He found a number of famous people already assembled, including two lady novelists, a Labour

---

¹ Combs was playing three-card Monte, a guessing game in which the dealer displays three cards, one of them a queen, turns them over, rearranges them and invites bettors to guess where the queen was. In this scam, the dealer arranges with a confederate to lose a couple of games and clumsily shuffles the cards, leading the mark to believe that he can win.
² Probably a play on *Light*, a Spiritualist magazine that published Conan Doyle's articles. The Styx is a river in Greek mythology that marks the boundary between Earth and the Underworld.

M.P., and Professor Foljambe, F.R.S.,[1] the eminent zoologist who had discovered the fallacy of the theory that it is impossible to say "Boo" to a goose.[2]

The medium opened the proceedings by a brief lecture on the objects of the séance, spoken with a pronounced American accent. Then he seated himself in the only chair the room contained, and his hefty assistant proceeded to tie him up with much grunting and straining over every knot.

The visitors were requested to sit on the improvised forms, and to take each other's hands. There was a slight diversion owing to Sherlog Combes sitting on a nail that had been left in one of the soap boxes. When all was ready the assistant switched out the lights.

For a few moments absolute silence ensued. Then a banjo thrummed once. As if this were a signal, a regular spiritual jazz band struck up. The room was filled with a medley of strange sounds. Instruments more or less musical seemed to be floating about in space, and twice Sherlog's bald head was smitten by a tambourine. Then the noise died away as suddenly as it had begun, and the watchers became aware of a shadowy phosphorescent figure standing before them.

"Who are you?" asked a voice.

"I guess Julius Caesar's my label, stranger," replied the apparition; and then added, rather inconsequently, "Take away that bauble!"

The illustrious Roman appeared to be a talkative spirit. He remained chatting for about ten minutes, during which time he gave a racy description of his landing in England in the year 1066 at the head of the Invincible Armada, and his defeat of the Britishers under the Duke of Marlborough at the

---

[1] Fellow of the Royal Society of London for Improving Natural Knowledge. What began in 1660 as a way for physicians and natural philosophers to meet and share knowledge grew to become a significant authority on scientific matters.

[2] An idiom that implies that the person is shy. Given the geese's reputation for viciousness, one wonders if this isn't just good sense.

battle of Bannockburn. Then he began to grow more shadowy and less phosphorescent, and ended by vanishing altogether.

"Keep you seats, ladies and gentlemen!" urged the hefty assistant. "There are more marvels to come!"

Again the banjo twanged, and several sharp raps rang out from the region of the door. Then once again there was silence. For fully a quarter of an hour the assembly sat and waited, but nothing else happened.

"Oh, dear, I am so frightened!" cried one of the lady novelists.

"Why don't they switch on the lights if it's all over?" demanded Professor Foljambe.

It was the Labour M.P. who first took action. Freeing his hands from the grip of his neighbour's, he plunged for the electric switch. The next instant the room was flooded with light.

In the centre stood the solitary chair, empty now, with the cords hanging limply upon it; but of the medium and his hefty assistant there was no trace.

"Strange!" murmured Sherlog.

He felt somewhat shaken, and longed for the soothing influence of a cigarette. His hand sought for the handsome gold presentation case he invariably carried, but to his surprise neither that nor anything else appeared to be in his pockets. He glanced at his companions, and noted the same bewildered expression on every face.

"What does it mean?" he asked, helplessly.

It was Professor Foljambe who took upon himself to answer. "It means," he said in solemn accents, "that all our valuables have been spirited away!"

"Good gracious!" said Sherlog, "I hope Dr. Potson never gets to hear of this."

Baffled

Another Adventure of the Dear Old Has-Been, Sherlog Combes

Anonymous

This is the second of two attacks on Conan Doyle's Spiritualist beliefs from London Opinion, *this time from the June 7, 1919, issue.*

The aged detective affixed his signature to the Unemployment Benefit form; and, wrapped in reverie and a dressing-gown, sank back into his chair. His violin lay amongst the littered breakfast dishes. A quid of cocaine, or a wad or tumblerful of it—I forget exactly how you take it—stood at his elbow. The hound of the Vilkerbaskes, wearing a bird-cage in lieu of a muzzle, spread itself over most of the hearth-rug. All these properties had to be there. How otherwise would you have recognised Sherlog Combes, the greatest living—if only just living—detective? His brow, like his financial outlook and the whisky he was drinking, was clouded. He had not had a case for years (like the wine and spirit merchants).

Suddenly a jarring tintinnabulation shattered the sylvan calm of Baker Street. An ordinary mind would have imagined that the belfry of a neighbouring church had fallen into the road, but to Combes' trained intelligence it could mean but one thing: the front-door bell. He removed his feet, and incidentally an oleograph of the Relief of Lucknow,[1] from the mantelpiece. His hawk-like eyes glinted. His hawk-like nose quivered. His hawk-like ears—no. Sorry, that won't do.

A lady entered hurriedly, without waiting to be an-

---

[1] During the Indian rebellion of 1857, the British Residency compound, consisting of six buildings over 60 acres, was surrounded by mutineers. Inside were 855 British officers and soldiers, 712 Indians, 153 civilian volunteers, and 1,280 civilians. They successfully defended the Residency against 8,000 mutinous Indian soldiers for 87 days before a relief force arrived to resupply the defenders, and another 61 days before they could be evacuated by the British army.

nounced. Her skirt and blouse were in the height of fashion, but her countenance was in the depths of despair.

Her voice was deeply agitated. "My husband—" she began.

"I understand perfectly," interrupted Combes. "You wish to tell me that your husband has disappeared. Maddened by the horrors of the super-tax[1] he has probably—"

"Nothing of the kind," said the lady. "My husband and I—"

"Say no more. I see it all. Home troubles. Domestic affliction, You are being blackmailed by a former admirer, who holds the *billets doux* which you, as a schoolgirl, flicked across the aisle to him in church."

"No, much worse. My husband and I and our baby—"

"Heavens!" cried Combes. "Your angel-child has been kidnapped. Four masked bandits, I presume, drove up in a black bassinette—"

"Please let me finish. We have been searching all over for—"

"Why didn't you say so at first?" snapped Combes. "A jewel robbery, of course, Madam, confide in me. It was I who discovered the great Californian Carbuncle in the Duchess's powder-box. It was I who—"

"No, not that."

"Well, what can I do for you? Perhaps your uncle has been found lying dead in the conservatory with an aspidistra[2] embedded in his brain?"

"No, no. Listen," said the lady in a weary voice. "I have simply come to ask you to find us a house."

---

[1] Britain funded the war by raising tax rates across the board in 1914 and 1915 while imposing an additional "super tax" on those who earned more than £3,000. By the end of the war, taxes became more progressive, imposing a larger burden on higher earners.

[2] Unlikely, or extremely ludicrous, as an aspidistra is a house plant commonly found in English boarding houses and middle-class homes. Better known as the cast-iron plant, due to its ability to thrive despite neglect, it became so identified with English respectability that George Orwell (1903-1950) used it as a symbol in his novel *Keep the Aspidistra Flying*.

"A house!" The detective's jaw dropped; not on the floor, you understand; it just dropped.

"Madam," he quavered in a voice broken with failure, "you demand the impossible. I have been a match for all the murderers, blackmailers, forgers and master-criminals in the world, but even I dare not tackle a modern landlord. I dabble every day in fabulous fortunes and missing millions, but London rents are beyond me.[1] I can find diamonds and rubies as easily as a conjuror fetches rabbits out of a hat; I can produce coronets and tiaras as quickly as a politician can abstract coin from a taxpayer's pocket; but a house! I am but human. With tief and grears — I mean grears and tief — I admit my powerlessness. I cannot find you a house."

With a low, gurgling cry, reminiscent of the last half-inch of water bidding a reluctant farewell to a bath, the lady fell forward in a swoon.

Combes gently raised her, and laid her on the sofa.

He swallowed the quid, wad, or bucketful of cocaine at one gulp, and, taking his violin from under the butter-dish, he drew forth, with ineffable pathos and a bow that needed rosin, the first haunting notes of "There's nae luck aboot the hoose."[2]

The lady swooned again. You cannot blame her.

---

[1] There had been a shortage of affordable housing before the war, which grew worse with a ban on construction imposed until after the Armistice. The extent of the problem was characterized by a cartoon in *Punch* which showed a couple on the street looking at a sign saying "This wall to let." The husband says, "What about taking this? We could at least hang our pictures."
[2] A midtempo Scottish country dance based on the poem by Jean Adam (1704-1765) about a sailor's wife lamenting when her husband's away at sea.

The Case of the Sinn Feiners

"Peter Todd" (Charles Hamilton)

Charles Hamilton (1876-1961) was not only a prolific creator of Holmesian parodies, but one of the most prolific writers of all time. Over a six-decade career, he wrote hundreds of stories in all genres under multiple pennames. Many of them were set at Greyfriars School and featuring his most famous character, the anti-hero Billy Bunter. In addition, Hamilton wrote 93 stories featuring Herlock Sholmes and Dr. Jotson. Written with a dry humor, these stories can reveal to the attentive reader a subversive attitude. Take, for instance, "The Case of the Sinn Feiners," published in the Aug. 28, 1920, issue of The Greyfriars Herald. *While Hamilton indulges in a few Irish stereotypes, he doesn't condemn Fenian attempts to win Irish independence and even sneaks in shots at British authority figures. Note also the nod to Sexton Blake, "the poor man's Sherlock Holmes," his assistant Tinker and the dog, Pedro.*

I.

"Pack your bag, my dear Jotson," said Herlock Sholmes, when I came down to breakfast one morning in our rooms at Shaker Street.

"We are going—" I began.

"To Ireland," said Sholmes. "You have just time to make your will and pay up on your insurance, Jotson. These little precautions are necessary — it is not as if we were merely going to Tartary or Timbuctoo."[1]

---

[1] *Tartary:* The region of central Asia stretching from the Caspian Sea and the Ural Mountain range to the Pacific Ocean and occupied by the Turko-Mongol peoples. The name was in use from the Middle Ages to the 20th century. It is now the location of modern-day nations collectively called "the Stans" (Uzbekistan, Kazakhstan, Turkmenistan, Kirgizstan, and Tajikistan), and Mongolia. Inspired by the Mongols, the region developed a reputation as a mysterious, exotic, and savage land. Tartar entered the language to describe a rough, intractable, and possibly violent person. *Timbuctoo:* An ancient city in Mali in west-central Africa. The city was established in the 12th century as a result of increasing trade across the continent. Its location in

"And our business in Ireland, Sholmes?" I inquired.

"You have heard of Sinn Fein, my dear fellow?"

"I have certainly heard the word, Sholmes. Is it a new breakfast food?"

"Nothing of the kind."

"A new parlour game?" I hazarded.

Sholmes shook his head.

"If you were a regular reader of the Daily Snooze, Jotson, you would know that Sinn Fein is the free and independent patriot party in the sister isle. If, on the other hand, you regularly read the Morning Ghost, you would be aware that Sinn Fein is the unpatriotic and traitorous party in Ireland. Like the little boy in the story, you pays your money and you takes your choice."[1]

"And the truth, Sholmes?"

Sholmes smiled compassionately.

"My dear fellow, all the news from Ireland comes in the shape of official reports or newspaper telegrams. There's no question of truth."

---

the African interior made the town (spelled also as Timbuktu and Timbuktoo) a byword for a mysterious, remote, and dangerous place. Today the city is the capital of Mali's Tombouctou Region.

[1] Newspapers in Britain wear their politics on their sleeve so vividly that a person can be judged by the papers they read. This is especially true in the case of Sinn Féin, the political group founded in 1905 in an attempt to create an independent Ireland. The name is taken from the Irish language for "ourselves" or "we ourselves," and was originally used by the Fenian Brotherhood, a group who advocated revolution to free Ireland from Britain. After the failed 1916 Easter Rising in Dublin, the Sinn Féin political party received overwhelming support in the 1918 elections and proclaimed an Irish Republic in 1919. A three-year guerilla war followed, ending in a truce in 1921. That December, the Anglo-Irish Treaty gave Ireland complete independence in home affairs, with Northern Ireland allowed to remain with Great Britain. Currently, Sinn Féin is a political party in the Republic of Ireland and the Northern Ireland Assembly. *Pays your money:* Probably of Cockney origin, the phrase means "the right of the choice is to the buyer," although according to William Safire in *The New York Times*, it also means nowadays "you made your bed, now lie in it." The phrase first appeared in an 1846 *Punch* cartoon.

"True!"

"My services have been called in by Dublin Castle,"[1] explained Herlock Sholmes. "Sinn Fein outrages have now reached the culminating point, or the patriot movement has now become formidable, whichever you like. Police-stations have been burned; policemen have been potted; banks have been robbed; life and property rendered generally unsafe — but that is nothing out of the common — the climax has now been reached."

"Good heavens, Sholmes! What has happened?"

"A distinguished official has been kidnapped by the Sinn Feiners!" said Sholmes.

My hand trembled as I dissected my kipper.[2]

This was, indeed, startling news!

"He was taken from his car, on the road near Ballybooze," said Sholmes. "He has disappeared completely, with his kidnappers. What their intentions are is not known. They cannot blow his brains out—"

"Why not, Sholmes?"

"I have mentioned that he is a distinguished official, Jotson. The feat would therefore be impossible."

"Most true!"

"But he is deprived of his liberty, and in all probability restricted to a meager diet of whisky and potatoes—"

---

[1] Just as a physical location in London, Whitehall, represents the seat of the British government, Dublin Castle was, until 1922, the place from which Britain ruled Ireland. A castle has stood on the site off Dublin's Dame Street since the days of King John (ruled 1199-1216). Since the 12th century, it was the royal residence for the Lord Lieutenant of Ireland, the monarch's representative in Ireland. The current building complex dates from the 18th century. Dublin Castle was handed over to Ireland's Provisional Government in 1921 with the signing of the Anglo-Irish Treaty. It is still used by the government of Ireland to inaugurate its president, for hosting state dinners and conferences, and as a tourist attraction.

[2] A whole herring that's been split from head to tail, gutted, and salted or pickled. Often eaten for breakfast. The flesh must be picked out from among the bones, hence Jotson's comment.

"Horrible!"

"However, I shall be there," said Sholmes carelessly. "Once arrived at Ballybooze[1] I do not anticipate great difficulties."

"You have a clue?"

"None!"

"Then how—"

"I am going to call on my friend and colleague, Bexton Stake,[2] and borrow his celebrated bloodhound, Squeedro," explained Sholmes.

"Ah!" I exclaimed. "You will show Squeedro something belonging to the prisoner, and he will follow the track—"

"Not at all."

"Then I do not see—"

"I do not expect you to, Jotson. Pack your bag, my dear fellow, and let us walk our chalks," said Sholmes.[3]

---

[1] At the risk of destroying the humor, note that "bally" was an ancient Gaelic word used to describe an administrative district, part of a rudimentary system of organizing and dividing the land that pre-dated the Norman invasions starting in 1169. Its meaning is unclear as the system varied across the island. Today the word means "townlands," and is the smallest administrative district. Bally also survives today in some townland names, such as Ballynamaddoo and Ballyjamesduff.

[2] A play on Sexton Blake, the popular fictional detective created by Harry Blyth (1852-1898) and modeled after Sherlock Holmes, even to the point of living on Baker Street. Blyth wrote the story for newspaper mogul Alfred Harmsworth's *The Halfpenny Marvel*, so his company owned the character. The popularity of the story led Harmsworth to hire writers to supply further stories (Blyth died in 1898 of typhoid fever). Since his debut in 1893, more than 4,000 stories have appeared, written by at least 200 authors, including John Creasey and Michael Moorcock, with numerous movie, TV and radio tie-ins. Among his many fans was a young Dorothy L. Sayers, who tried to write a Sexton Blake story that introduced Lord Peter Wimsey.

[3] The phrase actually means "go away," and not in a pleasant fashion. There are two origin stories to choose from. The aristocratic origin comes from the royal court. The serjeant-chamberlain of the royal household, needing homes to lodge the royal retinue, would chalk the doors of houses that were to be taken over. The inhabitants were therefore asked to "walk your chalk." Among the common people, according to several 19th century

On our way to the station we called in at the office of Bexton Slake, who was almost as famous a detective as Herlock Sholmes himself.

Slake was lying back in an armchair, examining an ordinary glass tumbler filled with some dark-coloured liquid, which he held tilted to his mouth. Strange gurgling noises emanated from the great detective's throat.

On his knee reclined the graceful form of the one and only Squeedro. Sitting on the floor, playing "noughts and crosses,"[1] was Slinker, Slake's handsome young assistant.

Without beating about the bush Sholmes stated his mission, and, having presented his friend and colleague with a fivepenny cigar[2] given him by a noted criminal on the previous evening, Slake readily agreed to allow him the services of his bloodhound.

An hour later we were en route for Dublin.

II.

The shades of night were falling fast — as I believe some poet has already remarked[3] — when we arrived at Ballybooze.

---

newspapers, walking the chalk was a challenge in the pubs or before the police to walk a straight line to show that you were sober.

[1] Also known in the U.S. as tic-tac-toe, a game that has been traced back to ancient Egypt.

[2] A very cheap cigar, since 5 pence in 1920 has the buying power of about 75 pence today.

[3] From the poem "Excelsior" by Henry Wadsworth Longfellow (1807-1882). Written in 1841, it opens: "The shades of night were falling fast, / As through an Alpine village passed / A youth, who bore, 'mid snow and ice, / A banner with the strange device, / Excelsior!" The rest of the short poem shows the youth resisting everyone's advice not to cross the pass, with each stanza ending with "Excelsior" (translated from the Latin as "higher" and meaning, in this case, "onward and upward"). The end of the poem finds him lying dead in the snow, "lifeless, but beautiful," and still clasping his "banner with the strange device." The poem was a massive success. It was set to music and sung in drawing rooms. Composer Franz Liszt (1811-1886) adapted it as a prelude to Longfellow's *The Golden Legend*. Thornton Wilder (1897-1975) referred to the poem and used Excelsior as the name of

It was a lonely village in the midst of the Tippleary mountains.¹

We put up at the village inn, which, for some reason unknown to us, had not been burned to the ground.

We retired to rest early. The night was an unusually quiet and peaceful one. Not more than five or six dead bodies were visible from the windows when we rose in the morning.

After breakfast Sholmes led Squeedro, the bloodhound, to the spot where the kidnapped official had been taken from his car.

I watched my amazing friend with keen interest.

I had expected that he would show the bloodhound some article belonging to the missing gentleman, but this was not Sholmes' method.

"As the kidnapped gentleman was taken away in a cart, he cannot have left a scent behind him, Jotson," he explained.

"True," I remarked. "But, in that case, I fail to see how Bexton Slake's bloodhound will assist you."

Sholmes smiled.

"Squeedro will follow the scent of the Sinn Feiners," he answered.

"But they are unknown—"

"Quite so."

"You have nothing belonging to them!"

"True."

"Then how—" I exclaimed.

"Patience, my dear fellow."

---

his New Jersey town in *The Skin of Our Teeth*, and it was parodied by A.E. Houseman (1859-1936) in "The Shades of Night" in which "A youth who bore mid snow and ice / A bird that wouldn't chirrup, / And a banner, with the strange device — / 'Mrs. Winslow's Soothing Syrup.'"

¹ In addition to being another drink pun — "to tipple" means to take a drink — it is also a reference to Tipperary. The Irish town inspired a music hall song "It's a Long Way to Tipperary" about an Irishman in London missing his hometown. It became a popular song among soldiers in World War I.

Sholmes drew a whisky-flask from his pocket. It contained Irish whisky.

Uncorking it, he held it to the bloodhound's nose.

Squeedro gave one sniff, and started off at a loping trot

Sholmes followed the bloodhound, and Jotson followed Sholmes.

across the mountain.

"Come on, Jotson!"

Sholmes followed the bloodhound, and I followed Sholmes, lost in wonder at the amazing sagacity of my astonishing friend.

The way was long, the wind was cold, but we pushed on rapidly, led by the unfailing Squeedro.

Over mountain and bog he led us, guided unerringly by the scent of Irish whisky.

Two hours later we arrived at the mouth of a solitary cavern. One glance at Sholmes's face was enough for the Sinn Feiners; they fled.

In the cavern lay a prisoner, who, by his expression of vacant imbecility, we knew at once must be a Government official.

"The kidnapped man, Jotson," drawled Herlock Sholmes.

Once more my amazing friend had succeeded!

Frank Richardson and fans in the 1950s.

The Master Mind

Dashiell Hammett

Sherlock Holmes was a product of his culture and times as seen in this attack on him by the future creator of Sam Spade. After spending seven years as a Pinkerton detective, with time out to serve in World War I, Dashiell Hammett (1894-1961) was finding his way as a writer. He wrote several pieces for The Smart Set, *including this one which appeared in its January 1923 issue. These were short fictional forays that let him experiment with satire and irony. His dominant theme was arrogance, whether from a woman who left her husband and child, a survey of great lovers who were more intent on loving themselves, and this piece, about a great detective who couldn't see the biggest crime of all.*

Wherever crime or criminals were discussed by enlightened folk, the name of Waldron Honeywell could be heard. It was a symbol — to the citizens of Punta Arenas no less than those of Tammerfors[1] — for the ultimate in prevention and detection of crime. A native of the United States, Honeywell's work had overflowed the national boundaries. Thirty years of warfare upon crime had taken to every quarter of the globe, and his fame into every nook where the printed word penetrated.

Bringing his work a singularly perspicacious intellect, and combining an exhaustive knowledge of both the scientific and more practical phases of his profession, he had reduced it to as nearly exact a science as possible; and his supremacy in his field has never been questioned.

He had punctured Lombroso's theories at a time when the scientific world regarded the Italian as a Messiah.[2] The

---

[1] A city at the southernmost point of Chile, north of the Strait of Magellan. *Tammerfors* is a city, now called Tampere, in southern Finland.
[2] Italian physician Cesare Lombroso (1835-1909) theorized that genetics determined if a person would become a criminal and that he could be identified through physical defects, such as fleshy or protruding lips, a

treatise with which he exploded the belief — fostered by no less an authority than the great W.J. Burns[1] — that Sir Arthur Conan Doyle would have made a successful detective, and showed that the mysteries confronting Sherlock Holmes would have been susceptible to the routine methods of the ordinary policeman, was familiar to the readers of eight languages. The mastery with which he unearthed and frustrated the Versailles bomb plot before it was well on its feet; the dispatch with which he recovered the aircraft program memoranda; his success in finding the assassin of the emperor of Abyssinia, the details of which were suppressed for some obscure political reason; the effectual manner in which he coped with the epidemic of postal robberies — these were matters of history, but in no way more remarkable than a thousand-odd other exploits in which he had figured.

Honors and decorations were showered upon him, governments sought his advice, scientists deferred to him, criminals shuddered at the sound of his name (one, who had avoided arrest for seventeen years, surrendered to the nearest policeman upon learning that Honeywell had been engaged to hunt him down), and his monetary rewards were enormous.

Early in 1922 Waldron Honeywell died, and left an estate consisting of $182.65 in cash, 37,500 shares of International Solar Power Corporation common, 42,555 shares of Cousin Tilly Gold, Platinum & Diamond Mining Company common, 6,430 shares of Universal Petroleum Corporation of Uruguay, S.A. preferred, and 75,000 shares of New Era Fuelless Motor Company common.

---

receding chin, or an uneven-looking face. Later in life, he abandoned atheism and, like Conan Doyle, became a spiritualist.

[1] William J. Burns (1861-1932) was a popular detective who moved from a career in the Secret Service into his own detective agency, and then to leadership of the Bureau of Investigation (1921-1924), the predecessor to the FBI.

The Mystery of the Murdered Major

James Thurber

Illustrated by Ray Evans

Born and raised in Columbus, Ohio, James Thurber (1894-1961) inherited his mother's zany sense of humor and flair for the dramatic. Attending Ohio State shaped his literary taste, including a fondness for Henry James, and introduced him to journalism. He became editor of the student newspaper and literary magazine, and developed his writing style by contributing to both. After spending two years in Paris as a code clerk for the U.S. Embassy, he got a reporter's job at the Columbus Dispatch. *Finding daily reporting dull, he branched out into comic observations, movie and play reviews, and feature stories.*

In 1923, he and illustrator Ray Evans were given a half-page in the newspaper's Sunday magazine. He wrote book reviews condemning the "sordid" sex portrayed in novels by James Joyce and D.H. Lawrence, and praised Willa Cather and his beloved Henry James. He also wrote 13 stories in "The Cases of the Blue Ploermell," one of the oddest Holmes parodies. Instead of cocaine, Ploermell indulged in animal crackers; in place of Watson was a Chinese servant. Maybe with the Roaring '20s in full swing, the Victorian world was passé. In any event, it represents an interesting curiosity that we get to see for the first time since it was printed.

Artist Ray Evans (1887-1954) was an illustrator and editorial cartoonist for the Dispatch *and contributed art to magazines including* Puck, Life, Judge, *and* The Literary Digest.

Published with permission of the Columbus Dispatch.

Blue Ploermell, the famous psycho-scientific detective, sat in his room, or rather in one of them, eating animal crackers.[1] They were his one vice, these little confections in the shape of bears

---

[1] No knows who invented animal crackers. They were created in Britain and imported to the U.S. in the late 19th century. Demand grew for them so American bakers began to produce them as well. Stauffer's Biscuit Co. in York, Pennsylvania, produced the first batch in 1871. In 1902, the National Biscuit Company named their cookies "Barnum's Animals," after the Barnum and Bailey Circus.

and lions and elephants and dogs and whatnot. The only time the noted mental wizard, with the attractively crossed eyes, ever showed the slightest trace of irascibility was when he ran out of animal crackers. His predilection for them was unaccountable, but charming. It added a kind of atmosphere to the man.

Gong Low, his Chinese servant, irised into the room, struck a brass gong, and irised out. It meant there was a visitor below. Ploermell indicated by gesturing slightly with a half-devoured buffalo that he would see the visitor. The man who came in was apparently greatly agitated. Ploermell arose, swallowing the rest of the buffalo, and waved the man to a chair.

"Major Preston was killed in his library yesterday afternoon, sir," the visitor said.

"By whom and what for?" asked Ploermell without hesitation.

"That's what I came to ask you," said the visitor, curtly.

"Did Major Preston have any enemies?" asked Ploermell, shoving the cracker box across the table where his guest could get at it.

"What the Dickens are these?" asked the visitor.

"Animal crackers," said Blue Ploermell.

"As far as I know, Major Preston did not have an enemy in the world," said the visitor, examining the little box of crackers.

"Tut, tut, man," said Ploermell, "he must have had an enemy. Do you intimate that some friend killed him? With what was the major struck down?"

"A heavy, blunt instrument."

"Ah, that again!" cried Ploermell. "We detectives will some day find that implement. It has caused far too many deaths already."

"He was struck just above the head," said the visitor.

"Ye — just above the head? You mean on the hat?"

"I mean on the crown of his head, of course," said the guest, irritably, shoving the animal crackers aside without taking any.

"Try those zebras," urged Ploermell. "This batch is lovely. Fresh. Just the right sweetness."

BLUE PLOERMELL, PSYCHO-SCIENTIST.

"Come, come, sir," said the visitor. "I want none of your animal crackers! What do you say about this case?"

"Have you read my book on 'Thuds'?" asked Ploermell. "In it I discuss thoroughly the various blows which produce death, unconsciousness and coma. There is a chapter which I think you will find enlightening on 'The Dull, Sickening Thud' — the very one with which, unless I am mistaken, Colonel Preston fell."

"Major Preston," said the visitor.

"It makes no difference now," said Ploermell. "Pray do not catch me up. I have written several chapters somewhere on military. But let us visit the room in which General-Major Preston was slain."

They found the major as the slayer had left him, strewn face down on the floor of his library.

"Turn him over so I can see who he is," said Ploermell.

"There can be no question of that," snapped the visitor. "This is the remains of my good friend Major Wolcott Preston."

"One can never be too sure," said Ploermell, eating a cow. "Be still now while I examine the room."

Finally he discovered, hanging in a corner, a parrot in a cage.

"Ha!" said Ploermell, "what have we here?"

"That's a parrot," said the visitor.

"Certainly, I know that. But what is he doing here?"

"Major Preston picked her up in the Boer war or some place.[1] Great pet."

"Talk?" asked Ploermell.

"Swears," said the visitor.

"Indiscriminately, or when annoyed?" asked the detective.

"Now and again," said the visitor. "It has a particular aversion to green, especially in neckties."

With a low cry, Ploermell sprang to Preston and examined his tie.

"Red," he muttered in chagrin. "Do you suspect the parrot?" asked the visitor, with asperity.

"Leave me alone in this room awhile," said Ploermell suddenly, looking from Parrot to Preston and other places — the visitor could not tell just where, on account of Mr. Ploermell's eyes.

Several hours later, the visitor, pacing restlessly up and down outside the room, heard a scuffle, cries and a metallic click. He burst into the room. Ploermell, his clothes awry, was

---

[1] Also called the Second Boer War (1899-1902), fought between Great Britain and two Boer states: the South African Republic and the Orange Free State. The Boers were Dutch and Afrikaan settlers in the eastern Cape frontier of South Africa who came there under the Dutch East India Company, but moved northward after the company failed and the British took over South Africa. The Boers defeated the British in the first Boer War (1880-1881), but lost their independence in the second.

standing above a figure which lay in a big chair. This man was disheveled and collarless and handcuffed.

"There," said Ploermell, "is your murderer."

"You mean Preston's?" asked the visitor.

"Exactly," said the detective. "Look." He held up a green necktie and a collar. "His." The sleuth felt in his pocket and drew out a rhinoceros. "This man passes this house regularly, wearing this tie. The parrot has seen it day after day and has cursed its wearer terrifically. Finally the man, in a rage, burst in through those French windows and killed Preston, believing him to be the curser. Today the man passed by again. The parrot swore at him. Naturally the man thought it was Preston's ghost and he stopped, staggered and turned pale. He would have swooned, but I went out and got him."

The detective sighed. "These rhinoceroses," he said, "are lovely. You miss a lot."

James Thurber.

The Teapot Dome Case

"A. Conan Oyle" (N.H.)

Decades from now, readers will hear about the Watergate scandal and say, "Oh, yeah, it was that ... thing ... about the election. And burglary. And wasn't somebody named Nixon involved?" Much like what we say today about the Teapot Dome scandal during Warren Harding's administration, if we learn about it at all.

But in its time, the Teapot Dome was just as notorious, just as hotly debated, and nearly as difficult for the public to puzzle out what was going on. The cast of characters was large, the crimes and nefarious doings varied (bribery, witness intimidation, perjury), and in the end, reputations were ruined, and "Teapot Dome" became the shorthand for presidential scandals until Watergate replaced it a half-century later.

At the center of the scandal were three oil-rich tracts of land owned by the U.S. government and intended to supply fuel to the Navy during a national emergency. Albert B. Fall, who was Secretary of the Interior under President Warren Harding, arranged to gain control of these lands, including one in Wyoming named Teapot Dome for its unusual appearance. He then secretly leased these fields to his friends in the oil industry in return for bribes disguised as loans and gifts, including cattle for his ranch. Word of these leases leaked and Congress began to investigate. Fall and his allies, including the publisher of The Washington Post, defended the contracts, claiming that the oil was unsuitable for the Navy's ships and that drilling in nearby fields were depleting the reserves. But Fall's displays of unexpected wealth made it clear something nefarious was going on. The scandal appeared to embroil President Harding when he died suddenly on Aug. 2, 1922. The investigations went on under his successor, Calvin Coolidge, and Fall went to prison for a year. Details about the scandal will be covered in the footnotes.

This is probably one of the oddest newspaper parodies ever. It was serialized a few paragraphs at a time on the front page of the Brooklyn Daily Eagle from Feb. 6 to April 3, 1924, and its existence as a Holmes parody was unknown until discovered for this book. The identity of its author, "N.H.," remains a mystery.

Sherlock Holmes snatched the evening paper from my hand. "Read no more, my dear Watson," he cried. "Those headlines are enough. We start for Washington in five minutes!" and he dashed into his dressing room.

I was throwing a suit of oilskins[1] into my grip[2] when the outer door opened. Upon the threshold stood a man of medium height, with dark hair and a closely cropped dark mustache. He held $24,700 in his hand. I recognized him at once.

"Mr. John T. King,[3] I believe?" was my greeting, when suddenly the visitor cast off his disguise, revealing the sharp features of Sherlock Holmes!

"Watson," said Holmes, as we sprang into the taxi, "did you notice anything unusual about our chauffeur?" I admitted that I had not. "He has, I observe, an oily skin," replied Holmes, significantly; "there is an oil spot on his cap, and his thumb has that peculiar flatness which comes only from long pressure on the bottom of an oil can. Do you follow me?"

We reached the station just in time to catch the Midnight Oil Limited for Washington. Holmes tore a dollar note in two and tendered half to the chauffeur, then carefully mislaid the part bearing the signature of the Treasurer of the U. S.[4] "Oil

---

[1] A fabric such as canvas or heavy cotton cloth that has been waterproofed with linseed oil.

[2] A rectangular container used for carrying clothes. Also called a suitcase.

[3] It is characteristic of this parody that we begin with a reference to an entirely different scandal. In January, William H. Anderson (1874-1959), the head of the Anti-Saloon League of New York, was convicted of forgery. He had taken $24,700 that a fundraiser earned collecting donations for the league and cooked the books to hide the theft. At his trial, Anderson claimed that the money came from a donor whom he knew only as "John T. King" and that he paid the $24,700 to "Henry Mann" for a publicity campaign. Oddly, there was a real "John T. King" who was not connected to Anderson. He was a wealthy businessman and Republican Party kingmaker who engineered Harding's nomination for president over much more popular candidates. There will be more references to Anderson as we go deeper into the story.

[4] Among the payoffs Fall had received was one for $100,000 in hundred-dollar bills which he used to buy land near his New Mexico ranch. It came

aboard!" shouted the conductor.

Hardly had the train started when Holmes sniffed the air. "Ah! An oil-burning locomotive," he whispered, nudging me in the ribs. I looked out of the window. It was a moonlit night and as the train roared over a bridge I saw upon the bosom of the dark, oily stream a drifting hat; on the band were the initials "W. G. McA."[1]

"McAdoo?" I cried, dragging Holmes to the window. "McAdon't," was the great detective's chuckling answer. I was somewhat puzzled. "Holmes," I ventured, "was that stream the Allegheny?" Sherlock Holmes smiled. "My dear Watson," he replied, "your geography needs dusting. That was the Oilegheny!"[2]

Holmes was still chuckling when the conductor approached, hoarsely demanding, "Oil tickets, please!" We quickly tore our tickets in two, handing the official the part minus the name of our destination.

"Where's the other half?" he growled.

"Mine," replied Holmes, calmly, "is in the Teapot on the breakfast table."

"And mine," said I, taking the detective's clue, "Is in the

---

from Edward L. Doheny, who was identified as "an old prospecting pal" of Fall and owned the Pan-American Petroleum and Transport Co., one of the companies leasing the oil reserves. Asked for proof that it was a loan, Doheny produced a promissory note but without Fall's signature on it. He testified that if he died his executors would press Fall for repayment, so he tore the signature off and gave it to Mrs. Doheny, who lost it.

[1] William Gibbs McAdoo, Jr. (1863-1941) was a lawyer, businessman, and politician who served as secretary of the treasury under President Woodrow Wilson (and married his daughter, Eleanor), founded the Federal Reserve System, and sought the Democratic Party's nomination for president during the 1920s. His quest for the nomination in 1924 was damaged when it was revealed he had received a legitimate $25,000 contribution from Edward L. Doheny, who had paid off Fall to get the oil leases. Despite that and an endorsement from the Ku Klux Klan, he nearly won the nomination.

[2] A pun on the Allegheny River, which flows past Pittsburgh and into the Ohio River.

Dome of the Penn Station."[1]

Holmes grasped my hand. "My dear Watson," he enthused, "you do me proud!"

The conductor signaled for the hot-air brakes.

The hot-air brakes, suddenly applied, drew sparks from the wheels, but the train slid on for some distance before stopping. "Oil on the rails, Watson," hissed Holmes.

"Oil out!" shouted the conductor. We jumped and found ourselves at a little oil tank station from which emerged Henry Mann.[2] The place was absolutely deserted.

Holmes quickly resumed his disguise, shifting to the medium height, dark hair and moustache of John T. King just as a water wagon rolled up and Brother Bill Anderson[3] alighted. The great detective shook hands with the great reformer, leaving $24,700 in the latter's palm.

I glanced up at the overcast Dome of the sky. "Looks like oil," I ventured.

"Capital, my dear Watson," grinned Holmes. "Capital, Washington, D.C.!" It was oil rather confusing.

When I lowered my eyes the $24,700 had disappeared, and I heard Mr. Anderson saying goodbye to Henry Mann.

"Henry is looking well," commented Holmes.

"Your eyesight, my dear Holmes, is far keener than mine," I admitted.

"My dear Watson," said Holmes, somewhat testily, "your memory is that of a witness in a Senatorial Investigation. You

---

[1] A reference to the expanse of arched glass over the main waiting room of New York City's Penn Station, which was destroyed in 1963 and replaced with Madison Square Garden.
[2] The non-existent publicity man to whom William H. Anderson claimed to pay $24,700 that he had taken from a fundraiser for the Anti-Saloon League of New York. See the "John T. King" footnote on page 284.
[3] The water wagon was a reference to drinkers who have "taken the pledge" to go dry during Prohibition (1919-1933). Calling Anderson "Brother Bill" refers to the religious aspect of the campaign against alcohol, since many churches add "brother" and "sister" to a first name to show acceptance and solidarity.

forget that I have assumed the character of John T. King. I see without being seen. Pray make a note of that, or, rather, a half note — a Doheny note, to be explicit."[1] And the great detective began to hum: "Do-he-ny-fa-sol-la — do you follow me?" It was somewhat confusing.

"And now, Watson," added Sherlock Holmes. "I detect the approach of the conveyance I ordered in the name of John T. King when we were put off the Washington train."

"How did you order it?" I inquired.

"My dear fellow," was the rather bored reply, "I ordered it by radioil!"

It was truly a curious equipage which drew up at the platform: a cut-glass coach fashioned in the form of a water-wagon and decorated with scenes from Andersen's Fairy Tales. The coachman, whom I recognized at once as Santa Claus, was seated in a witness chair holding the whip hand over a team of 24,700 white water rats.

The jolly old driver touched his hat to Holmes. "Good evening, Mr. King," he said. "Where to, sir?" It seemed a bit fantastic.

"To Washington," ordered Holmes as we seated ourselves in the coach, which was comfortably lined with $1,000 bills.

"Pretty soft, Watson," murmured the great detective, producing an oil lamp and lighting his long-stemmed brier pipe. "I observe, my dear fellow," said Holmes, "that you are admiring the pipe lines."

Santa Claus whipped up his team of white water rats and

---

[1] The first of the oil reserves surrendered to private interests were in California. Edward L. Doheny (1856-1935) was an "old prospecting pal" of Fall's and the owner of the Pan-American Petroleum and Transport Company. During 1921, Fall and Doheny began making preliminary arrangements for leasing part of the Navy's oil reserves.

In November of that year, Doheny made what he and Fall would later claim was a loan to Fall. Doheny had his son draw $100,000 in cash from the son's account, wrap the bills in paper, place them in a little black bag and deliver it to Fall in his apartment. Doheny later testified that he had received a note from Fall for the money, eventually producing a note whose signature had been torn off.

we dashed away over the well-oiled roads, while Holmes began to recite:[1]

> 'Twas, the night before Christmas
> And oil through the land
> Not a good boy was failing
> To hold out his hand.
>
> Oil good boys who never
> Had done a wrong thing
> Expected a visit
> From old "John T. King"—

"I don't quite follow you," I broke in.

Sherlock Holmes ignored my interruption. He continued his recitation:

> When out on the lawn
> There arose such a clink
> Of coin that they knew
> It must be "Mr. Kink."
>
> Of medium height,
> With "dark hair" and moustache,
> And bearing a basket
> Brimmed over with cash
>
> Yet modestly keeping
> Himself out of sight.
> They knew at a glance
> It was "John T.," all right—

---

[1] Based on "A Visit from St. Nicholas." It was once thought to be written by Clement Clarke Moore (1779-1863) but literary detectives point to Henry Livingston Jr. (1748-1828) as the author.

Suddenly the coachman pulled up his team.

Our coachman, Santa Claus, got down and spoke to Holmes: "Better put on your oilskins, Mr. King, we'll soon be in Washington, D.C. In fact, we are even now in the District of Calamity."

"What is that reflection on the Government Offices?" queried the detective.

"That," confided Santa, "is the Teapot Domebell oillumination. It's 100,000 scandal power. Mebbe we'd better drive round by the Department of the Interioil and give Dr. Watson, here, a look at the Teapotomac and the celebrated Albert Fall, dried up at present."[1]

"Ah!" said Holmes, "the Moneyhaha Falls, eh. Watson?"[2]

---

[1] Despite his delicious middle name of Bacon, Albert B. Fall (1861-1944) was a bitter enemy to anyone who obstructed his pursuit of political power. Settling in New Mexico as a result of a respiratory illness, Fall became involved with Oliver M. Lee, a landowner who used hired muscle to back Fall's political career as well as to rustle cattle. Fall, in return, acted as his attorney in legal matters, including defending Lee in the disappearance and presumed murder of a rival attorney and his eight-year-old son. When former sheriff Pat Garrett, famous for killing Billy the Kid in 1881, came to the area to investigate Lee and was himself killed, Fall defended the accused killer.

Fall went on to become senator from New Mexico after it became a state, resigning in 1921 to become Harding's secretary of the interior. Convicted of conspiracy and bribery, Fall served only one year in prison, then entered a comfortable retirement. Of the two men accused of bribing him, Edward L. Doheny was acquitted (and, adding insult to injury, foreclosed on Fall's home over that $100,000 "loan"), while Harry F. Sinclair was found guilty of contempt of court and sentenced to six months in jail and a fine.

[2] Minnehaha was the fictional Native American woman who loved Hiawatha in the 1855 epic poem "The Song of Hiawatha" by Henry Wadsworth Longfellow (1807-1882). Later in the story, Watson will use the poem to tell the history of the Teapot Dome case. The poem begins:

By the shore of Gitche Gumee,
By the shining Big-Sea-Water,
At the doorway of his wigwam,
In the pleasant Summer morning,

We drove rapidly along the banks of the Teapotomac, past the noted Albert Fall. I was but faintly impressed.

"How high was it?" I asked Holmes.

"About $100,000," he snapped.

The coach stopped abruptly.

"Hands up!" came a woman's voice, and a good-looking girl opened the coach door and covered us with an automatic. "Which of youse gents is Johnny King?" was her query. I indicated Holmes. "Slip me them 24,700 smackers," she said.

The great detective smiled. "My dear young lady, I've just had a meeting with Mr. William H Anderson and—"

The highwaymaid lowered her gun. "Excuse me, Jack," she interrupted. Suddenly the gun girl asked: "did youse see anybody wit' Willie Anderson?"

I was speechless, but Sherlock Holmes spoke up: "Madam," he said, "whom did you meet on the road before we came along?"

The holdup woman thought for a moment. "Nobody," she answered. Holmes placed the tips of his fingers together and regarded her with a triumphant smile. "My dear young woman," he murmured, "that was Henry Mann!"

"Out o' luck," groaned the robberess. All of a sudden she pointed her weapon at me. "Who's that bird?" she demanded. For a second Holmes hesitated, then he answered smoothly: "He is a prominent lawyer who has never had any connection with oil interests."

"Quit yer kiddin'!" shrieked the lady. "There ain't no sich guy!" And she aimed the gun at me, glared at the great detective and pulled the trigger. There was no report!

But her shriek startled the white water rats; they started off at a rattling good pace. It was oil over in an instant. Sud-

---

Hiawatha stood and waited.
All the air was full of freshness,
All the earth was bright and joyous,
And before him, through the sunshine,
Westward toward the neighboring forest

denly Holmes spoke: "Did you notice anything odd about that gun, Watson?"

"It didn't go off," I ventured.

"Precisely so," agreed Holmes. "But why? Because the mechanism lacked OIL! That eliminates the girl from the Teapot Dome mystery."

"Then she," I cried, "was none other than the Bobbed Hair Bandit!"[1]

"The Boob Hair Bandit, my dear fellow. You observed how easily she was hoaxed."

"Foiled," I agreed.

The great detective held up a warning finger. "Never use that word," he said sternly. "It has oil in it." Sherlock Holmes refilled his pipe. "We shall soon arrive at our destination, but meanwhile we might pass the time pleasantly by reciting some popular poems. Suppose you give us 'Barbara Frietchie.'"[2]

Oilways willing to humor my eccentric friend, I began:

---

[1] Celia Cooney (1904-1992) a laundry worker from Brooklyn, became a media darling when, along with her husband, Ed, she robbed 10 stores during 1924 before she was arrested. Depending on the newspaper, she was portrayed as a modern woman gone wrong, a libertine, or an example of police incompetence. Celia and Ed were sentenced to 20 years in prison and paroled after seven. They had two boys who weren't told of their parents' criminal past until she died.

[2] Based on the poem by John Greenleaf Whittier (1807-1892). Barbara Frietchie (1766-1862) was a real person, a Union supporter living in Frederick, Maryland. According to the poem, when Confederate forces under Gen. Thomas "Stonewall" Jackson passed by her house, he saw Frietchie's American flag and ordered that it be fired upon. The 90-year-old Frietchie waved at them in defiance and, in Whittier's words, "Shoot, if you must, this old gray head. / But spare your country's flag," she said." Jackson ordered the flag to be left alone. It's questionable whether the incident really happened, or that the event was combined with other flag incidents. It can be said, at this late date, that there were incidents of nobility and courtesy on both sides during the Civil War, and conclude that "Barbara Frietchie" falls into the category of "fake, but accurate."

"*Up from the meadows rich with oil,*
Spouting high from the Guv'ment's soil
The clustered gushers of teapot rise,
But Senator Walsh, bigosh, gets wise –"

"That's all wrong," I objected.

"It's oil right," contradicted Holmes. "Pray proceed." So I went on:

'Round about them leases creep,
But not a bird lets out a peep
Till that fair morning in oily Fall
When Walsh lets out an awful bawl—

"Your oilocution is remarkable," encouraged Holmes. "Pray resume."

I continued:

Forty gushers that got in right,
Forty gushers with prospects bright,
Shook in the morning wind.
A leak somehow,
Somewhere, and then—
Wow, WOW!

"Not so good, Watson," criticized my companion, "but go on." I tried the next verse:

Up rose friend Albert Fall right then,
Bowed by his hundred thousand yen.
Bravest of all in Washington.
He signed up the leases one by one
And then set pretty for quite a spell,
But DOGGONE, Albert, you never can tell—

Although the verses I was so glibly reciting seemed unfamiliar to me, Holmes insisted that they were quite right for the present.

"Don't you know any more?" he urged. So I obliged:

Up the street came the probers' tread.
Walsh of Montana writing of head.
Under his mustache, left and right,
He asked, "is Al B. Fall in sight?"
"Halt!" The oil-skinned ranks stood fast;
"Subpoena!" Out blazed the question's blast;
It shivered the Teapot into hash.
It rent the oil can with seam and gash.
Quick as it fell in spots remote
Doheny caught up a tattered note
He leaned far out of the witness chair
And shook it forth in the oily air:
"That's half the note of which we've read,
"But where's the other half?" they said.

Our coach stopped abruptly. "Here we are, Watson," cried Holmes. I sprang out to find myself in the heart of Washington. We dismissed our curious vehicle, which instantly vanished in a cloud of suspicion.

I observed that our hostelry bore a signed letter "The Boiling Teapot" and a crude picture of the same dome in oil.

"The place," explained Holmes, "was formerly called 'Oil Drop Inn.'" It was just about closing time and as we hurriedly entered, we felt a distinct shock, accompanied by reverberations.

"That, I deduce," said the great detective, "was either Ed Denby[1] closing up or Frank Vanderlip[1] shutting up. But here

---

[1] Edwin Denby (1870-1928) was secretary of the navy under presidents Harding and Coolidge from 1921 to 1924. Denby laid the groundwork for the Teapot Dome scandal by getting President Harding's approval to move control of the navy's oil reserves to Albert Fall's Department of the Interior. Denby had to resign as a result of his role in the scandal.

we are—"

"Here we are, Watson," repeated Holmes, as he stepped to the desk and registered as John T. King. I signed the name of Henry Mann. The detective greeted the night clerk. "How are the folks, oil well?"

The clerk made a despondent gesture. "Oil sick," he replied, adding the information that the best rooms were already taken by retiring Cabinet Officers.

A happy group of Common People in the grill were singing. "Yes, we have no subpoenas."[2]

Holmes ignored them and, microscope in hand, proceeded to scrutinize the lobby.

"It is covered," I observed rather proudly, "with linoleum!"

"With petroleum," corrected Holmes. "Or, if you prefer, oilcloth."

Suddenly the tramp of many feet drew us to the window. A number of prosperous-looking citizens were marching in the direction of the Senate, each carrying a folded paper and a traveling bag covered with Florida or European hotel labels.

"Hah!" I whispered. "Returning witnesses who thought they wouldn't come back!"

"My dear Watson," corrected Holmes, "be more concise and say, 'Parade of the Wouldn't Soldiers.'"[3]

When I recovered, Holmes was at the telephone calling the Navy Department.

"Is Mr. Denby out?" he asked. I did not hear the answer, but Holmes inquired, "when do you expect him out?" Distinctly I heard the reply, "March 10."

"Many tanks," said Holmes in a gushing manner.

---

[1] Vanderlip (1864-1937) was a banker and journalist whose advocacy of the public's right to know about the scandal led to his resignation from many company boards.
[2] Sung to the tune of "Yes, We Have No Bananas," a hit song popular in 1923. It was the sole hit co-written by Frank Silver (1892-1960) and Irving Cohn (1898-1961).
[3] A reference to the "Parade of the Wooden Soldiers," a popular march written in 1897 by German composer Leon Jessel (1871-1942).

Hardly had Sherlock Holmes hung up the receiver when I saw a body of men moving at double time toward the capital. Their heads, I observed, were fairly bursting from their hats.

Calling Holmes, I ventured a conclusion. "These," I said, "are Volunteer Witnesses; or shall I say Natural Gushers?"

The great detective patted me on the head with an oil can. "My dear Watson, you are oil informed, but you are improving. Think again."

I thought. Suddenly I cried, "are they Know-It-Oils?" Holmes blew his police whistle.

In response to the detective's blast on his police whistle a platoon of bootleggers rushed into the lobby. I recoiled, but a look from Holmes made me realize the danger of any action.

"There's oil in recoiling, Watson," he whispered. "Have you forgotten my warning?" And he calmly opened the window and, placing his finger to his lips, produced an excellent imitation of the drawing of a cork.

Instantly a dozen members of Congress came running in. "Scofflaw-makers," commented Holmes.

Just then Wayne B. Wheeler walked in and the Congressmen fled. The night clerk approached Holmes. "Mr. King," he said, "the room reserved for Atty. Gen. Daugherty is still unoccupied, if you care to take it temporarily."

"Come, Watson," yawned the detective, "let's turn in. We'll have an exciting day tomorrow unless I'm much mistaken. I've just received a very cautiously worded telegram from Frank Vanderlip."

"What does he say now?" I asked, excitedly.

"Not a word," replied Holmes.

"And he didn't say anything over the 'phone?" I persisted. "Is his lip cracked?"

"That would be a wise crack," replied the great detective, drawing his automatic.

Holmes fired twice and I fell once. I arose at the count of nine.

"I merely disposed of Henry Mann, my dear fellow," he

said soothingly. "And now, Watson, while I smoke and think, you could help me greatly in solving this oil problem if you would oblige with some of your recitations. Suppose you try that one about the little busy bee?"

The great detective settled himself comfortably on a chandelier and I began:

How did the busy Albert B.
Improve each shining hour?
He made the oil flow fast and free,
But now it's turning sour.

"I spoiled it," I groaned.

"There you go again, Watson," scolded Holmes, "using words containing OIL. You'll get a subpoena yet. But your little recitations are quite up to date and help to relieve that boredom inseparable from the study of an oil well problem."

"And now," added the great investigator, "if you will first give me a bit of 'Hiawatha,' I'll give you a brief history of the Teapot Dome case."

I selected a stanza at random:

"In the oil fields of Wyoming.
On the famous Dome called Teapot,
Ed Doheny, oily riser,[1]
Stood upon the lid at daybreak;
At the crack of dawn he stood there.
Stood pat on the Dome of Teapot –

My "Hiawatha" seemed oil mixed to me, but I did not dare say so to Holmes, who called for another stanza, so I reluctantly resumed:

---

[1] As mentioned in the above footnote for "Doheny note," Edward L. Doheny (1856-1935) owned the Pan-American Petroleum and Transport Company and gave Fall $100,000 for leasing the Navy's oil reserves to his company.

Ed Doheny got up oily,
Very oily in the morning,
Put some leases in his pocket,
Waived a note above the Teapot.
At the great magician's bidding
Oil came dashing forth in barrels,
Gushing from the magic teapot,
From the famous Dome called teapot,
In the oil fields of Wyoming –

Holmes checked me with a question: "how many verses do you get on a gallon of oil, Watson?" He asked. That made me mad so I started another stanza:

"But a lot of oil's been going
O'er the dam since that spring morning,
Quite a lot of oil, believe me,
And the chill of Fall has fallen
On the famous Dome of Teapot.
While upon its somber summit
In the circle of the Searchlight
Ed Doheny stands and mutters,
Talking to himself in this wise:
'Where did Albert Fall from off of?
Fall from off the Dome called Teapot.
On the Gov'ment Reservation
In the oil fields of Wyoming?'"

"Great, Watson," cried Holmes. "Although I fear the facts in the case escape you. In other words, you're something of a Domebell, but—"

"but enough of 'Hiawatha' for the moment," continued Holmes, "and now I shall keep my promise to give you a brief outline of the Teapot Dome mystery to date."

He swung himself from the chandelier to the curtain pole

and, assuming an attitude of complete relaxation with the tips of his fingers touching the toes of his shoes, the great detective was about to begin when I thought of another fragment of "Hiawatha" and began:

"Oh, the short and cruel questions,
Oh, the long and oily answers,
In the weary oil inquiry,
In the long investigation —

The great detective drew his automatic and fired three times. I fell twice, then arose and brushed myself off with the whiskbroom I always kept suspended about my neck. I knew my eccentric friend used only blank cartridges, but I never failed to fall when he fired. It pleased him and did me no harm.

"Don't let me have to shoot you again for some time, Watson," said Holmes, "as I want to give you a brief history of this Teapot Dome mystery to date.

"It seems that the Republicans, one of our oldest and wealthiest families, were gathered around the tea table one winter afternoon enjoying their tea and plums and congratulating themselves on the happy state of the family fortunes and the brilliant prospects for the future. In other words, they were sitting pretty. Do you follow me?"

I shook my head in the negative, so Holmes resumed: "the phonograph was playing 'In a Cozy Tea Room' and 'I am Sitting Pretty in a Pretty Little City.' They were, as you know, in the beautiful small town of Washington, D.C. Do you follow me?

"I'm afraid not," I answered, "although it seems quite oilementary-"

"There you go again!" barked Holmes. "When you can't find words containing oil you invent them. You will get yourself subpoenaed in spite of my warnings. Still, being an obscure person, you may never be drawn into this Oil Inquiry. I shall now proceed with my story of the Case."

"As I explained, the Republican family were sitting pretty

around the tea table, which was covered with a napkin—"

"A doily," I suggested, and Holmes went on:

"With a doily upon which was embroidered the figure of a joyous Elephant."

"Apparently everything was oil to the mustard, when suddenly there came the sound of a heavy Fall, the Teapot boiled over and to the horror and consternation of the family, the happy home was filled with the unsavory odor of OIL!"

"Then, to their amazement, they saw that oil was gushing from the Teapot and smearing the Elephant, which, I may add, was the pride of the Republican family."

"Imagine, Watson," continued Holmes, "the shock to the entire Republican family! Old Cabot Lodge, Republican, seems to have been rendered temporarily speechless by the catastrophe, while others lost their tempers, which are still missing, thereby adding to my problem. Still others became panic-stricken and in their frenzied efforts to stop the flow of oil, merely succeeded in splashing it over each other, including Edwin Denby, Republican, the sailor son of the family, who was obliged to remove his Naval uniform and change to civilian clothing."

"Young Calvin Coolidge, Republican, who was sawing wood at the time, seems to have kept his head and to have called for assistance. However—"

"However," Holmes went on, "the amazing teapot continue to spout oil, and the Democrats, another old and respected family living across the road from the Republicans, rushed into gloat, I fear, rather than to help.

"There seems to be a feud between the two families, each claiming that the other is an aggregation of nitwits unfit for public office. Be that as it may, Tom Walsh,[1] Democrat, in a

---

[1] Sen. Thomas Walsh (1859-1933) represented Montana as its senator from 1913 to 1933. For two years, he chaired the committee that investigated Albert Fall's granting of the oil leases. His committee uncovered Edward L. Doheny's loan of $100,000 in cash to Fall that provided the smoking gun. Up to that point, thanks to the disappearance of requested records, there

praiseworthy attempt to get at the bottom of the mystery, lifted the lid entirely off the Teapot, and blooey – you know the result. Even Willie McAdoo, Democrat, the pet and pride of the family, did not escape the ensuing splash. Do you follow me?"

Holmes's question woke me from a sound sleep. "Watson," he added briskly, "just give a brief summary of the facts as I have just related them, in rhyme, if possible.

I lost no time in beginning:

"The Midnight Wire of Paul McLean."[1]
"Listen my children and you shall hear
Of the midnight messages, plain and clear,
Which told how a certain apricot,
Knowing the winter was growing hot,
Talked to an apple homeward bound,
But not while the servants were around."
"You mentioned only Fall fruits," interrupted Holmes.
"Yes," I agreed, "but mostly the oily varieties."
"Pray go on," said Holmes, with an apologetic gesture.
"He said to his friend, where the cherries grow
Out of the golf course in the spring,
See Zev peel peaches and let me know,[2]

---

was no evidence how Fall became so rich so quickly. Then Walsh uncovered Doheny's loan, and this led to Fall's downfall.

[1] A parody of "Paul Revere's Ride" by Henry Wadsworth Longfellow (1807-1882). This 1860 poem popularized the story of how Revere, during the American Revolution, rode from Charlestown to warn the Minutemen in Medford, Lexington, and Concord that the British troops were coming. Although the poem contains numerous historical inaccuracies, they were made intentionally by Longfellow for poetic effect.

The McLean in the parody poem is Ned McLean, the owner and publisher of *The Washington Post*, who participated in the cover-up of the Teapot Dome scandal. To keep informed, he sent and received telegrams in a code acquired from the Bureau of Investigation, in which fruits substituted for his allies' names. One such message ran: "Just talked with apricot and believe he has the thing well in hand. He advises for your interest not to talk about peaches or apples with anyone or in front of servants."

[2] A champion thoroughbred racehorse and inductee into the National Mu-

*Or else tell Mary or John T. King,
But don't say cherry or mention peach
Until you have notified gob – Palm Beach,
Cherries and peaches may be right,
But Duckstein shall not ring tonight."*

Just then the telephone rang violently.

"That's Duck now," whispered Holmes excitedly. I listened in as Holmes held the receiver.

"Helloil," said a pleasant voice. "Zev hocusing frankfurter's encyclopedia, but neckties are swimming on wrong track."

"Well, well!" answered Holmes, "that's fastidious carburetors for hobgoblins, isn't it? But did you chance to observe any oyster stamps lurking about the ticket office?"

"Mary didn't manicure the goldfish in the weather report, because the sun burns," came the prompt answer.

Holmes hung up the receiver.

"That last word," I cried, "did you get it?"

"Right, Watson," shouted Holmes, "it was burns – that could have been none other than my only rival, Bill Burns, the great detective."

"Bill Burns[2] is a bit jealous, I fancy," explained Holmes,

---

seum of Racing Hall of Fame. Zev was owned by Harry F. Sinclair, one of two oilmen who bribed Albert Fall.

[1] William O. Duckstein was married to Jesse Duckstein, private secretary to Ned McLean, the owner and publisher of *The Washington Post*. An agent of the department of justice, Duckstein was hired by McLean to spy on the investigation and pass on anything they uncovered. Duckstein was also hired by Harry Daugherty to work for the Bureau of Investigation (a precursor to the FBI) as a G-man. This gave him access to the BOI's codebooks, which he used to send coded messages to McLean on a private telegraph wire set up in McLean's Palm Springs home (sample message: "Zev hocusing imagery commensal abad hosier lectionary. Clot prattler lamb jaguar roved timepiece nudity," which translated to "Zeveley believes investigation is progressing entirely in your favor. He doesn't think much of Walsh as a cross-examiner.").

[2] Through his participation in several high-profile cases and savvy publicity, William J. Burns (1861-1932) was one of the best-known lawmen of his

"because I have been called into the case—"

He was interrupted by a series of loud, crackling reports outside. We rushed to the window and saw the sky illuminated by sparks and flashes from the telegraph wires.

"A brilliant electrical display," I remarked.

"Quite so," agreed Holmes. "Someone evidently trying to obtain 'easy access to the White House'; and Watson, if you will hand me a copy of 'Mother Goose' that you will find in my grip I shall send a code message to Ned McLean.[1] 'Mother Goose,' you know, is the secret code used by the juvenile division of the Department of Justice, and no one has ever discovered what it meant. There is no written explanation. It's a simple code in the head," concluded Holmes as he vigorously blew his nose.

Holmes turned the pages of "Mother Goose" until he came to page 44. "Ha!" He exclaimed, "here is just the thing." I produced a pencil and telegraph form in the great detective dictated:

McFat, Fern Beach:

---

time. He led the investigation into the bombing of the *Los Angeles Times* building in 1910 that resulted in two arrests and convictions. Thanks to his relationship with Attorney General Harry Daughtery, he was selected to lead the Bureau of Investigation. At Daughtery's orders, the BOI investigated Sen. Thomas Walsh in retaliation for his investigation into Fall. Burns stonewalled a subsequent investigation of the BOI's role in the scandal and his agents attempted to intimidate newspaper editors who attacked the bureau. In 1924, Burns was forced to resign by Daughtery's successor, and J. Edgar Hoover took his place. As part of a reform movement, the BOI was renamed the FBI. In 1927, during Harry F. Sinclair's trial for his role in the Teapot Dome scandal, he hired Burns' agents to follow the jurors. Burns was convicted of contempt of court, but it was reversed in a Supreme Court decision.

[1] Edward "Ned" McLean (1889-1941) owned and published *The Washington Post* (1916-1933) before he was declared insane and committed to a psychiatric hospital. A friend of Fall, McLean lied to Sen. Walsh and the committee, saying that he was the source of a $100,000 loan to secretary of the interior to hide that it actually came from the oil companies. This revelation provided a major piece of evidence that led to Fall's arrest.

The man in the wilderness asked of me,
How many apricots grew in the sea?
I answered the principle, as I thought good,
As many as bathing suits grew in the wood."

"What name shall I sign?" I asked in some confusion.

"One moment," mused Holmes. He turned to page 41. "Sign Mary—".

"Which Mary?" I stupidly inquired.

"Mary, quite contrary," snapped the detective.

At that moment there was a crash of glass and four missiles came through the window. They proved to be an apple, an apricot, a peach, and a cherry.

"Ha, Watson!" ejaculated Holmes, examining the fruit with his microscope, "you know what this means? All the Principles are in season!"

"In season?" I repeated, dumb as ever.

"My dear fellow, those are code words meaning out of luck; do you follow me?"

I didn't, but I lied clumsily. It seemed the thing to do in an oil case. Holmes drew his automatic.

"What oils you, Watson?" he asked sternly. "Have you sent that code message to Fern Beach?"

I still held it in my hand, so I replied, "certainly."

Holmes regarded me with admiration. "Watson, you'll be an oil magnate someday," he said. "Is that a duplicate message you have there?"

"No, sir; that's the original," becoming confused and blurting out the truth; but instantly I recovered myself. "I gave the duplicate message to one of those two messenger boys," I stammered.

"Which one?" quizzed the great detective. He was trying to catch me in the truth.

"The original one," I replied. Holmes persisted: "and where is the duplicate messenger?"

"In duplicate," was my clever answer, as I tore the telegram in half and rang for two messengers.

"Watson, why didn't you send that message without lying about it?" asked Holmes.

"Because it isn't done, sir," I replied.

"Quite so," agreed Holmes, "but I think you have reversed the procedure, which is, I observe, to send the message first and tell the whopper afterward. Do you follow me?"

"I can't remember," I muttered. "But here comes the messenger with the answer to our wire, and if there is nothing to conceal, the reply will be in safer. Am I right?"

"What did you say?" inquired Holmes.

"I can't remember," I said boldly. I had now been nearly a week in Washington.

The messenger who brought the reply to my wire was disguised as a movie fan. He wore a brown fedora, a four-in-hand tie, gloves and tan shoes. Over his grey business suit he wore an overcoat, and to complete the illusion he came on a dead run.

Holmes seized and read the message aloud:

Everybody, Wash., D.C.
Sing a song of peaches,
A pocket full of rye.
Four and 20 apples
Baked in a pie.
When the pie is opened
The apricots will sing
Isn't that a telegram
For John T. King?"

Holmes slipped the message under the rug when the bogus movie fan wasn't looking.

Suddenly a man entered the room. From the oil can which hung on his arm he produced a subpoena and handed it to me. "That service for you," he remarked. "And look at the calls I got to make before lunch!" flourishing a copy of *Who's Who in Washington* and a bulky volume entitled *City Directory*.

Hardly had he departed when a letter carrier on an oil burning bicycle rode in and handed Holmes 85 Special Delivery letters. Each one was from an Investigating Committee requesting him to act as a special investigator. He promptly wired 84 acceptances. "It would be too much to accept all," he said. I rushed for my luggage.

While Holmes proceeded to disguise himself as a basket of fruit, I quickly changed into a suit of oil skins of semiformal cut, and placing an oileander in the lapel of my coat I taxied to the Capitol.

I found an unbroken line of witnesses moving in and out of the building. It seemed that a witness, having testified that he didn't remember, went outdoors to refresh his memory, and, after again getting in line, went back for another try. One old fellow told me he was making his 19th trip and couldn't yet recall what kind of toothpaste he used in the fall of 1901.

Fortunately one of the witnesses who had been in line for three days left his place to get a shave and I slipped into the vacancy.

A few hours later I was in the witness chair and the questions and answers began:

"Dr. Watson, between the summer of 1919 and the spring of 1924, you have used words containing oil?"

"I couldn't help it, sir!"

"Did you not, on the morning of Aug. 8, 1920, say that you hated to SOIL another collar?"

I was about to answer when a huge basket of fruit was brought in and placed upon the table. One of the apricots appeared to wink at me!

"Careful, Watson," hissed a voice from the basket.

It was the inimitable Sherlock Holmes!

At this point the witness chair was removed and a daybed substituted. I made myself uncomfortable and the questioning was resumed:

"Dr. Watson, have you bought any oil stock?"

"Positively not."

"When did you buy it?"
"In the autumn of 1922."
"Give the exact date."
"April 1, 1925."
"From whom did you purchase it?"
"It was a gift."
"What price did you pay for it?"
"$985.50—"

Suddenly a messenger boy removed the basket of apples, peaches, cherries, and apricots. The basket of fruit, which was Sherlock Holmes in disguise, got by without arousing suspicion, everybody taking it to be a code telegram.

Suddenly my questioner asked:

"Dr. Watson, who presented you with this gift of oil stock for which you paid $985.50?"

"Mr. John T. King."

"Dr., you are, I believe, a bachelor."

"Yes, sir."

"And to whom did you give this stock?"

"To my wife."

"When?"

"Shortly before I got it."

"When was that?"

"I can't remember."

"And the date you have forgotten, doctor?"

"February 31st, 1922."

"You are excused until Thursday."

As we paused for breath a bulky envelope was placed in my hands. It bore the letterhead "Departure of Justice" and contained a code message from Holmes:

"The peach is red, the cherry blue. The apple is sweet and the apricot, too."

Which, decoded, read:

Dear Doc —
  I am now working on the following cases:

The Teapot Dome Case.
The Sign of the Fourflushers.
The Adventure of the Flying Check Stubs.
The Whiskey Warehouse Mystery.
The Case of the Mysterious Million.
The Man with the Bulging Hip.
The Fight Film Funny Business —

My reading of Holmes's message was stopped for:
"Now, Dr. Watson," thundered my inquisitor, "where were you on the afternoon of March 1?"
"Looking at the fight picture."
"When was this?"
"On the evening of Feb. 16."
"Where were you at that time?"
"Right in front of the lunch wagon."
"Were you alone?"
"No, sir, I was not."
"Who was with you?"
"Nobody."
"Did you have any conversation?"
"Yes, sir, quite a discussion."
"Watson," said Holmes, as we sat smoking in our barracks (we were now quartered in one of the vast cantonments for witnesses), "Watson, I believe I have unearthed the most amazing sensation of the whole inquiry."
Holmes carefully closed the door and whispered: "I cannot be certain as yet, but I think I'm on the trail of a witness who has absolutely no charges to make against anybody!"
It seemed unbelievable. "Are you sure? I cried.
"Absolutely, Dr. Watson."
"Positively, Mr. Holmes?"[1]
And quite naturally we burst into a spirited duet:

---

[1] A reference to the catchphrase "Positively, Mister Gallagher? Absolutely, Mister Shean!" a line from a popular vaudeville comic song by Edward Gallagher (1873-1929) and Al Shean (1868-1949).

*Oh Dr. Watson, oh Dr. Watson,
You've a head like one of these old Teapot Domes.
When upon the witness stand
Your evasions have been grand;
You're a liar, Dr. Watson—
You're another, Mr. Holmes!*

At this moment the siren on the Capitol sounded the first call for witnesses, and we rushed out and joined our respective companies, already forming on the parade ground. Soon we were marching up Pennsylvania Avenue to the stirring sounds of "Walsh Me Around Again, Tommy."[1]

The long columns of witnesses diverged to the various investigations. My battalion halted and stood at "Rest" and soon my number, "927," was called and I mounted the witness stand.

Another mattress was placed on the daybed.

"Now, doctor," said "Sen. Quizzem," "when you are answering my questions you can lie more comfortably."

The first query was, as we British say, a fair crumpler:[2]

"Did you possess a corkscrew in 1917?"

"No, sir, I did not."

"Did you keep it in the pantry?"

"That was my custom."

"Do you know Miss Moxie Stencil?"

"I have known her for years."

"When did you first meet her?"

"I never had the pleasure of meeting her."

---

[1] A reference to "Waltz Me Around Again, Willie," a popular song from 1906. It was popularized by Billy Murray (1877-1954), a tenor who was one of the most popular singers of his time. When his crooning style declined in popularity, Murray switched to singing in animated cartoons. Two of his songs, "You're a Grand Old Rag," and "Shine On, Harvest Moon," can be heard in the video game *BioShock Infinite*. "Tommy" is, as we've seen above, Sen. Thomas Walsh, who led the Senate investigation into Teapot Dome.

[2] A crumple is actually slang for a cravat, a neckband favored by a military organization called the Croats, light cavalry forces from eastern Europe.

At this point the bulletin was read into this record stating that Harry Daugherty[1] denied having resigned from the Potomac Ma-Jong Club.

The evening of Friday, March 28, was a sad one in the great encampment of witnesses. Never shall I forget the date, unless called to the witness stand. Attorney General Daughtery resigned very suddenly and his exituary notices were in all the evening papers.

Demobilization of the 17th and 18th Corps of the Grand Army of Witnesses had already begun. These organizations were composed of three-months men, who were now being mustered out of the service and transferred to the Witnesses Reserve Corps. Great fires were burning, in which tons of notes, data, and memoranda were being destroyed, while the departing volunteers were mournfully singing:

"Way back to private life and business
Sadly I roamed;
Far from the witness chair I wander
And far from the Teapot Dome!"[2]

It was a sad night for those who had so much to say and now couldn't say it.

---

[1] Harry Daugherty (1860-1941) was a failed Ohio politician and influential figure behind the scenes. His role as Warren G. Harding's campaign manager led to his appointment as attorney general (1921-1924). He was a member of the "Ohio Gang," consisting of Harding's friends and political allies who followed him to Washington and subsequently began enriching themselves. While nothing was ever proved about Daugherty, he was forced to resign by President Calvin Coolidge after Harding's death.

[2] A parody of "Old Folks at Home," more popularly known as "Swanee River," an 1851 minstrel song written by Stephen Foster. Despite the singer's longing for "the old plantation" and crying out "Oh, darkies, how my heart grows weary / Far from the old folks at home," it became the state song of Florida in 1913. They did change "darkies" to "brothers" however. In 1978.

Intelligence Service

"Z. 4.999"

Illustrated by "RVG"

Translated by Bill Peschel

In 1066, the Duke of Normandy crossed the English Channel with his army, and, as William the Conqueror, became the first Norman king of England. England has never forgiven France ever since. For centuries, this rivalry played out on numerous battlefields, and it wasn't until the rise of a unified Germany that the two antagonists put aside most of their differences in the face of a common enemy.

But an alliance doesn't necessarily mean friendship, and the two nations remain united in their bemused contempt for each other. Take this story, for example, published in the Dec. 13, 1925, issue of Le Matin *("The Morning News") of Paris.*

Whitechapel,[1] 5:49 p.m. Behind the docks, the light from the electric globes glitter on the small street like diamonds in

---

[1] A neighborhood in London's East End. Its location near the docks on the Thames made it a popular place for immigrants. The Jack the Ripper murders took place there in the late 1880s.

the thick fog.

Strong smells of gin and rotted grains rose from the sheds whose feet bathed in the Thames. In the middle of the stream that cuts the street, a woman in a feathered hat waits for the statuesque policeman to escort her to the night court.

I enter the small pub. To keep from being noticed, I disguised myself as a Hawaiian general. I place on the table my cocked hat, my chewing gum and the secret code of the British Admiralty I just bought at the nearest bookstore.

After a second the man entered. He was dressed in a checkered Inverness cape,[1] and he puffed scrolls of smoke from the blond tobacco in his briar pipe. He also carried, I was to learn later, very compromising documents. The man's light blue eyes were piercing and disturbing. They searched the room until they stopped on me.

"I know you," he said with a Scottish highland accent. "You were born in Belleville,[2] as evidenced by your mountain shoes; your father was an arthritic metal smelter; because you have your ears widely spread, you have failed twice obtaining your bachelor's degree; and you like cherries soaked in *eau-de-vie*."[3]

I was amazed; he had just dissected my life like a bitter almond. I looked at him, stunned.

"Are you determined to work with us?"

"Yes, sir," I replied.

---

[1] A weatherproof sleeveless coat with an added short cape from which the wearer's arms emerge. It was developed in Scotland in the 1850s and underwent modifications in the length and design before it reached its final form. Although Holmes typically wore an Ulster coat in the books, he was portrayed with the showier cape in Sidney Paget's illustrations.

[2] The French word for "beautiful town" is used by at least 10 places in France, as well as a fictional location for the French animated movie *The Triplets of Belleville* (2003). In this case the narrator is probably from the Paris neighborhood on the east side of the city. It was founded as an independent municipality (called a commune) after the French Revolution, and was annexed by the city in 1860.

[3] Literally translated as "water of life," it is a colorless fruit brandy.

"Let's speak in French," said the man with a strange smile. He lowered his voice. "Let me introduce myself. I am Sherlock Holmes."

"The Great Detective."

"Simply 'The Detective' will do; the smartest man in Britain, presently chief of the Intelligence Service of His Majesty's Army. Your country concerns us. France is secretly rearming and, as the vulture flies, London is too close to Paris. We need vital information about your strategic points."

"How much do you pay?"

"One thousand pounds down and another thousand pounds upon delivery."

"Done. What do you desire? I have on me the number of soldiers who guard the Elysee Palace,[1] the plunger from a rapid-firing "680", and a model of the Republican Guard's regulation boots."[2]

"We know all that; we need more important military intelligence." The man spoke in a low voice. As he whispered these grave words — I must confess — he nervously pricked his left forearm with a Pravaz syringe[3] and with his right foot

---

[1] It has been the official home of France's president since 1848, but before that its history mirrored the fortunes of the French royalty. Designed in the French classical style and built in 1722 for an aristocratic family, it was bought by King Louis XV for his mistress Madame de Pompadour. The monarch sold it after her death in 1773 to the court's banker, one of the richest men in France, for his use as a country home. In 1787, it was sold to the Duchess of Bourbon, who named it the Élysée Palace, after the Elysian Fields, the equivalent of heaven in Greek mythology. After the French Revolution, the palace was confiscated and turned into a business offering food, drinking, dancing and gambling. In 1808, it was sold to Emperor Napoleon Bonaparte, and after his final downfall after the battle of Waterloo, it was returned to the Duchess of Bourbon, who sold it to Louis XVIII. The most notable event in the palace since then occurred in 1899, when 58-year-old President Félix Faure died of apoplexy while having sex with his 30-year-old mistress.

[2] A tool used to regulate the explosion time of a shell after firing. An explanation for the "680" could not be found.

[3] Charles Gabriel Pravaz (1791-1853) was a French orthopedic surgeon and

beat the march of the First Scottish Grenadiers.¹

"I want to know," he said, "where is the Eiffel Tower. Then, I want to know where I can find the Opera railway station. Finally, I need to know what the cannon sounds like at the Palais-Royal.²

"Good God!" I said, my teeth chattering, "you're not pulling your punches! What you're demanding is not simple."

"Take it or leave it, but I advise you to take it, because if you leave, my poor arthritic son, there is a good chance that you'll finish your days in the lowest dungeon in the Tower of London."³

"I accept, but you must pay me the advance."

"Here!" He handed me a thousand pounds in sixpence coins.⁴ By the time I counted my money, he vanished, or

---

inventor of the hypodermic syringe.

[1] A non-existent unit. There may be Scotsmen in the Grenadier Guards, a long-serving infantry regiment in the British Army, but no specific unit by that name is on its roster.

[2] *Eiffel Tower:* Probably the most famous symbol of Paris, the tower was considered a failure by artists and intellectuals when it was built for the entrance to the 1889 World's Fair. More than 7 million people visit it every year. It is named for the engineer and designer Gustave Eiffel (1832-1923). *Opera*: A railway station in the 2nd arrondissment of central Paris. Named for the Place de l'Opéra Square. Nearby lies the Palais Garnier opera house, the home from 1861 to 1875 of the Paris Opera. Apart from its architectural and musical merits, it is also known as the setting of the novel by Gaston Leroux (1868-1927) *The Phantom of the Opera* (1910). *Palais-Royal:* A former royal palace located next to the Louvre in the city's 1st arrondissement. It was built for Cardinal Richelieu (1585-1642) in 1639 and became royal property upon his death. It is now used by the Ministry of Culture and the Constitutional Council.

[3] A castle located on the banks of the Thames in central London. The White Tower was built by William the Conqueror in 1078. More buildings and two concentric rings of walls and a moat were finished by the late 13th century. The Tower has served as a mint, an armory, records office, a prison (1100-1952), and is currently the repository of the Crown Jewels of England. During the 16th and 17th century, it imprisoned nobles, some of whom were later executed for treason.

[4] A coin from the old British monetary system. It is also called a tanner or half-shilling (since a shilling is 12 pence). Worth about a pound today,

maybe he metamorphosed. Because from that moment on, my steps were dogged by an Italian organ player from Barbary playing Toselli's serenade night and day.[1]

I was part of the "Intelligence Service." To reflect the important role I was going to play, I virtuously swallowed a cocktail, a cocktail mixed from equal parts shame and pride.

I crossed the English Channel and rented near my field of operation in Paris a boiled-egg shop to convince my neighbors that I was an honorable merchant. I stuffed my display with fake eggs and hired accomplices: two nurses for the cannon of the Palais-Royal, a paratrooper for the Eiffel Tower, and a fake naval officer whose uniform was similar to that of the employees of the subway.

Dressed in their colorful coats, my henchmen reconnoitered their targets. Meanwhile, I enjoyed the high life at the expense of the Intelligence Service. I had mistresses, a sedan, washable gloves and vermeil cigarette holders.[2]

In the end, my fun became the ruin of me.

Holmes' advance represents a substantial fortune. It's also a substantial weight, since £2,000 in half-shillings weighs 500 pounds.

[1] A popular piece of classical music, better known as Serenata "Rimpianto" Op.6 No.1. Enrico Toselli (1883-1926) was an Italian concert pianist who performed all across Europe. His elopement with Archduchess Louise of Austria in 1907, a few years after she deserted King Frederick Augustus of Saxony, caused a scandal. Their marriage, however, ended in divorce in 1912.

[2] *Sedan:* A passenger car that has three compartments for the engine, passengers, and cargo. The name is derived from a sedan chair, a box with poles front to back that was carried by porters. The word was first applied to vehicles in 1912, although they existed as early as 1899. *Washable gloves:* While the properties of goatskin used to make chamois gloves make them washable, advances in tanning and treatment of other hides led to the advertising of gloves that could be washed in gasoline or warm water and soda. *Cigarette holders:* When women took to smoking in greater numbers after 1900, this fashion accessory was invented to keep falling ash off their clothes (hence the unusually long lengths), reduce staining of the fingers, gloves and teeth, cooled the smoke and kept the lips from tearing the thin paper. Men took to them as well but preferred the shorter lengths.

One fine morning, Sherlock Holmes appeared in Paris. We met in the shop, where I updated him about our operations. The paratrooper could not reach the Eiffel Tower because of the demolition work at the Exposition Internationale des Arts Décoratifs,[1] the fake officer had been bottled up fr eight days at the Madeleine,[2] and the nurses were deafened by the Palais Royal's cannon and I had to drive them to the hospital.

The most intelligent man in the United Kingdom looked at me angrily, then suddenly bursting into a mad laugh, he whistled in a beautiful key. Two French agents entered the store and dragged me to the depot.

As if failing in my mission wasn't bad enough, it turns out Sherlock Holmes was in cahoots with the Pointed Tower.[3]

---

[1] The style known as Art Deco debuted at the International Exhibition of Modern Decorative and Industrial Arts in Paris. From April to October 1925, more than 16 million people visited the 15,000 exhibitors from 20 nations. It was a celebration of Modernism in art, design, and architecture. The Eiffel Tower could be seen from the exhibition, especially after the Citroen company decorated it with 200,000 lights that displayed patterns of shapes, circles, the signs of the zodiac, and the company's name.

[2] A subway station in the 8th arrondissement of central Paris. It is one stop west of the Opera station. Although it bears the same name as the traditional small cake that inspired Marcel Proust to write *Remembrance of Things Past*, the subway stop was named for the L'église de la Madeleine, the Neo-classical church consecrated in 1842 to Mary Magdalene.

[3] [Original footnote] La Tour pointue (The Pointed Tower) in French slang means the Préfecture de police de Paris, 36, quai des Orfèvres (police headquarters in Paris) because of the pointed tower above it.

The Rollo Boys with Sherlock in Mayfair; or Keep It Under Your Green Hat

Corey Ford

Illustrated by Gluyas Williams

There were always books written to appeal to children, such as The Swiss Family Robinson *(1812),* Tom Brown's Schooldays *(1857),* Little Women *(1869), and* The Adventures of Tom Sawyer *(1876). But it took the appearance of cheaply printed and cheaply priced "dime novels" to launch the genre of boys' adventure stories, where youthful enthusiasm, imagination, and cleverness were championed. Heroes such as Frank Merriwell, Frank Reade Jr., Tom Swift, and the Rover Boys were sunny optimists who built fabulous machines, explored exotic parts of the world, and defeated bullies and villains.*

These stories were the target of Three Rousing Cheers for the Rollo Boys *(1925), the first book by humorist Corey Ford (1902-1969). In each chapter the boys embarked on a different adventure where silly things happen. For example, in one story, after the boys and their sweethearts are shipwrecked on a desert island, Ford describes what happened next:*

> *"'What shall we eat, though,' complained Dolly. She had no sooner spoken than a second wave carried up a table and a full set of dishes, and rapidly spread places for seven, handing each of the castaways a French menu as it departed down the beach. 'Dat old devil sea,' muttered Captain Blossom, as a third wave rolled apologetically up the beach with some butter, which the second wave had apparently forgotten. And he continued to shake his head and mutter as more waves drifted in after supper and washed the dishes."*

In the chapter below, Ford introduced the boys to two popular literary figures: Sherlock Holmes and Michael Arlen, the author of the best-seller The Green Hat *(1924). An Armenian by birth, Arlen (1895-1956) emigrated to Britain where he launched his literary career with his romances about Britain's Smart Set, the young generation* who passed through the war years unscathed and had time and money for idle frivolities.

The Green Hat told the short, tempestuous life of Iris March, the doomed last member of an aristocratic family, who recklessly drove a yellow Hispano Suiza luxury car and sported a green cloche hat. The novel shocked readers with its frank discussion of sex — at least frank for its time — which included Iris' declaration that she wanted sex and didn't care much who she did it with. Her life of joyous abandon was marred by Gerald March, her alcoholic brother, and her first husband, "Boy" Fenwick, who committed suicide "for Purity" — in particular his bride's lack of same. In the end, she dies tragically in an auto accident.

The story was illustrated by Gluyas Williams (1888-1982), an American cartoonist whose skilful depictions of the sophisticated wealthy class appeared frequently in The New Yorker.

"My dear Rollo Boys," said Sherlock Holmes, as he lounged over the test tubes in his long purple dressing gown, his pipe clamped between his teeth and the visor of his detective cap pulled down over his eyes, "I am seeking to ascertain the chemical elements of Purity." He held up two empty test tubes to the light, shook them, and poured the contents into a glass globe. "I should say they are about two parts of fiction to one of truth," he concluded slowly, examining the glass globe, which was empty, "and the rest merely impotence."

The three Rollo Boys were seated about the fire in their dressing gowns, the visors of their detective caps pulled down over their eyes, and their pipes clamped between their teeth. Silence fell over the little room, picking itself up again and rubbing its shins with an ill-concealed oath as it limped through the door.

Outdoors the windows were being washed by an autumnal rain, named Tony.

"You may have wondered that I should have sent for you to come here," said Sherlock Holmes slowly, as he emptied the contents of the globe and stirred the remaining vacuum reflectively. "But perhaps you can tell me what is needed."

"I should say, well, about a pony of brandy,"[1] murmured

---

[1] American slang for one fluid ounce of spirit, smaller than a shot of liquor

Tom Rollo absently, with one eye on the contacts of the globe.

"It is in connection with the strange mystery of the Mayfair Suicides," explained the detective, ignoring the fun-loving Rob's remark as he drained off the vacuum and threw it away leaving only the hole in space where the vacuum had been.

"You probably read in the *Evening Standard* this morning that one 'Boy Fenwick'[1] was found lying in the courtyard of the Hotel Vendôme, dead of a shattered reputation. He had fallen, it appears, from his bedroom window on the third floor. Iris March, his beautiful young wife, had been asleep, had suddenly awoken, if there is such a word, to a sharp feeling of solitude, had happened to look out at the dawn. ..."

"What came next?" gasped Dick Rollo.

"*Four trailing dots!*" hissed Sherlock Holmes, and removed the hole, leaving only the space.

"The Sign of the Four!"[2] cried Harry; and the three Rollo Boys stared at each other in horror. "But why—why—?"

Sherlock shrugged. " 'Boy died,' she said, 'for Purity!'"

And so saying, he seized the contents of the space where the hole had been which had been left by the vacuum, removed the contents, removed *that*, and held the result up to the light. "I have discovered *Purity!*" he cried.

"But you have nothing there!" ejaculated Tom.

"Precisely," laughed Sherlock Holmes diabolically, as the doorbell rang. "But if I am not very much mistaken, and I have never been mistaken except in the following cases," naming them, "this is the very lady now of whom we were speaking. It always is," he added by way of explanation, as he drew aside the window curtains and pointed to the long, low, empty battle chariot before the door, like a huge yellow insect, open as a

---

(1.5 oz.). Bartenders who use pour spouts in their bottles measure their pours by counting out loud so each word could be clearly understood. For a pony, they count to four; for a shot, to six.

[1] As noted in the introduction, he was the husband of Iris March who killed himself "for Purity."

[2] A reference to the second Sherlock Holmes novel published in 1890.

yacht, it wore a great shining bonnet, as supplied to his Most Catholic Majesty. (Ed. Note: It was an automobile. Ans.)[1]

"The lady is tall, not very tall, but short, her face is small as a lady's handkerchief provided she hasn't a cold, wearing a light brown leather jacket, and as they would say in the England of long ago — she is fair. To be fair, to be sad ... why, is she intelligent, too? And always her hair dances a tawny, formal dance ... may I have the next? I promised Lord Eggleston. But ... on her cheek, under the shadow of a Green Hat which she wears bravely, *pour le style*."[2]

"My God, Sherlock!" cried Dick, amazed by the man's extraordinary powers of deduction, "how can you tell all that?"

"Oh, I read the book," snapped Sherlock Holmes, as the door opened and our visitor entered.

"I've always wanted," said the voice of the Green Hat. One could not see her face, because the full moon does not rise over El Dorado till Thursday. One murmured thus and thus. She murmured: "You know, vaguely. ..."

"Of course, vaguely," said Sherlock Holmes. She sat in the deep wicker armchair. People named Elmer always sit in deep wicker armchairs. Superficially; but, then, God help us all! "I wonder." Who said that?

"Who said what?"

"I wonder."

"Perhaps you are right," she replied; and her hand smelled dimly of that scent whose name I shall now never know. She too belonged then to the scent-whose-name-I-shall-now-never-know School. "Why?" she said. "But, really ... "

She looked at him through a pair of opera glasses, upside down, and then she wound her watch, but one did not know. One never knew. Even if one wrote it ... Or even why ...

"Women," he said, "are—"

---

[1] Abbreviation for answer. This sentence is a good example of Arlen's writing style, which came to be called Arlenesque. Ford will continue to poke fun at Arlen's style for the rest of this story.

[2] A French phrase meaning "for the style," or to be stylish.

"You are not a bad woman, Iris March. You are just bad grammar."

"Of course, *women*. But —"
"Then how should I say 'women' — ?"
"You should make a dash after them," suggested fun-loving Tom merrily.
"Am I," she cried suddenly, "real? I must know. Am I thus,

or else thus? Do I wear this hat for the style (*pour le style*)? Am I — style? *His style?*" She shuddered. "Am I vacuity, or Mencken,[1] or both?" Her eyes were spoonfuls of the Mediterranean. *"Do I exist?"*

The clock struck twelve. What of it?

"You are not a bad woman, Iris March," said Sherlock Holmes kindly. "You are just bad grammar."

Chrysanthemums bloom in September; and they say that the Americans will "tell the cock-eyed world." Phut! one never knows. People with prominent left ears — *qu'est-ce que c'est que ca!* (what is it that it is that that?[2]) — one prefers turnips.

"Boy died," she said, "for Purity. And there's Gerald. ..."

"My God! Not Gerald. ... "

" ... " she replied, and was gone. Phut!

"The Sign of the Four!" gasped Dick, as the Rollo Boys stared at each other in horror. "We are not a moment too soon!"

"To the rescue!" cried Sherlock Holmes; and, seizing their magnifying glasses, the Rollo Boys set out in hot pursuit.

CHAPTER NINE

As swiftly as possible (which is not any too gosh-darned swift) the Rollo Boys and Sherlock Holmes advanced down their intricate maze of twisted phrases, similes, and winding allusions, trying to find their way through the mystery of Mr. Arlen's style. Now and then their eyes watered as a loose adjective whipped their faces; and once Dick caught himself in the nick of time from stepping into a deep insinuation directly in his way. On both sides little bypaths lured them from their

---

[1] H.L. Mencken (1880-1956) was an acerbic journalist and cultural critic. At this time he edited *The American Mercury* magazine and wrote columns for *The Baltimore Sun* newspapers. *Vacuity* means empty space or empty-headedness.

[2] The phrase is an idiom that means simply "what is that?". Since an idiom is a group of words whose meaning cannot be deduced by translating the individual words (such as feeling "under the weather" or "missing the boat," Ford was having fun by literally translating it.

main course, but they continued resolutely ahead, reading neither to the right nor to the left. Once a deep chasm between two chapters loomed before them, and they only crossed the gap by grasping at a hidden meaning. Once a break in the narration yawned at their very feet. Once Dick yawned himself. ...

"Pray God we are not too late!" prayed God Sherlock Holmes as they followed down the trailing dots to the little group that stood clustered about the open window of Gerald's bedroom, on the third floor of Shepherd Market.[1]

"It's awful," said one. "You see ..."

"Exactly," said the lady of the Green Hat. "And he —"

"Quite," replied one; for Gerald was not. "Gerald died," explained the lady of the Green Hat, as Sherlock Holmes and the Rollo Boys arrived at a run and stared at the open window at the sidewalk below, "for Purity!"[2]

---

[1] Not a residence as implied in the story, but a square in the Mayfair area of central London. A popular location for writers and artists, Shepherd Market was Michael Arlen's home, and he set much of *The Green Hat* there.

[2] The characters in *The Green Hat* debate what purity is and what it meant to Boy Fenwick, who killed himself in Dauville, France, by leaping from a window. What it means is never explicitly said; one character says "That might mean anything, and so of course we all took it to mean the worst thing as regards Iris." While this may seem unusual to modern readers, this gives you an idea of the distance between what was publishable in our time versus the years following World War I.

For those who don't want to plow through *The Green Hat*, here's a section from Chapter Three in which the narrator discusses purity with his friend, Hilary. It is not only a succinct summary of the situation, but there is an unexpected shout-out at the end:

"It seemed to me that it was, to say the least, rather hasty of a young man to die 'for purity' in connection with a girl of twenty. Hilary, in two thousand years we have discovered only one caddish way of getting to Heaven, and Boy Fenwick, like many "idealists," has taken it.'

"'You probably don't realise,' said Hilary, oh so reasonably, 'the depths of sudden despair — in decent people.'

"'But I thought we were discussing human beings!' And, as regards human beings, one couldn't help thinking that a girl who had confessed that her lover had died 'for purity' was purer than the lover who had not been able to live for it. Boy Fenwick's death had an air of getting away with

Well! but one can count to ten. You Americans would say: "It is a wow!" She was saying: "... and in the heart of the dandelion a tiny little rose." There is one for you. For that matter, there is one for Burbank. "Who?" asked Holmes.

"Hilary ..." she replied wildly, "and Guy ... and Napier ... and old Sir Maurice ..."[1]

"The Sign of the Four!" gasped Dick, and the Rollo Boys stared at each other in horror.

"Cripes! all of them?" ejaculated Tom.

"Hark!" cried Sherlock Holmes; and all the Rollo Boys pricked their ears except Harry, who had had his ears pricked by an old gipsy woman when he was a baby.[2]

From afar came the mysterious punctuation: "... . ..."

"S O S!"[3] gasped Holmes, and the Rollo Boys set out in hot pursuit.

CHAPTER NINE[4]

There was a rhythm. There was syncopation. It had a beat,

---

rather a good thing. He had destroyed the girl by exalting himself — for purity! How did boys come to have the infernal conceit of setting themselves up as connoisseurs of purity? And he had taken care to leave his corpse in such a position as best to foul the fountains of his young widow's womanhood. Sir Arthur Conan Doyle ought to speak to him about it."

For those who don't want to read *The Green Hat*, your editor included, it is revealed that after Boy, madly in love with Iris, finally marries her, he discovers he has syphilis, a sexually transmitted disease for which (in 1925) there was no safe and effective treatment. It wasn't until 1947 that penicillin was proved to treat the disease.

[1] These are all characters from *The Green Hat*.
[2] In the 1920s, the popularity of ear piercing declined in favor of clip-on earrings. It seemed like only sailors and gypsies pierced their ears. For a long time, anyone who wanted their ears pierced had to go to their family doctor or hold "piercing parties" at home. It wasn't until the later part of the 20th century that commercial outlets appeared that offered piercings.
[3] Holmes is incorrect. In Morse code, the international distress signal is three dots, three dashes, and three dots. Contrary to popular belief, the letters do not mean "save our ship" or "save our souls." It's simply a code word that is easy to remember and to send.
[4] [Ford's footnote] No; it isn't an error.

like a policeman. Instant, unforgettable, unforgivable, it throbbed like a sore thumb. There were many green dresses: red, blue, pink. The women had white oval faces, small breasts, black eyes, thin arms, and husbands named George. Everyone's husband is named George; and there you are. Or there. I see you, behind the clock.

"Quick!" hissed Holmes. The King of Spain was eating salted almonds.

Silently the three Rollo Boys and the detective drew on the red and green checkered pants, the bright gold epaulets and cocked hat, the long blue beard and spectacles; and thus completely disguised as head waiters they wandered unnoticed toward that table ... (which table? How should I know; listen what he's saying. I know, but Mama — Ssssh!)

Hilary said: "Life is, life being what it is, life ..."

Sir Maurice started: "We are the damned victims —"

Guy and Napier said nothing. They were somewhere else. They were never in Buffalo either.

"— of a literary style," finished Guy; and Napier said thus and thus.

They walked arm in arm to the window. Everyone walks arm in arm to the window, or goes to the Boston Symphony and wears dress shields.[1] "Iris ..."

"The Sign of the Four!" croaked Dick, as the Rollo Boys stared at each other, slightly bored as a matter of fact.

"We die," announced the four, standing on the window sill, "... you first, Hilary? After you, Guy. No matter ... 'for Purity!'" They lit a cigarette. ...

"We are getting warmer!" gasped Holmes, mopping his brow as the Rollo Boys set out once more in hot pursuit.

CHAPTER NINE[2]

"Iris ..." rose to their lips. "That car's gone mad!" They

---

[1] Replaceable moisture-absorbing pads that were applied to clothing to wick away sweat. They act as an alternative to antiperspirants, and are very useful in an era where laundry had to be washed by hand.

[2] [Ford's footnote] Just go with the flow.

swept headlong around the corner. "Iris!" Holmes sobbed. "Stop her, Arlen! Stop her! Not that —"

She poised on the sill of the third-story window. "I die," she said, "for Purity —"

"For purity of what?" shrieked Tom.

"For purity of grammar," she replied, as she held her nose and jumped. People yelled. ... The Rollo Boys were on the sidewalk and Holmes stooped and picked up the Green Hat. Beneath it on the sidewalk there was only a great, jagged, dripping stain ... only a mixed metaphor. ...

"Michael Arlen!" cried Dick, leaping into the swarm of eager parodists, humorists, and newspaper columnists who had already gathered about the nonchalant novelist in their midst. "Wanted for the murder of those Charming People!"

"Not at all," smiled Arlen suavely, as he elbowed his way through the rapidly increasing crowd of imitators and burlesquers, and set off in the direction of Southampton. "There has been no murder. All good Arlen characters when they die simply go to America!"[1]

"Not at all," smiled Mr. Arlen. "There has been no murder."

---

[1] Ironically, Arlen himself will move to America during World War II. He had been living in France with his family since 1928, but moved back to Britain when war broke out in 1939, where he wrote newspaper columns and published a novel and joined the Civil Defense. Objections were raised to his appointment in the House of Commons because he was a Bulgarian

"Three rousing cheers for the Rollo Boys!" shouted the relieved citizens at Mayfair, tossing their green hats in the air and cheering lustily. The cheers were given with a will; and the contents of that will, and how it affected the fortunes, not only of our young heroes, but also of the author and his publishers, will all be related in the next volume of this series, to be entitled:

"And Here Let Us Say Good-by; or, Beer and Light <u>Winesburg</u>."

And here let us say Good-by.

Good-by.[1]

Time magazine cover featuring
Michael Arlen, 1927.

---

and his novels were vaguely objectionable. Arlen responded by resigning and moved to America, where he lived until his death in 1956.

[1] Ford is aping the traditional way most Rover Boys adventures ended.

The Adventure of the Missing Hatrack

Frederic Dorr Steele

Illustrated by Frederic Dorr Steele

On the courthouse steps in Boston, American Mercury editor H.L. Mencken (1880-1956) sold a copy of his magazine and was arrested. Inside the magazine was a story called "Hatrack." It was about a part-time prostitute who services the church-going men in her small town. The story contained no curse words or unsavory descriptions, and there was nothing glamorous or salacious about Hatrack, who was given that nickname for her Olive Oyle-like physique. But because "Hatrack" offended the New England Watch and Ward Society, the magazine was banned in Boston, and later by the post office.

That's just one backstory behind "The Adventure of the Missing Hatrack," by Sherlockian illustrator Frederic Dorr Steele. The other story involves the Players Club, a social group founded in New York City in 1888 by Edwin Booth, the popular actor and brother of actor and Lincoln assassin John Wilkes Booth. Steele was a longtime member of the club, known for his skill with a pool cue and given the nickname "The Little Giant." He was also the editor of the Players Bulletin magazine, in which this story appeared in its Oct. 15 issue.

"The Adventure of the Missing Hatrack" is a curious mix of inside jokes about its members, combined with a fun poke at the censorship battle that became another skirmish for free speech in the U.S.

Steele (1873-1944) was an artist and freelance illustrator who worked for many of the top magazines. But to Sherlockians, he's best known as the American Sidney Paget. Basing his Sherlock on stage actor William Gillette — who made a career out of portraying Holmes on stage — Steele illustrated the stories that later appeared in the U.S. editions of The Return of Sherlock Holmes and The Casebook of Sherlock Holmes.

It was on an evening in October 1926, that Mr. Sherlock Holmes made one of his rare visits to The Players.

Many years had passed since the great man had come to

Gramercy Park,[1] and the faithful John McDonald at the door did not at once recognize the tall, spare figure looming before him in the fading light.

"What name, sir?" he asked.

For answer Holmes silently handed him the familiar fore-and-aft cap.[2]

"Can it be — Mr. Holmes?" gasped McDonald in an awe-stricken whisper. Overcome by his agitation, he sank on a bench. The hall boys, coming to his assistance, saw that his hair was quite white.

Ten minutes later Sherlock Holmes was seated at his favorite table in the southwest corner of the grill-room.

"All is as usual, Watson," he said genially. "It is indeed good to be back again in these dear surroundings, which your touch has made more beautiful than ever."

"You do me too much honor, Holmes," I replied. "As Chairman of the House Committee I try to—"

Holmes interrupted. "I observe you have added the wielding of the cue to your other accomplishments."

"Holmes, you are astounding!" I said. "I rarely play pool, but it is true that I did play just a frame or two today. But how could you know?"

"Elementary, my dear Watson, elementary. A faint but distinct odor of Lillian Russell talcum powder aroused my suspicions, and they needed no further confirmation than the little blue chalk-mark near your left shoulder."[3]

---

[1] A private park in the Gramercy neighborhood of New York City, established in 1844. Access to it is limited to the neighboring residents who pay an annual fee to get a key to the gate.

[2] Conan Doyle never described Holmes wearing the iconic deerstalker cap. It was up to illustrator Sidney Paget to depict Holmes sporting it (along with the Inverness cape) in "The Boscombe Valley Mystery" (1891). The look was adopted by William Gillette for the *Sherlock Holmes* play, which in turn was imitated by Steele in his illustrations. As its name implies, the cap was worn by hunters, and the long brim at each end was designed to shed water.

[3] Russell (1860/1861-1922) was one of the most famous actresses and sing-

"My dear Holmes, it is marvellous."

"Attention to detail, Watson, is—"

Suddenly the insistent peal of a bell was heard from an upper floor. Holmes' austere face broke into one of its rare smiles. "I am glad to hear that my friend Marcosson has returned."

"You are right again," said I in astonishment. "He is even now entertaining the Pope and Premier Mussolini in the private dining room."[1]

"How restful this old room is!" Holmes resumed. "And is it not a pity that crime and madness can lurk in so peaceful a spot! I had hoped, my dear fellow, to spend a few completely idle hours here, listening to the innocent prattle of my actor friends, but it was not to be. Certain important persons have asked me to look into some strange events here. Books have mysteriously disappeared from the library and reappeared in unexpected places. A story called 'Hatrack' has been brutally cut out of a magazine. No man's private copy of *La Vie* is safe.[2]

---

ers of her time, celebrated for her buxom beauty and talent, for being married four times, and for being the mistress of wealthy businessman Diamond Jim Brady (1856-1917). She was also not shy about making money off her name by endorsing products such as Coca-Cola and a line of beauty products marketed as "Lillian Russell's Own Toilet Preparations." She and her manager could be careless at times, such as when her signature appeared below the statement: "I have taken three bottles of Lydia Pinkham's Compound and feel like a new man." She was among the first celebrities to endorse a politician, endorsing Theodore Roosevelt in 1912 alongside *Sherlock Holmes* actor William Gillette.

[1] Isaac Marcosson (1877-1961) was a magazine editor and author. He was also noted for his interviews with famous men and women, which makes it appropriate that he would sit down with Pope Pius XI (1857-1939), in his third year of his papacy, and Benito Mussolini (1883-1945), in his fourth year as Italy's prime minister.

[2] La Vie Parisienne ("Parisian Life") was a sophisticated risqué literary humor magazine. While the contents were relatively mild, it published illustrations of scantily clad women in tasteful poses, which was enough for General John J. Pershing to warn U.S. soldiers from buying the magazine. This didn't stop them from taking home copies of the magazine after the war. After the war, postal authorities banned the magazine at least once

A man named Banning has appealed to me for protection; the poor fellow is beside himself."¹

He paused and lighted his briar.

"And that is not all. A person called Girardot has been seen talking in low tones with a waiter and pointing to a plate of food.² The word 'poison' was overheard. There are sinister forces at work, Watson. I am told that Frank Warrin, the solicitor, has lost a pound and a half through worry.³ My friend Allen McCurdy has begged me to look into the case. Indeed I expect him to meet me here."⁴

At this moment that individual appeared and joined us at table. The great man greeted the newcomer kindly, and McCurdy, his brow knotted with anxiety, plunged at once into the recital of his suspicions.

"The Hatrack is not the only thing, Mr. Holmes!" he said vehemently. "Can you explain to me why George Middleton persists in playing Kelly?⁵ You can't tell me the money power

---

from being sent through the mail.
¹ Kendall Banning (1879-1944) was a poet and magazine editor who had his share of run-ins with the censors. As editor of "Snappy Stories," a pulp magazine aimed at a male readership, he fought the Boston Watch and Ward Society – the same group that banned "Hatrack," for a story he published. As part of his campaign, he privately published in 1926 a collection of innocuous nursery rhymes with censorious black boxes placed over words at random.
² Etienne Girardot (1856-1939) was a stage and film actor. He played Lord Fancourt Babberley in the first U.S. production of *Charley's Aunt* in 1893. The suggestion of murder predates by a few years Girardot's role as the coroner in the Philo Vance movies starring William Powell.
³ Frank Lord Warrin (b. 1883) was a New York City lawyer who in 1918 acted as a technical advisor to the Americans during the peace negotiations at the end of World War I.
⁴ A club member renowned for his ability to make a masse shot, a trick shot that makes the cue ball spin around a ball. He was also a disputatious member who, according to a book about the club: "could always be relied upon to take the opposite side to your own in any proposition." There's no doubt that it's him in Steele's illustration, knocking the table in front of Sherlock and shouting "Tell me that, Mr. Holmes!
⁵ A playwright, director, and producer, Middleton (1880-1967) was instru-

isn't behind him! This trivial game is only a cloak to conceal some damnable plot. Doesn't his mind keep wandering from the game? And how about those trips away for a rest? How do we know what is going on in Bermuda? And why does Paul McAllister wear those whiskers?[1] Tell me that! Why does A. E. Thomas try to pass himself off as Augustus Thomas?[2] And Owen Meech![3] Does anybody believe that is a real name? Why does Oliver Herford have no telephone address?[4] Why, I say,

---

mental in forming the Dramatists Guild to renegotiate an agreement in which the theatre managers received 50 percent of the stock and picture rights for any plays they produced. In January 1926, 131 dramatists agreed to form a closed shop and draft an agreement to present to the producers. Middleton was known at the club as "Desperate" George after an incident at the pool table. During a game, seeing his ball trapped and with a big pot at stake, he closed his eyes and left it to chance. His blind shot won the match. When he was asked how he figured out the right shot, he admitted: "I took a desperate chance." *Kelly:* Kelly pool was a popular game in the first half of the 20th century, and it was played often at the Players. Also called "pea pool," it is played with the standard set of 16 pool balls and 15 smaller numbered markers called peas or pills. The peas are placed in a opaque bottle and each player secretly draws one pea. The number on it is the numbered ball they must sink to win the match.

[1] An American film actor (1875-1955) who appeared in 37 movies between 1913 and 1940, including *Beau Geste* (1926), *She's a Sheik* (1927), and *Noah's Ark* (1929). As the story implies, he had an impressive beard.

[2] Augustus E. Thomas (1857-1934) was a playwright best known for being among the first playwrights to base his plays on American history. He also directed five movies, including *The Jungle* (1914), based on Upton Sinclair's notorious 1906 novel.

[3] A stage actor known for his character roles in Shakespearian plays. In real life he had an abstracted air which led to one memorable incident in the pool room. Absorbed in looking up a number in the telephone book and sensing the presence of a strong light over the table, he proceeded to lay the book down on the table's green felt in mid-game. The players were too astonished to object. They were also curious: Would his conscious mind surface and realize where he was? The answer: No. He found the number, picked up the book, and left the room.

[4] English artist and writer (1860-1935) whose family emigrated to the U.S. in 1876. His work appeared in magazines such as *Life*, *Harper's Weekly*, *The Masses*, and *Punch*. He was also noted as a wit. When the Episcopal priest Bishop Henry Potter (1834-1908) lamented that his nephew had

"TELL ME THAT, MR. HOLMES!"

does John Phillips wear rubbers?[1] What does Russ Whytal conceal in that umbrella that he carries on pleasant days?[2] If you keep your eyes open you will see three men who call themselves Drew, Denny and Schmidt huddled together.[3] What, I ask you, is the subject of those conferences? Why did Cy Nast spend all that time digging in walls and monkeying with the electric wires?[4] I tell you there are things going on

---

married an actress, Herford reassured him saying "I wouldn't bother about it, Bishop. You know actresses happen in the best-regulated families."

[1] Magazine publisher (1861-1949) who co-founded the muckraking *McClure's* magazine that published Ida Tarbell's expose of the Standard Oil trust and Conan Doyle's short stories and articles. "Rubbers," it should be noted, refers to a type of latex overshoe that is worn over the dress shoe and not what you're thinking.

[2] Actor and playwright (1860-1930).

[3] John *Drew* (1853-1927) was considered the leading matinee idol of his time. He is also the uncle of John, Ethel, and Lionel Barrymore, which makes him Drew Barrymore's great-great uncle. He was also the third president of the club. George K. *Denny* was an actor and one of the club's directors. Arthur P. *Schmidt* (1846-1921) was a music publisher.

[4] Cyril Nast (1879-1966) was advertising manager of New York Edison Co. He was the son of cartoonist Thomas Nast.

that we don't know anything about!'

During this tirade Sherlock Holmes sat quietly, his deep-set eyes bent on the Gramercy stew as though to penetrate its inmost secrets.[1] "These singular incidents of which you have told me," he said at length, "whose meaning is so baffling to the simple mind of the actor, artist or literary man, are plain enough when—"

At this moment a tall, raw-boned stranger stalked into the room leading a small ferret-like animal.

"Mr. Brian Hooker, I believe,"[2] said Holmes, extending his hand in greeting. "It is good of you to respond to my summons, and I note that you have brought the animal with you."

"Anything to oblige!" drawled the stranger, with the rich twang of the Connecticut Yankee. "Yes, sirree. I guess no keener or stauncher cheese-hound can be found in all New York."

"I thank you, Mr. Hooker," said Holmes affably. "My purpose will be disclosed without great delay. Clearly, gentlemen, the time has come for action. John, bring me the latest copy of *La Vie Parisienne*."

With the magazine clutched in his talon-like hand, Holmes led the way down to the billiard room, which was now deserted save for two weird figures. One of these sat in semi-darkness on a high chair and when addressed as "Dick"

---

[1] A dish from the Gramercy Tavern and Beer Hall that operated at 129 East 18th St. for more than 150 years. It is now occupied by Pete's Tavern. It is not the same as the Gramercy Tavern that opened on East 20th Street in 1995.

[2] Poet, lyricist and librettist (1880-1946). His 1923 translation of Edmond Rostand's *Cyrano de Bergerac* was used by Jose Ferrer (1912-1992), who won a Tony award in his 1946 Broadway version of the play, and an Oscar in the 1950 film adaptation. His affection for the free-lunch counter at the club was well-known and led to his nickname Cheese Hound. One afternoon, a member walked in with a letter demanding to know where Hooker was. A fellow member said, "I will arrange it," lifted the cover of the cheese plate, and placed the letter there. No sooner had he replaced the lid when Hooker came down the steps, marched to the bar, and lifted the lid on the cheese plate.

"No stauncher cheese-hound can be found in all New York."

moaned slightly.[1] The other stood in a corner near the water

---

[1] Elevated chairs, akin to tall bar stools with arms, are a common feature of pool rooms. They allow for spectators to sit high enough to watch the action on the table. Of the 14 members named Richard in 1926, the strongest candidate by far is newspaper editor Richard Lloyd Jones (1873-1963). When he was editor of the *Tulsa Tribune,* he hired his cousin Frank Lloyd Wright in 1929 to design his new home, which contains a billiard room. His admiration for Lincoln would later lead him to help preserve the Lincoln farm in Hodgenville, Ky., as a national historic site.

Also telling is that the longtime member was referred to as "Dick" in a long anecdote — the only one involving a Richard — in the club's 50th anniversary book. When Jones was 14, he stayed with a friend in Chicago. Edwin Booth was performing in a play, and since he was a friend of the family,

pitcher and silently regarded the party.

Holmes proceeded to a small table on which lay a plate of partially consumed cheese. Lifting the cover, he picked up a fragment of the substance and rubbed it vigorously on the fresh and lovely magazine.

"Really, Holmes," I protested, "as Chairman of the House Committee[1] I fail to understand —"

"You always fail to understand, my good Watson," said Holmes with a touch of asperity, as he placed the magazine on the table beside the plate. "We will now return to the grill-room and await developments.[2] And, Reggie," he added, addressing the silent figure, "keep your eyes open!"[3]

Richard attended the performance. That day, he woke up early. A statue of Abraham Lincoln by sculptor Augustus Saint-Gaudens (1848-1907) had been installed recently in Lincoln Park, in a ceremony attended by 10,000 people, including the president's grandson, Abraham Lincoln II (1873-1890), who later died from a blood infection caused by a cut on his arm.

According to the book:

"It was a beautiful bright morning and the Park was deserted. Dick looked at the statue for a time. As he turned back along the path he had come by, he heard the click of horses' hoofs on the entering road. A carriage rolled up and halted. A man alighted and walked toward the tall bronze figure. He stopped midway and gazed at it for some time. Then with bared head went nearer and looked up into the face of Lincoln long and intently; bowed his head awhile, Dick said, as if in prayer; finally took a flower from his coat and laid it on the pedestal at Lincoln's feet.

"As he walked back to the carriage he turned around once, with hat in hand and arms half extended — a sort of gesture of appeal. Then slipped into the carriage and drove away, leaving the place deserted save for the hidden boy in the shrubbery who was thrilled by what he had seen. For he knew the man was Edwin Booth."

[1] The group charged with overseeing the club's operations.

[2] A room in the basement containing tables where food can be served, as well as a pool table where Mark Twain played with the club's co-founders.

[3] Probably Reginald Bathurst Birch (1856-1943), whose illustrations of Little Lord Fauntleroy in the 1886 novel by Frances Hodgson Burnett started a fashion craze that condemned boys to wearing ringlets, black velvet suits adorned with lace collars, and matching knee pants. *The Players' Book* celebrating the club's first 50 years recalls him "at 82 or 83, still erect and slender, still the perfect pattern of the boulevardier, with immaculate

For perhaps three hours we sat waiting in tense silence. There was no sound in the dimly lighted grill-room. Hourly, August, the sturdy watchman, passed silently through the house, carrying his heavy black weapon. Holmes, his nerves as always under iron control, gave no sign of emotion save that from time to time he rose and hurled a plate through the window on to the piazza.[1] I made no comment on this, for by custom considerable latitude is allowed to our honorary members.

At last there was the faint sound of a footstep on the floor below, followed by an ugly tearing or ripping. Like a tiger Holmes sprang from his chair and was the first to reach the downstairs room. Prostrate beneath the table lay the unfortunate magazine. It had been brutally attacked and its mangled innards streamed out on the floor.

"You know my methods, Watson," said Holmes, briskly. "The miscreant has evidently risen to the bait, but I fear he has taken alarm and fled. Quick, Hooker, the cheese-hound!"

The trembling animal sniffed at the cheesy remains and strained at its leash, barking furiously. Holmes' voice rang out sharply. "Now we shall see what man or devil can have done this thing. Release him!"

With a mighty bound the hound sprang toward——

[The next installment of this gripping mystery serial will not appear in an early issue.]

---

manners, waxed moustache and Inverness coat, and still to be seen now and then at the bar, but always, always standing, awake or asleep, not infrequently the latter.

[1] The word has two definitions that could apply here. It could be either the balcony that runs across the front of the club, or Gramercy Park across the street.

Expert Assistance

James J. Montague

James J. Montague (1873-1941) was a newspaper reporter, humorist, and poet whose verse was published in papers nationwide. After a stint at a Portland, Oregon, newspaper, he was recruited by William Randolph Hearst in 1902 to go to New York City. Reluctant to go, Montague asked for double his salary — to $60 a week — and was shocked when he got it. He stayed with Hearst's New York American *and* New York Evening Journal *until 1919, when he jumped to Joseph Pulitzer's* World. *Over his 25-year career, he produced more than 7,500 poems. Many of them were tied to the news of the day, including this one, which was discovered in the Jan. 29, 1929, edition of the* Seattle Post-Intelligencer, *about Holmes and his creator.*

> In Conan Doyle's creative youth
> He gave the world an able sleuth
> Who brought to light the hidden truth
> Concerning craft and crime.
> No mystery was too profound
> For this lean-visaged human hound,
> By mental synthesis, to sound
> In half a fortnight's time.
>
> When gems were lost, or men were slain.
> Sometimes for spite, sometimes for gain,
> In good King Edward Seventh's reign,[1]
> And dread spread far and near,
> The baffled coppers scratched their domes,
> And called in Mr. Sherlock Holmes,
> Who read a few old tattered tomes
> And made the whole thing clear.

---

[1] Holmes' career spanned the reign of Queen Victoria (1819-1901) as well as that of her son "Bertie" (1841-1910), and with "His Last Bow," the reign of George V as well. But poetry makes its own demands and attention to it must be paid.

7But now, when spooks and spirits foil
The wit of even Dr. Doyle;
When, as he burns his midnight oil,
He sees them near and far;
When through his country home they stray,
Half-formless shapes of foggy gray,
He owns he really cannot say
Just who and what they are.

I wish the doc would resurrect
That keen deducing intellect,
And have those spirits tagged and checked,
And either jailed or shot.
For I am sure that in three shakes,
And with no guesswork or mistakes,
He would turn them up as fakes,
If Dr. Doyle cannot!

James J. Montague

The Mystery Than Which

Rupert Hughes

Rupert Hughes (1872-1956) lived a life full of wide-ranging experiences. Before he became an Oscar-nominated screenwriter and director, he had been a globetrotting researcher for the Encyclopaedia Britannica, served as an officer in the Mexico border service and the U.S. Army in World War I. In New York, he was a successful best-selling novelist, playwright, and biographer — his book on George Washington in 1926 revealed the man behind the mythology. Selling his novels to Hollywood studios lured him to the West Coast. His first marriage ended in a divorce trial in which his wife testified that she had "seen Mr. Hughes kiss nearly every woman who came into our house," and that he "boasted openly of his illicit relations with other women." But he is best known as the uncle of an 18-year-old boy whom he introduced to the movie business: future billionaire Howard Hughes.

This story appeared in Morrow's Almanack and Every-day Book *for 1930, with the following introduction.*

Whose novels have had millions of readers, who would have been burned to a crisp in Chicago, for his biography of George Washington, had the cow kicked over another lantern.

"Among the uniquer murders I have known, the Affaire Klaus was far and away — oh, farther and awayer — the uniquest."

The Master mystery-monger was speaking, and I, being merely his Quick-Watson,[1] asked:

"What made this Affaire so especially unique, Master?"

"Ah, that takes a bit of tellin'."

"So long as it takes no longer than that," I said, "I can still catch my train, which leaves in exactly three minutes." We were in the Grand Central Terminal[2] at the time and the Mas-

---

[1] Probably named for the phrase which appears in so many of the parodies: "Quick, Watson, the needle!"

[2] A commuter rail terminal at 42nd Street and Park Avenue in Manhattan. Opened in 1913, it was named for the New York Central railroad which built it. Still in use today, it is the largest train station still in operation in the U.S.

ter, sniffing snow in a backhanded manner[1] and giving himself self a deft shot in the arm, to the amusement of the throngs, began:

"Old Johann Klaus — no relation to Santa of that ilk — was just the man you'd expect to be findin' murdered in his library. Fearin' such a fate at the hands of his dissipated and impatient nephew, he had had the library torn out of his house and what he quaintly called a 'set'n' rum'[2] substituted. Even that gave him little comfort because he had a feelin' that his nephew was ready to murder him in any room in the house or his property in order to acquire his property. The nephew was a hard drinker."

"Still," I put in, watching the train-gate anxiously, "many drinkers have soft hearts."

"And hard arteries," laughed the Master with that arch drollery of his, which he concealed except for a merry twinkle in his eye, and a habit of jabbing one in the ribs with his elbow while emitting loud guffaws.

"But jokin' aside," he resumed, "old Klaus was afraid of his nephew, and the last person he was known to speak to was the chief constable."

"My train is going. Good-by," I said.

"Don't interrupt!" he retorted, putting his foot on my suitcase and his elbow on my shoulder:

"As I was sayin', the old man was sayin' to the local Dogberry,[3] 'Chief, I'm goin' home tonight with a mort o' money.[4]

---

[1] A reference to sniffing cocaine off the back of the hand, like snuff. Snow was one of its many contemporary slang names alongside coke, happy dust, and candy.

[2] Sitting room.

[3] The comic night constable character from *Much Ado About Nothing*. Used as slang, it refers to a particularly stupid constable or magistrate.

[4] While more commonly known as death, derived from the Latin word *mors,* or *mort,* it appears most often as a root word related to death, such as mortuary, mortician, and mortality. In this instance, there is a second definition that seems to have come from another source as an English regional saying to mean "an abundance of." The phrase has been traced to

I'm buyin' a farm off a man who won't take a cheque. I want you should put a guard around my set'n' rum. Tell your men to saw off their shotguns and peel their eyes, for somethin' tells me I may never see another rosy-fingered dawn gently dror aside the misty curtains of jocund day.'[1]

"The constable did as he was told, but the old man never reached home. He was found foully murdered on the way, lying in a pool of blood. But you have a train to catch. I'll solve the mystery in the next installment."

"You'll solve it now," I answered with unsuspected vim. "You've lost me my train, and I have an hour to kill."

"Too bad it isn't a rich uncle," the Master roared. "But jokin' aside, old Klaus was dead and the mort o' money was conspicuously missin'. Rememberin' his words, the chief pursued and — to everybody's amazement — caught the nephew red-handed and red-nosed — gorgeously drunk.

"There was blood on his clothes. His fingernails were full of it. His shoes were caked with blood and mud which chemical analysis showed to be the same mud and blood in which the old man lay.

"He had in his possession the entire mort o' money except what he had spent acquiring his hot, cross bun.[2] His fingerprints conformed exactly to the numberless fingerprints sprinkled all over the scene of the crime. He was thrown into a cell. The grand jury indicted him without leaving the room.

---

many English counties, including Sussex, Kent, Lincolnshire, Devonshire, and Cornwall, so it's difficult to tell how it came into the language.

[1] There are two classical references combined in the same sentence. *Rosy-fingered dawn* comes from Homer's *Odyssey*, where the poet uses that phrase some twenty times to describe the new day. The second half is a Shakespearian reference drawn from *Romeo and Juliet* (1597). When Romeo prepares to leave Juliet after their wedding night, he says "night's candles are burnt out, and jocund day stands tiptoe on the misty mountain tops." *Jocund* means cheerful and lighthearted.

[2] While there are many euphemisms associated with bun, this one refers to an obscure one from the late 19th century for a state of drunkenness, as in "having a bun on."

Court bein' in session, for once, his trial began forthwith."

"Master," I gasped spellbound, "this is indeed a mystery. Then they called you in, of course, to solve it."

"No, they refused my services and went ahead."

"Who sprang to the defence?"

"Nobody. The defendant swore he was at a distance from the crime courtin' the young and innocent Miss Sarah Kringle."

"Aha, the woman in the case!"

"But not for long. Sarah swore she hadn't seen the Nephew for weeks and hoped he'd swing."

"This suspense is killing me," I panted. "'Who saved him in the dramatic court-scene?"

"Nobody. The jury brought in a verdict of guilty."

"I can't bear it. Who confessed?"

"Nobody, except the Nephew, when he learned the Governor wouldn't commute, reprieve, or pardon."

"The poor man perished to shield another! Quick, Master, the answer. Who was it?"

"Nobody."

"Then whom do you suppose committed — pardon me! Who do you suppose committed the crime?"

"The Nephew indubitably."

"Hell's bells, Master! Where's the mystery in that?"

"This is America, my boy. The mysteries are many and all unique. They suspected the guilty man; they caught him at once; they gave him a prompt trial; he was not a foreigner, or a poor and homely defective; yet, it was not the jury but the murderer that hung. He was a red-blooded 100 percent typical American killer. And they killed him. Did you ever hear of anything like that?"

"Master, you are marvelous," I confessed. But I was sorry I had missed my train.

Appendix

The Adventure of the Whyos (1894)

In his remaining years, Mark Twain devoted his energies to dictating his memoirs, a monumental outpouring of stories and opinions that he told, not in chronological order, but as they came to him. Although he embargoed them for a century, excerpts were printed in his lifetime. The Mark Twain Project at the University of California, after years of careful, meticulous work, published the Autobiography in three volumes.

But not everything has been collected. Around 2000, I bought a box of old papers at a warehouse auction in Carlisle, Pa. There was nothing about the box that suggested there were treasures within. It contained a jumble of handwritten papers, receipts, advertising circulars, crumbling newsprint, and other ephemera. As an amateur historian, I'm fascinated by such mundane papers. It certainly held no value to its original owner, who had scrawled "BURN THIS" on the side.

An examination of the pages, however, revealed that they were nothing less than Mark Twain's tales of his adventures with Sherlock Holmes and his circle. Dictated to a secretary as part of his autobiography, he chose for some reason not to publish them. Apparently, the box was given to his longtime maid Katie O'Leary. Instead of following instructions, she took the box home. Perhaps she frugally intended to use the paper to light her household fires. Eventually, the box was sealed and stored and passed through the family over the years until it was disposed of in Carlisle.

At least, that's my story, and I'm sticking to it.

The first story, "The Adventure of the Whyos," was published as an ebook single in 2011. The rest of the stories appeared in the back of volumes in the 223B Casebook series that were published over the next eight years. All of them, including this one, were collected and published in 2018 as The Casebook of Twain and Holmes. Since "Whyos" never made it into one of the 223B books, it seemed appropriate to print it here. I hope you enjoy it.

In the late spring of 1894, Mark Twain and I were getting along as well as two cats in a burlap bag. I was bankrupt. Henry Rogers, my good friend and the financial wizard behind Standard Oil, had convinced me to close my publishing concern, Webster & Co., and I was obliged to assume responsibility for its debts. I was a pauper, same as my father was fifty years before, and confirmed the old saw to those who knew the family back in Hannibal that "the apple doesn't fall far from the tree." People who knew me as Mark Twain expected tall tales and japes, and what they got instead was Sam Clemens, who held him responsible and was in no mood for jollity.

I had to close the house in Hartford that I had designed and lived in for nearly 20 years.[1] To live more cheaply, my family went to Paris. When I saw to the publishing house's corpse to the burial yard, I followed on the *SS City of New York*. The journey took a week, and I spent the whole of it in my stateroom, smoking cigars and immersed in my misery.

The ship docked in Southampton where Weatherwax shanghaied me. He was a florid bruiser-turned-business tycoon I was acquainted with in Hartford. He had read in the papers about my bankruptcy and my travel plans, and he wired me to expect him. He had a problem and needed my help.

Warned by Weatherwax's telegram, I laid low in my cabin and intended to plead ignorance of his cable as well as smallpox, but he bribed his way on board and barged in, acting like the wretched course of my life had been fated solely for the purpose of coming to his aid. I was overcome. The fight was not in me. My bags had been packed in anticipation of leaving at Le Havre six hours later, so he ordered them unloaded and bundled the whole of us into his growler.

Like me, Weatherwax had spent time in Nevada, but unlike me had struck it rich. A decade amid Eastern society had

---

[1] Twain tended to conflate dates in his memoirs. Webster & Co. was closed in April of 1894, while Twain closed the Hartford house a year later after the failure of the Paige typesetting machine, at a loss of between $3 million and $5 million in today's currency.

refined him; when he bit the end off his cigar, he opened the window before spitting out the stub. He set fire to the remainder and said, —

"Chloe's been in a bad way since you saw her last, Twain."

I winced at the mention of that cursed name. He said, —

"She's taken to her bed a week ago."

"My sympathies." I had known Chloe since she was a playmate to my daughters and thought she had the most sense in the family.

He explained that he was in England to get his only daughter knotted in matrimony to a fellow named Rannulph Winthrop, the son of a genuine copper-bottomed gold-plated English lord, only she wasn't having any of it. We were on our way to Chalkhills, his lordship's estate down the coast, where the lawyers were hammering out the contract, and he hoped that I could stop by and talk some sense into her.[1]

"I was afeared his lordship would call the match off, but he said he'd like nothing better but to carry on. Said it was obvious that the youngun's were meant for each other; Chloe just don't know it yet."

I eyed him critically. Was he a humbug or a hypocrite? I had met many aristocrats on my previous visits to the mother country, and if Rannulph's father was like them, Lord Winthrop had the morals of an imbecile and was chronically short of cash. Even if it meant his son marrying a near-corpse, Winthrop wasn't about to let pass this gold mine. Weatherwax poured smoke into the closed carriage like a steamship be-

---

[1] It was the fashion at that time for newly-rich Americans to marry their daughters into the aristocracy. The year before, Cornelia Martin wedded the 4th Earl of Craven in New York City. The Martins' bragging in the press about the wealth of the earl — whose demonstrated his interest in the ceremony by wearing boots with rolled-up pant legs — triggered a riot at the wedding. A side door into the church was found unlocked, and the public flooded in, disrupting the event and stealing anything that wasn't nailed down. The Martins fled to their home overseas, but the incident didn't deter them from seeking publicity. By their social-climbing standards, Paris Hilton and the Kardashians are pikers.

hind schedule and said, —

"Problem is, she's taken a dislike to Rannulph. You know what happens when a girl gets a notion into her head. Takes dynamite to blast it out."

He prattled on in this fashion, and I regretted my decision to join this fool's crusade. The carriage filled with smoke, and I had the notion of using it to screen my exit from the vehicle, but I decided against it. I wasn't as athletic as in my youth, and leaping from a speeding carriage no longer held any charm. Weatherwax let loose another chimney full of smoke and said, —

"I told my Chloe that it was her duty as a daughter to obey. Rannulph's as good as the next man, right Twain?"

"Assuming the next man was Jack the Ripper," I wanted to say, but the pressure in me was building like an overheated boiler. My concerns weighed heavily on my conscience, and it had been too long a voyage. Weatherwax fired another cannonade and said, —

"Don't know what to do. She's a girl, you know. We talk to her and talk to her. The lawyers are still tussling over the contract — and won't it make your eyes start to read the details in the Herald. Titled aristos are short on the market. Dukes and marquises have vanished, so viscounts are holding firm and asking for the moon — and getting it. You wouldn't believe what a mere baron without a castle would ask! Why —"

I fantasized shooting myself. Unfortunately, I missed, and instead, said, —

"Yes, yes, but what about Chloe? What's the matter with her?"

"Don't know. Doc won't say. Consumption, English cholera, the yim-yams. She's having trouble keeping her food down. I swear she's getting thinner by the day."

"So what do you want me to do?"

"Talk to her. Make her see reason. She loved playing with your Suzy and Clara. She looks to you as an uncle. She'll listen to you." He leaned closer. He had a glint in his eye that I used to see in the sharpest cards at the poker table. "I realize I'm keeping you away from your family when you're — I mean, I'll make it worth your while if you can swing this deal." And then he tapped the side of his nose and tipped me the wink.

Oh, how I wanted to tear him to pieces! In my palmier days, I would have raged at his effrontery. But I knew my financial situation, and while Livy has been the calm rock of reason, I still have to look to the family's future. So I denied my better nature and nodded as my conscience writhed.

Then he grew silent and worked his jaw some while the coastline rolled by. A notion arose that he was working up a head of steam to say something, and finally, he said, —

"This is strictly between us, Twain. We didn't meet out West, but I feel I can tell you things I can't tell a man like Beecher or Howell back in Hartford.[1] They're too refined for such sordid matters."

"And I'm a crude hayseed."

"Please! Please, Mark. I'm sorry. I didn't mean to insult you. But you know what I mean. I can tell you things."

He paused, then delivered his line like an actor on the Bowery stage, —

"Mark, I'm being blackmailed."

I gasped. I felt it was expected, but I sucked a large cloud of smoke that tickled my lungs, and I spoiled the effect by hacking into my handkerchief. Weatherwax pounded my back until the spasm passed and said, —

"A week back, Lord Winthrop's house was burgled. I thought they hadn't touched us, but a few days later, I got this note." He pulled a crisp half-sheet out of his pocket.

It read, —

"We found these prety notes. His lordship

---

[1] Henry Ward Beecher (1813-1887) was a prominent clergyman and social reformer. He was the brother of Harriet Beecher Stowe, a neighbor of Twain in Hartford. William Dean Howell (1837-1920) was a literary critic and friend of Twain.

gits the rest of the stash unless you put £100 on the sundial at the Grecian folly at sundown. Tell no-one.

"The Whyos"

"They had taken from Chloe's jewelry box letters she had written to some boy in Hartford."

"Who?" I couldn't help asking.

"I don't know! I never knew of this in the first place. She said it was a Lionel and that she had met him at church. She said the affair ended three years ago, and they returned each other's notes. But instead of burning the letters, she kept them! They sent a page from them with this demand."

As he blew on, I worked through the families we knew who might have a Lionel, but a candidate failed to appear. "It's no crime to fall in love," I said.

I swear Weatherwax blushed. It did not suit him. He said, —

"The . . . sentiments . . . were, well, I don't have to spell it out to you, do I, Twain? Even if his lordship didn't mind, if the New York papers got ahold of these, it would cause an uproar! You remember the Martin fiasco, don't you? They were forced to leave the country, with the papers hissing their spite at them."

"Did you pay?"

"Of course I paid! Cleaned me out of ready money. I had to send to Coutt's for more. I received the rest of the letter in next day's post."

"So your troubles are over."

Weatherwax's face grew red and he said, —

"But that's just one letter! They've got the rest. This gang will either bleed me dry or expose my daughter. I'm trapped, Twain, no two ways about it."

In the ordinary course of events, the prospect of extortion would have cheered me up considerable. I wasn't looking forward to playing Dutch uncle with the girl, but not even a broken-down pauper lecturer like Mark Twain was expected to play policeman. Help needed to be called in. But I knew only one man in England who would qualify, and after our last adventure, when I came within an inch of perdition, I swore that I'd rather let a tribe of Apaches skin me, or reread *The Deerslayer*,[1] before I darkened his threshold.

Then a vision of Chloe arose before me, and I knew I had no choice. I grumbled, —

"Weatherwax, I have this friend who might help . . . "

When Weatherwax heard of my proposal, he ordered the carriage to stop at the next station and shoved me onto an express to London. He would continue on to Chalkhills and talk his lordship into giving me room and board. I wired my family that I was delayed while he bought the ticket. It rankled me not to pay for it, but I swallowed the lie that he was obliged to do this because of the favor that I was doing him, not that I had no more on me than my name, a moth-destroyed purse and a stack of debts.

It was night by the time I reached that great metropolis, and the hansom cab bearing my remains to Baker Street rang on the cobblestones with that musical cadence familiar to all of London's visitors. The woman let me in at 221B and the moment I stood at the base of the staircase, I knew he was at home. The stench made my eyes water. My nose refused its duty. I climbed into the sulfurous haze and, at my knock, was ordered to open the door.

Sherlock Holmes was deep into one of his chemical experiments. He brusquely begged me to park my corpse in the spare bed until he was finished. His rudeness when his mind was otherwise engaged was well-known to all, so I took no more offense than usual. I was exhausted from my long day's

---

[1] From Twain's essay "Fentimore Cooper's Literary Offenses": "In one place in *Deerslayer*, and in the restricted space of two-thirds of a page, Cooper has scored 114 offences against literary art out of a possible 115. It breaks the record."

journey and quickly fell asleep amid the stink of bubbling gases and the clink of test-tubes.

I dreamed of Hell.

Holmes' mood improved dramatically with the coming day. He greeted me with the warmth born from our long association — reluctant on my part — and called downstairs for breakfast.

I like and admire the English, but my affection cannot extend to their cooking. It was designed by a remorseful Puritan hoping to achieve a state of grace by scouring the innards. And an English breakfast cooked by a Scot landlady must be intended as revenge for the occupation of her native heath.

We ate the kippered herrings and the grilled mess of tomatoes and bread and drank the strong coffee. I laid the case before Holmes and tried to make the mystery as enticing as my powers of speech could make it, but I needn't have worried. He said, —

"I have business that needs attending to in that part of the country. Are you familiar with the Whyos?"

His question startled me. Holmes has that nasty habit of asking questions to which only he knows the answer. But he couldn't dog me with this one.

"They're a gang of New York ruffians, found in the Five Points area."

Holmes nodded. He got up and searched among the line of scrapbooks on the wall until he pulled out one newspaper-sized volume. "One of the biggest," he said, opening the cover. I glanced over his shoulder and marveled at the stories culled from the city's newspapers. He said, —

"This concern has been in operation since your Civil War, and they have covered the range of criminal activities. At one time, they dominated Manhattan so thoroughly that other gangs needed to ask permission to operate there. Their crimes ranged from theft and extortion to murder. One of them even went so far as to carry a menu of their services."

He tapped his finger on a crudely-handwritten half-sheet

that described such choice selections as "Punching $2," "Ear chawed off $15," "Shot in leg $25" and "Doing the big job $100 and up."

He closed the book and slid it back into its place on the shelf. "They're nearly finished as a major criminal force in New York, but it appears some of their number are attempting to rebuild their fortunes by exporting their expertise to our country. I suspect they may have a hand in the job I was hired for. We'll go down today. Are you willing to accompany me?"

"Of course. But where's Watson? Is he coming?"

He shook his head and the regret in his voice was apparent. "After my affair at Reichenbach, he returned to his practice and is there yet, dealing with consumption and dropsy and the membranous croup. Yet, if I know my man, he'll sell his practice soon and rejoin me at Baker Street."[1]

We left Baker Street and boarded the train at Waterloo accompanied by a stack of newspapers. I never saw a man who had such an appetite for news as Holmes. London was a great town for newspapers, too, with at least a dozen of them in all flavors. Our journey was quiet as we smoked and read, but presently he shoved the stack aside and we talked. He wanted to hear my views on the great financial panic of last year, when a number of railroads collapsed. Credit became as hard to find as a banker's smile, and no less than sixteen thousand businesses went under, one of them being mine. Holmes was a good listener, and when I had finished describing the panic on Wall Street, crowded with investors watching their fortunes disappear with each swipe of the chalkboard, he refilled his pipe and said, —

"A number of my countrymen had invested heavily in those railroads and suffered severe reverses as a result. Unfortunately, I expect we'll see more of these shocks. It was a shot across our bow when events in Argentina could cause a bank

---

[1] Which Watson would do three months later, unbeknownst to him at the time with Holmes' assistance, as recounted in "The Adventure of the Norwood Builder."

like Barings to fail.[1] But let us turn our minds to more profitable uses. Your news about events at Chalkhills was most welcome. Several country homes in that area have been robbed. The gang strikes when the home is empty or held by a few retainers. The valuables small and large are carried away, from the plate and paintings to furniture and statuary. This could be our best opportunity to get a line on this gang."

"How do the Whyos tie into this?"

"That remains to be seen. Even after Moriarty's fall, the Empire has more than enough experienced thieves for there to be no need to import more."

"And what about the extortion?"

Holmes smiled as toward a child asking where the sun goes at night. He said, —

"I won't fail you on that count. Surely a solution has already presented itself to you."

A caustic reply came to my mind about Holmes' indulgence in stagy jim-crack, but I bit it back. I can't stand this supercilious claptrap, but Holmes is a genius at what he does, and genius must be served. I'm sure people say the same about me.

A cart was waiting for us at the station. A young man in the rough clothes of the drover's trade transferred our bags and with a courtly "Arfter yew, gents," bade us to climb aboard. Holmes said, —

"You must be Rannulph, Lord Winthrop's son."

A grin split his face at being found out, and he offered his hand to shake. "Right as rain, sir. How d'yer guess?"

"The hands can tell much when one knows where to look. They are rough from use, but well-cared for. The nails are trimmed and squared, not thick and chipped. Your face is fair, telling me that either you are not out in the sun much, or you

---

[1] Holmes was referring to the Panic of 1893, when overinvestment in railroads and stock manipulations had thrown the United States into a recession. The warning shot had been fired as far back as 1890, when Baring Brothers, England's largest banking house, collapsed due to overextended loans to Argentina.

take care to wear that wide-brimmed hat when you are. This is confirmed by your tanned hands that end at the sleeve. Finally, you also bear a Roman nose, the hallmark of the Winthrop profile."

Rannulph chuckled as he parked himself on the bench in front of us and picked up the reins. He said, —

"That's as good a trick as any I seen on the stage. Helping out on the estate helps us keep an eye on the workers."

"What do you raise?" Holmes said.

"Mostly barley and potatoes. Quite a lot for this area. We set up a shipping concern to export the lot up the coast, even to France. I oversee that end."

I said, —

"The workers must appreciate the attention that you pay to their welfare."

"Oh, they hate it. They took great offense when I took to joining them in the fields. Complained to the governor, they did, when they caught him between routs, rides and revels. Now, I don't help 'em as much with the real work and they chalk the rest of it up as 'the young master's queer touches.'"

We drove on in silence as the town gave way to fields. Hoards of midges swarmed us. We swatted our hats at them for a time before giving up and letting them feast.

Holmes said, —

"I understand that you and Miss Weatherwax are engaged to be married. My congratulations to you both."

Watching his back gave me no clue to his mood, but the quiet stretched far longer this time.

"Ah, weel, that has not happened, yet. Early days."

"Negotiations can drag on with so much at stake, but I'll wager they'll resolve themselves to everyone's satisfaction," Holmes said.

"Maybe," he said. "The governor wants the estate to stay on a sound financial footing. We just disagree on the means. Here's the turn into Chalkhills, gents. Mind your hats, the ride's going to be a little rough."

That's when the first ruts hit the axles amidships. We jostled about, our teeth banging and clashing, until a branch road turning toward some barn-like buildings took the ruts with them. Rannulph apologized; the combination of a rough winter and recent rains turned the road into muck and repairs had not commenced. Emulating the great detective methods, I concluded that whatever the source of his lordship's fortune, it did not lay with concrete or paving stones.

Weatherwax had been anxious for our arrival. He popped out of the mansion's front door at our approach, and arranged with a servant to move our luggage to our rooms. His lordship was out shooting, so Holmes asked Weatherwax to convey us to the invalid's room at once.

We followed Weatherwax through a maze of corridors and great halls until we reached the bedroom wing. Before the final door, he muttered, —

"I only hope that harridan isn't guarding the bedside."

What a pitiable sight! The shades were drawn and the gas lamp by the bed was the merest flicker. Chloe lay under the sheets, her eyes closed, her cheeks hollow and her eyes rimmed in red. Her hair spread like damp seaweed across her pillow, like Ophelia pulled from the brook. A small band of gold set with a single pearl on her left hand was the lone spot of cheerful color over the dismal scene.

Holmes crept to her bedside and gazed at her in that peculiar fashion that always gave me chills. A serpent eyeing his prey could not have been more still. He said, —

"Part the curtain, Clemens, if you would."

I did, but only for a moment. A sliver of light crossed Chloe's face and she flinched and cried, "No, no, leave the oysters be, for the love of God!"

Her outburst startled me so I slapped the heavy drapes closed. The door to a connecting room opened behind us and a young woman, slender as a reed and quick as a whippet, strode in and hissed, —

"What is all this? Who are you?"

Weatherwax spoke harshly and said, —

"This is Mr. Holmes and Mr. Twain. I asked them—"

"Oh, for shame, Mr. Weatherwax! Don't you recall the doctor's instructions?" She shooed us toward the door like she was herding a flock of geese. "No visitors and no disturbances. It could be fatal!" Chloe chimed in with a terrible moan and her babble pursued us as we fled. At the door, I looked back to see the woman dabbling at Chloe's forehead with a damp cloth and murmuring soothing words.

Weatherwax closed the door and Holmes gently led me away. I was horrified. Chloe looked far worse than I expected, and a dread rose in me that her time was near. It brought vividly to memory the suffering of my son, Langdon, dead these many years.

Weatherwax fumbled with his watch and turned to view its face by the light of the window. He stood there quietly for a moment with only the ticking of the hall clock for conversation, then he wiped his brow with a spotted red handkerchief and said, —

"Hotter than Hades in there. Come on, let's go see his lordship."

I linked his arm with mine and said, —

"She'll recover. She's young and vital."

Holmes — as unaffected with emotion as usual — asked, —

"Who was that young woman?"

"Her? That's Lord Winthrop's daughter, Judith. She's been looking after Chloe. That's her bedroom she came roaring out of."

"Is she solely responsible for Chloe's care?" Holmes said.

"She hovers over her like a mother hen when Dr. Conover's not here."

"Is he the local man, then?"

That roused Weatherwax. He said, —

"I should say not! He's one of the most eminent physicians in London, from Harley Street itself, with fees to match! Take a look at his latest bill."

Holmes glanced at the paper and I caught a glint of understanding in his eye. He handed it back and said, —

"Then she must be in very good hands. Now, I think it's time to beard the lion in his den."

His lordship was seated before the library fire, fresh from a morning spent massacring his kingdom's waterfowl. Since his wife died a few years back, he had been free to indulge his many hobbies involving the slaying of various beasts. He had been happy to leave Judith to run the household. It gave him the double the savings from treating a trusted family member as an employee while not having to dish out cash for a wedding dowry. All this galloped through my mind while watching his valet engaged in removing Winthrop's boot, which had not been scraped of bits of the countryside. His lordship assisted by pressing his still-shod counterpart against the man's backside.

Batting away the few midges that followed us inside, I mentioned my purpose in being there and introduced Holmes as a particular friend, here to advise me on the best way to solve the problem, keeping his true purpose under a bushel basket.

Winthrop repeated Weatherwax's arrangement to put us up for the night, and we accepted. He added, —

"I don't have to tell you gentlemen how anxious I am to have this wedding come off. I'm sure Mr. Weatherwax will richly reward you for your trouble."

Holmes said, —

"Your concern for your son's future wife is admirable, sir. Between the negotiations and the recent burglary, the strain must be burdensome. May I ask if any progress had been made in locating the gang?"

Lord Winthrop shook his head and said, —

"Constable Noakes is excellent only at chivvying the drunks and investigating the burning of hayricks."

We were interrupted by a servant bearing a coil of paper on a silver tray. Winthrop passed the strip through his fingers and I recognized it as a stock-ticker tape with the latest prices. He frowned, then he fixed me with his eye and said, —

"Mr. Clemens, you're from New York."

I admitted I was familiar with the metropolis.

"A fascinating city. I have not been there myself, but both Rannulph and Judith have visited friends there. You know Mr. Jay Gould. His railroad stock is profitable to buy, I believe."

I cannot fathom why a foreigner would assume that a resident — or in my case, a visitor only — to a city of over a million souls would be on good terms with them all. I said, —

"Men like Gould, Vanderbilt and Morgan don't enter business to lose money, but I can't say that's true for anyone who joins them."

He fumed at this, then rose and excused himself to get sluiced down before tea. Judith came in, and his lordship suggested that she show us about the place.

British mansions tend to be built on the notion that giants may someday decide to take up residence. We wandered amid soaring ceilings and oversized furniture. With Holmes' encouragement, Judith regaled us with the family history, mostly honest, and a complete description of the bric-a-brac. Her knowledge of furniture, its designers and provenance of the better pieces, was encyclopedic. We ended the tour in the billiard room, where she suggested we might relax before dinner.

This suited me something powerful. I had a table installed in my home in Hartford, and there is no better exercise to be found. I'm sure there are billiard parlors in heaven.

In England's better homes, a proper billiard room contains two tables, one for snooker and another with holes in it for the honest American game. While Holmes sat in a chair and smoked his pipe, I racked the balls and Weatherwax and I stroked for lead. But my heart wasn't in it. My concern for Chloe affected me, so much that my eye was off and Weatherwax was able to run the table and pocket a side bet I could ill-afford to lose. I was grateful when Holmes interrupted the transaction and asked Weatherwax for a list of Chloe's complaints. He said, —

"Fever, weakness in the limbs, sensitivity to light, headache, great fatigue, cramps, loss of appetite. She's been unable to keep down her food. You heard her babbling of oysters. She's like that when the fever's on her."

"What has Dr. Conover to say about this?"

"He prescribes what he calls blue pill and black draught and says that the disease will declare itself in a few days. Then he presents his bill."

He sat back in his chair and relit his pipe. "Let us turn to this threatening letter. How did you receive it?"

"By mail three days ago. A servant from the hall fetches the bag from the post office and Judith parcels it out at lunch."

"And it contained this note," he pulled the sheet Weatherwax had given me in the carriage, "and part of a letter?"

"That's right. It never occurred to me they were, well —"

"More than acquaintances. Yes, I understand. Have you talked to Chloe about it?"

"No, Judith forbade it. The doctor ordered complete rest."

"Do you still have the letter? I must see it."

The man shambled off, looking wretched. I shot a game in the ensuing silence while Holmes paced and smoked. He was cogitating hard, and I knew to let him be. He stopped and said,—

"A very pretty problem this is, Clemens."

"I'm glad you think so," I said with asperity. "A girl's dying and you're entertained. Her funeral will be the high point of your social calendar."

He idly rolled one of the balls on the table. "Oh, I don't think it'll go that far. I have a theory, but I need a day or so to pull it together, two at the outside."

I slammed the stick on the table.

"Confound you! Talk sense."

He put his hand on my shoulder like he was calming a skittish colt and said, —

"Miss Weatherwax is shamming, Clemens. Did you remark her face?"

"You saw her only for a moment."

"You see, but you do not think," he said in that superior way of his. "You shined a light on the truth, and a literal one at that. There was kohl under her eyes and a touch — the merest touch — of slap on her cheeks to emphasize the cadaverous effect. And one does not normally see smears of makeup on the pillows. You saw my Hamlet on the New York stage; I made the application of make-up a specialty of mine, and wrote a monograph on the subject. With the proper tools, Clemens, one can bring the dead to life and life to the dead."

I was so overjoyed at the news that I forgave Holmes his monstrous ego, and it was there that I blundered terribly. Weatherwax came in bearing the note for Holmes. He looked so miserable that it wrung my heart. As usual, Holmes ignored everything going on around him. He took the note to a French window and searched it intensely, so I laid a hand on Weatherwax's shoulder, and to comfort him, I said, —

"Put your mind at rest, Weatherwax. Holmes here has determined that Chloe's not sick at all. She's —"

"Twain!" Holmes said. But it was too late, as I realized what that meant.

Weatherwax pumped my hand and said, —

"So that's her game. Thank you, Twain. We'll see who's shamming who—"

Judith encountered Weatherwax in the doorway, and he threw her the most terrible look. She was perplexed, but recovered and came to me and apologized most prettily for ordering us out of the sick-room. I assured her that I had been thrown out of worse places with less courtesy. I introduced her to Holmes, who was still studying Chloe's note by the light of a window.

Then Weatherwax returned, rubbing his hands with the air of a man who had performed a full day's work to his satisfaction and said, —

"That's that. I conceded the last few points. Chloe is now officially betrothed."

Judith turned pale and cried, —

"But her illness—"

"A sham, Twain assures me. Right, Mark?"

I babbled that I was guessing, but my stock sank rapidly under Judith's furious look. Holmes said, —

"I'm afraid that's true."

Judith said nothing but she played with a small pearl ring on her finger, and her look said it would please her if I had the courtesy to fall dead of apoplexy.

"I must inform Chloe," she said and left. Weatherwax said,—

"And I must tell my wife and see to the packing. Chloe's to be married in six weeks in New York and there's a mort of work to be done."

The door closed and it was left to Holmes to complete my humiliation:—

"There must be something in the American character that encourages babbling. Your lack of discretion makes me long for my Watson."

Holmes abandoned me in the billiard room, saying he had to move fast before we left the next morning. I spent the rest of the afternoon playing and smoking, but my heart wasn't into either pleasure. Afternoon tea held no charm for me, so I did not attend.

Then I heard a voice behind me. "May I join in?"

Chloe had walked into the room and picked up a cue stick. She looked frail as a reed, but she had scrubbed color back into her cheeks. But she still seemed weighed by her circumstances.

We did not play a game, but scattered the balls across the table and took shots as we saw them. We discussed Suzy and Clara and remembered happier times in Hartford, the tea parties and parlor concerts we held, and the hikes through the fields. I looked inside her for the bright flower of a girl that I knew, but she was gone.

Weatherwax's charge hung like a dark storm cloud over us. I had to, as the Bard said, screw my courage to the sticking point to bring up the subject and said, —

"Your father means the best for you, you know."

She knocked a ball across the table and into the corner pocket. I had long suspected that she and the girls had been practicing in my office while I was away, and her skill with the stick confirmed it. She said, —

"What do you think of Rannulph?"

"He seems like a fine lad," I said. "He has less of Lord Winthrop in him than you fear."

"Do you think I should marry him?" She turned to me for an answer. Her wide, brown eyes searched mine for any sign of humbug, as she did when she was a child, which meant, at the risk of repeating myself, that I had to lie like a congressman.

"Yes."

She held my gaze and then turned to study the table.

"Our minister in Hartford told us that families negotiated marriages in Jesus' time, like with Joseph and Mary."

"Yes, that is true."

"Do you think they were happy?"

"I do."

She shot again, a two-bank shot that failed to find the side pocket. As I bent over to return fire, she said, —

"Are you happy with Livy?"

I scratched, and she laughed with the cruelty native to girls.

"I'm sorry, Mr. Clemens. I didn't mean to corner you with such a personal question."

"Nonsense." I retreated to the table to pick up my cigar. "I can tell you that she is the light of my life. Without her, I would be a tramp miner. Or tramp writer."

"So she lifted you from the gutter and showed you the stars," she said. "But if Rannulph is as good as you say he is, I won't have as much work to do."

"Oh, I'm sure he has his faults. All men do."

She nodded as if I had confirmed her suspicions. The faint clamor of the dinner gong sounded. "I must leave you to your game and dress for dinner."

"Until then, Miss Weatherwax."

"Until then, Mr. Clemens."

Dinner that evening would have tried a saint's patience. Winthrop and Weatherwax kept up a fair rumble over the virtues of American versus English horses. Judith was glum and picked at her plate. Rannulph ignored me, since I was responsible for his future unhappiness. Chloe and her mother were civil to me but felt no obligation to sparkle. At one point, Weatherwax caught my eye. He nodded to Chloe and smiled at me. It had the feel of a pat on the head for being a good little boy.

To tell the truth, my feelings were in a tangle. Fulfilling my charge did not please me. The marriage would go forward, thanks to my — Holmes' — intervention, but I did not feel like celebrating. There was an ache in me without a clear source or cause.

Holmes walked in between removes and was in disgusting fine spirits. He joined in the men's talk about Shires and Morabs, Dale Ponies and Morgans like he had spent his life in the saddle.

The talk had turned from horses in general to Lord Winthrop's in particular. There was a particularly fine colt called Polestar he had his eye on for running at the Chester races.

Chloe said, —

"Lord Winthrop, I know so little about horses so I hope you can educate me. How can you be so sure this colt will run well?"

The old duffer preened at being able to act as an authority. "Because his bloodlines are sound, Miss Weatherwax. He was sired by Melbourne, out of Seaweed, both splendid runners."

"So you investigated the horse's parents?"

With a condescending chuckle he said "that's a pretty way of looking at it."

"Then may I ask after your bloodlines, sir?" A puzzled look crossed his face. "I ask on behalf of myself. If I am a filly charged with begetting an heir and a spare, I think I have a right to know. Is there insanity in your family? imbecility? Any whelps that needed putting down, lest they weaken the bloodline?"

The air around the table was charged. Mrs. Weatherwax, a female doppelganger of Mr. Weatherwax, cooed, "Oh, my," while his lordship's face turned beet red. Rannulph continued to dine as if he hadn't heard a word, while Judith cocked her head as if she were hearing an unusual birdcall.

"Pray, tell us, my lord," Chloe continued. "What are your qualities? I can see from your legs that you're not much of a runner, and your temper indicates you throw your riders too often. Were they bred out of your son?"

"Miss WEATHERWAX—" he said.

"Chloe, leave the table!" Mr. Weatherwax thundered. "Twain, what the hell are you braying at?"

I couldn't help it. I had been trying to suppress an outburst, but I had been flushed from the bushes, so I laughed my heart out. While Lord Winthrop sputtered his objections, tears sprang from my eyes and I slapped the table until the glasses chimed.

"Chloe's got you there, Lord Winthrop," I finally choked out. "And I think she has a point."

"Twain — " Weatherwax growled. "We agreed, — "

"Oh, stuff your agreement," I said. "Chloe," and I kept my face as straight as a card sharp. "You should marry who you want. Marry Polestar, if you like. I daresay he'd prove a fit husband."

"She'll marry Rannulph Winthrop," Weatherwax emphasized and raised his glass to him. "And no amount of rude behavior will change that."

"Hear, hear," Lord Winthrop said.

"And Twain," Weatherwax said. "Don't think you'll get one dime out of me."

"I wouldn't touch your tainted money," I said.

"That's right! Tain't yours at all!" He brightened at that. "Hey, I made a funny! Lord Winthrop, is it time for the port?"[1]

It was a relief when the cloth was drawn and the ladies excused themselves. In disgrace, I begged off an evening of claret and cigars and tottered to bed. Not that they were demanding that I stay. My propensity for speaking out of turn overwhelmed my reputation as a storyteller. Not that I minded, because speaking my piece greatly eased my tattered soul.

Still, it was an unhappy Sam Clemens who sat smoking in bed that night, writing a memoranda of the day's events. The ghost of my publishing house rose before me like the deceased Marley. I missed the comfort and counsel of my Livy, as well as my daughters. It seemed that everything I touched turned to ash, and I was not looking forward to resuming my journey tomorrow leaving Chloe stranded in a marriage unwanted by everyone except the fathers. I closed my notebook, extinguished my cigar, and lay back, but, as usual, sleep would not come to relieve my sorrows.

Blinking in the dark, my despair sunk as far as regretting disappointing Holmes, even if he does scrape my soul like a healthy conscience.

Then, a woman's shriek sent lightning down my spine. I leaped out of bed and was tucking my nightshirt into my pants when Holmes came to fetch me.

We tracked the hullabaloo to Chloe's sick-room. The place was a mess, with clothes thrown everywhere and the furniture tumbled about as evidence of a great struggle. Lord Winthrop

---

[1] Years later, someone commented to Twain that his Standard Oil friend Henry Rogers "is a good fellow. It's a pity his money is tainted." Twain replied, "It's twice tainted. Tain't yours and tain't mine."

was berating the maid with a letter in his hands and demanding answers, and she replied between sobs that she heard the sound of breaking glass and found the room empty and the French doors hanging shattered on their hinges.

He spotted us and charged, waving the letter in his hands and said, —

"These damned scoundrels kidnapped Miss Weatherwax!"

The note read, —

"We have the gurl. Will send word how much to have her back in one peece.
"The Whyos"

"What is this 'Whyos,' what? what?" his lordship demanded. I explained as best I could — leaving out the blackmail scheme — as he went on with the hellfire and damnation over the broken glass and the damage to the room, before returning the harass the maid some more.

I walked to the sideboard, where stood a decanter and glass filled with a clear liquid. Next to it was a plate in which were floated several sheets of brown paper. The midges had found the open door, and I slapped at them, causing several to join their mates floating in the water. Holmes was on his hands and knees by the French doors, nosing over the glass shards with a magnifying glass. Behind him stood Weatherwax, white-faced and bearing a candelabra in a shaky hand that was dripping wax. He said, —

"We have to do something. We must call the police."

Winthrop ordered the maid to inform the head butler, then joined me at the sideboard. He picked up the glass and said, —

"It'll take an hour for Noakes to get here, but we have to act now." He was about to take a drink when, from the floor, Holmes spotted him out of the corner of his eye. He shouted "No!" and flipped his lens at Lord Winthrop. It caught the glass at the stem and dashed it from his hand. He whipped around in anger but Holmes spiked his guns.

"It would be worth your life to drink that," he said. "Come, Clemens. There's not a moment to lose."

We ran onto the terrace and raced for the stables where we secured two horses from the sleepy stable boy. I said, —

"Holmes, what happened?"

"You just witnessed the denouement of your revelation. More fool I was not to have anticipated this, but logic cannot always deduce the ways of the heart. Let's ride, Clemens. We have to get there before it's too late."

"Too late for what? Chloe's been kidnapped."

Holmes had mounted and was off as I shouted, "What are you on about?" after him. Cursing a streak that would have horrified Livy. I mounted my horse and followed.

We pounded down a road that moonlight had turned into a river of silver, past shrubbery turned into glowing fantastical shapes. I had not galloped like this for years, so the first mile racked my bones and panic tightened my grip on the reins. We reached the coast road and turned toward Southampton. Our screws were thundering at a steady pace so I could lift myself in the saddle and looked about. Over the cliff to one side could be heard the rumble of the surf. On the other side, the rising moon illuminated the rolling fields of flax.

When we reached town, Holmes slowed his horse to a trot, giving me a chance to catch up. The chase had proved as beneficial as any tonic. Everything had been forgotten — my decrepitude, my financial worries, my failures. I was on an adventure, like Huck and Jim floating down my beloved Mississippi, and I must have sounded like a boy again when I said, —

"Where to, Holmes?"

"The wharf."

Even though it was late, there was still great activity as stevedores worked to load and unload their cargos. We rode past the slips and, at every boat, Holmes asked if any passengers had boarded within the last half-hour. All said no until we reached the steamer Lochinvar. Smoke poured from her stacks, and the mate of the watch said she was bound shortly for America. A half-crown bought us permission to come aboard and directions to their cabin.

At the door, Holmes said, —

"Do you have your gun?"

I told him it was at the wash.

"Then be on your guard for anything. They're desperate."

He knocked and sang out in a Boston accent that the captain would like to speak with them.

The door opened to reveal a tall, thin man in a moustache and bowler. He gasped and tried to close the door, but Holmes pushed in. The man raced for the table and pulled a pistol from a Gladstone bag, but Holmes twisted it from his hand. In two swipes, he pulled off the hat and moustache.

"Judith," I cried.

A connecting door opened and Chloe entered. It was an improved edition of the young woman I saw at dinner. The color was high in her cheeks, and her smile of welcome was charming. Kidnappings proved very agreeable to her. She said, —

"Hello, Mr. Clemens, Mr. Holmes. How lovely of you to see us off."

Holmes bowed and said, —

"Miss Weatherwax. You led us on a merry dance. I'm glad to see you've dropped the masquerade."

She laughed and said, —

"Oh yes! I was so looking forward to home again. How did you see through it?"

"Your extortion note spoke very clearly. Despite the misspelled words, the hand that wrote 'Grecian folly' could not be from a New York gang member. And I doubt that a Whyo would charge for blackmail five times the going rate for 'doing the big job.'"

Chloe said, —

"I apologize on their behalf, Mr. Holmes. I knew it was all the cash father had at hand."

I said, —

"What do you need the money for?"

"To pay Dr. Conover," Judith said. "He helped us so much with his lengthy treatment of Chloe's illness. It was only right to compensate him for his trouble. But now that we need the money for our passage, I'm afraid he'll never receive it."

Holmes said, —

"Don't worry about your friend. He's been billing your father at thrice the going rate for a Harley Street physician."

"How did you learn of our scheme?"

He pulled from his pocket Chloe's note to Lionel. "This love note. The ink is much too fresh for a three-year-old letter, and the paper bears the same watermark as the extortion and kidnapping notes."

Chloe laughed again, and, despite the trouble she had put us through, it did my heart good to hear her. Her mood turned serious, however, when a sailor knocked at the door and said it was time to cast off. She said, —

"Must we go with you?"

Holmes said, —

"I'm afraid so."

"But we meant no harm."

"This is about more than fleeing an unwanted attachment. My job was to unmask the Whyos and their connections on this side of the Atlantic, and I have done so."

He looked at Judith, but she stood firm and straight as a willow reed with a damn-your-eyes impudence.

He said, —

"There's no further need for dissimulation. The scheme was simple: the gang would steal from country homes, ship the swag to America in the guise of lawful goods and sell it there. But they needed someone with shipping connections, someone who knew where the treasures were located and who could be trusted not to preach on them. The coastal connection was vital to the solution, so I concentrated there, looking for large unexplained shipments of goods. I eliminated all of the ports but this one, and Clemens' call for help provided an ideal opportunity to visit this area.

"I must admit it was fortune that brought us to the right door. The only question was which family members were involved. You and your brother have been to America; your father had not. You're knowledgeable about the furnishings; your brother has the shipping connections. And, just to make sure, I visited your outbuildings down that rutted road before dinner and found the spoils of—."

Holmes' story was interrupted by another knock at the door. The sailor said, —

"Stay or leave, makes no matter to us. But if you stay, you gotta pay."

We took charge of the women and went off to roust the local constabulary. Holmes told Noakes that Inspector Lestrade was expected down from Scotland Yard by the first train to take control of the proceedings. Judith was arrested, and Chloe asked to stay behind to keep her company. As it was the shank of the night, we agreed, but not until I gave her a hug and informed her of where we were staying in Europe. There was more I wanted to say, but after the excitement of discovery had faded, it was clear she was worn to a nubbin.

We rode back slowly to the house on horseback, the moon lighting our way. The sea breeze picked up, keeping our cigars alight and whipping our smoke away.

I despise the moment in stories when the Great Detective is sitting high, wide and handsome, and prepared to reveal all to his adoring acolyte. After expending thousands of words in murder and mayhem, it seems obscene to take any pleasure in the wrecks of people's lives. That may suit a man of Watson's sheep-like demeanor, but we Westerners are made of sterner stuff. But as I mused over the events of the day, I came to an understanding. We were placed on this Earth to question, and the need for answers can become overpowering. I just didn't know how to ask.

But Holmes was an old hand at this game. He waded in

and said, —

"It was a near-run thing in Chloe's bedroom, Clemens. You remark the paper in the basin? That was flypaper. Soaking it in water brings up the arsenic. His lordship would have been dissatisfied with his drink if I hadn't intervened."

I wished now I hadn't been told that. I said, —

"She meant to destroy herself."

"Until Judith interrupted with an alternative. She convinced Chloe to flee, packed what they could and tumbled the room to make it look like a kidnapping. Judith probably lashed out at the French doors for a touch of verisimilitude. But as the blackmail scheme was a fraud, I reasoned this probably was as well. Besides, the ladies took care not to crush the glass into the carpet, as it would have been if a gang of men had stomped into the room after kicking open the doors."

"And the boat to America, how did you figure that?"

"Logical inference from the available data."

"You mean you guessed."

Holmes ignored my jibe. He was in full lecture mode, which cannot be interrupted by any act short of dynamiting. "They had two choices: flee into England or away by boat. The authorities would be sure to watch the roads, the ports, and the railways, whereas no one would enquire after a couple seeking passage to the states."

"And the disguise?"

"Final proof of her criminality. She was prepared to flee before she entered Chloe's bedroom, probably as a result of my appearance. My name is not unknown in the criminal underworld, Clemens, and showing up on her doorstep made her suspicious. She used Chloe's affection for her, combined with your blowing up their scheme to derail the wedding plans, as a means of escape. Which was fortunate for Chloe's sake. Perhaps— ," he mused, "she used the disguise in her dealings with the gang. A minor point, but worth investigating."

We smoked quietly for awhile until I said, —

"Holmes, was it necessary to have Judith arrested?"

"Would you rather they sailed to America?"

"I'd rather Chloe was happy and away from her grasping, social-jumping scoundrel of a father."

"With only a few pounds between them?"

"I would have given her Rogers' address at Standard Oil. He would have seen after them on my word."

"And her brother? should he get away as well? Clemens, this gang robbed mansions of tens of thousands of pounds worth of goods."

"Oh, who cares a flip about the gee-gaws of the rich! You unmasked them. That should be plenty."

"I don't believe the owners or your public would agree."

I brooded about that. It seemed like Chloe was back where she started. Holmes — blast his genius for mind-reading — must have understood what I was getting at, for he clapped me on the shoulder and said, —

"Don't feel bad for Chloe. She won't be marrying after all, and I imagine that Mr. Weatherwax would be most grateful to us for being saved from the consequences of a scandalous match."

"Only to make another for her; perhaps with an even worse character."

"The answer to that is a closed book at present," he said solemnly, the ass. "We have a more pressing concern with the welcome we'll receive at Chalkhills. Will Lord Winthrop keep his promise to let us stay after unmasking his children as part of the Whyos gang, or must we doss somewhere else? It will be an interesting test of the English capacity for politeness."

Afterwards

This was the first story in the TwainLock series, published on the Amazon Kindle in 2014. What I had forgotten until I looked through my notes recently was that I had written it in 2001. So what follows is a recreation, based on the printed evidence, of how I came to pair an American humorist with a fictional British consulting detective.

It all began in a sparsely decorated two-room basement apartment outside Harrisburg, Pa. I had moved there in 2001 from South Carolina to take up a copy editing job at a newspaper. While my wife stayed behind to take care of the kids, ages 11, 4, and 2, a dog and four cats, and sell the house, it was my job to go to work and hunt for a new place to live. That left me with a lot of time on my hands. I had no TV and dial-up Internet access, so I had plenty of time on my hands. Stimulus #1 for creativity: boredom.

The previous year, I had reviewed two collections of Sherlockian pastiches edited by Marvin Kaye. These books planted the seed for this series. The central conceit behind *Resurrected Holmes* was that a wealthy collector paid enormous sums to famous writers to concoct a pastiche story based on Watson's untold tales. So we got John Gregory Betancourt writing "The Adventure of the Amateur Mendicant Society" in H.G. Wells' voice and Kaye inhabiting Rex Stout to pen "Too Many Stains (The Adventure of the Second Stain)." *The Confidential Casebook of Sherlock Holmes* imaginatively mingled the great detective with P.G. Wodehouse, Ida Tarbell, Consuelo Vanderbilt, and even Conan Doyle.

So with all these mash-ups in my head, eight years before Seth Grahame-Smith took it to the profitable extreme with *Pride and Prejudice and Zombies*, I decided to throw together Twain and Sherlock. Twain is one of my favorite writers, as my much-handled copy of the two-volume *Unabridged Mark Twain* proves.

It wasn't the first time Twain had appeared in print as a detective. Peter J. Heck wrote six novels in the Mark Twain mysteries, two of which I have: *Death on the Mississippi* and *A Connecticut Yankee in Criminal Court*. In those stories, Twain took on the Sherlock role, with his fictional secretary, Wentworth Cabot, acting as his Watson.

As I looked through them, I wondered: Could I do something like this as well? And what if I could tell it in an authorial voice, like the writers in *Resurrected Holmes*?

Only one way to find out.

To make it more challenging, I decided to not just tell the story in Twain's distinctive voice, but I would set it against both men's chronology. In short, I decided to play the Game.

For those of you who aren't members of the Baker Street Irregulars, or who aren't Holmesians, let me explain. It consists of a group hallucination adopted by members of Sherlock Holmes fandom.

There are a few rules. First, Sherlock Holmes existed. Dr. Watson existed. The characters in the canonical stories existed. Conan Doyle existed, but merely as Watson's literary agent.

Second, all of these stories took place sometime in the historical timeline of Britain. But when? That's the beginning of The Game.

Sometimes, Watson made it easy. In "A Scandal in Bohemia," he firmly states the story began "on the twentieth of March, 1888." Other stories are more vague, with perhaps the mention of the month, or a reference to the season, or to Watson's marriage. It's up to the Sherlockians to look at the evidence, pick a date, and make a case for it.

The chronology is not the only thing Sherlockians argue about. There's the question of Watson's wives. He mentions two, and the first one by name. Who was the second wife and when did they get married? Some speculated that he even married a third time. The questions can even go into some weird areas. Dorothy L. Sayers, a notable mystery writer herself, postulated that Watson wasn't a man, but a woman!

For my purposes, I decided not to play that part of the game. I had enough to do already! Sherlockian Les Klinger put together a fine chronology, so I adopted it. (If you want to see how deep the chronological rabbit hole goes, I heartily recommend Brad Keefauver's "A Basic Timeline of Terra 221b (https://basictimelineter-ra221b.blogspot.com/p/a-basic-timeline-of-terra-221b. html) I took R. Kent Rasmussen's *Mark*

Twain A-Z with its detailed timeline and combined the two.

Writing the first story was easy. It was inspired by the forced marriage of Consuelo Vanderbilt to the Duke of Marlborough. I had written a mystery novel set at the Biltmore Estate in Asheville, N.C. It had been built by George Washington Vanderbilt, the grandson of Commodore Vanderbilt. This led to a lot of reading about the Vanderbilts, the Gilded Age, and the marriage market in which American robber barons acquired titles for their family by bartering their daughters to English aristocrats.

Once all that was settled, the writing came easy. It was the perfect combination of background knowledge and storytelling. I sent it off to the major mystery magazines — *Ellery Queen* and *Alfred Hitchcock* — and it came rocketing back with printed rejection letters. So I put it in a drawer and forgot about it.

Flash forward a dozen years. I'm at the Pennwriters convention. My first book, *Writers Gone Wild*, had come out, and I had given a talk on marketing. This earned me a seat at the book-signing table, and by chance I was seated next to Jonathan Maberry, the best-selling thriller novelist.

During a pause between signings (long for me, short for him), we talked about stories, and I mournfully mentioned the "Whyos," tucked away never to be seen by anyone.

Now, Jonathan is a pro. Writing is his business, and he attacks it with all his energy at his command. I had barely launched into my lamentation when he shot out the obvious question: "Why don't you publish it yourself?"

I suspect my brain short-circuited at the obvious logical answer. "I can do that?"

"Sure. Publish it for the Kindle." And then he turned to greet another wave of his fans, and I was left to think "why not?"

Which seems to be the motto for the entire series. Whenever I wondered if an observation was too audacious, if a plot twist too unbelievable, I ended up asking, "Why not?" and did it. I hope you enjoyed the stories.

About the Editor

Bill Peschel is a former journalist who shares a Pulitzer Prize with the staff of *The Patriot-News* in Harrisburg, Pa. He is also a mystery fan who runs the Wimsey Annotations at Planetpeschel.com.

The author of *Writers Gone Wild* (Penguin), he publishes through Peschel Press the 223B Casebook Series of Sherlockian parodies and pastiches and annotated editions of Dorothy L. Sayers' *Whose Body?* and Agatha Christie's *The Mysterious Affair at Styles* and *The Secret Adversary*. An interest in Victorian crime led to the republication of three books on the William Palmer poisoning case.

Peschel lives with his wife, Teresa — whose books are published through Peschel Press — in Hershey, where the air really does smell like chocolate.

Visit Bill at Peschel Press (www.peschelpress.com) or his personal website at Planet Peschel (planetpeschel.com). He can be reached at peschel@peschelpress.com or write to him at Peschel Press, P.O. Box 132, Hershey, PA 17033.

The Complete, Annotated Series

Available in Trade Paperback and Ebook editions

Return to your favorite novels by Agatha Christie & Dorothy L. Sayers with added material exclusive to these editions!

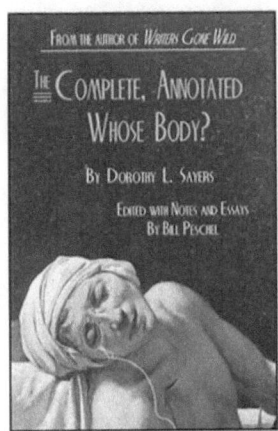

The Complete, Annotated Whose Body?
Dorothy L. Sayers

Sayers' first novel introduces the witty Lord Peter Wimsey investigating the mystery of the body in the bath. Three maps and essays on notorious crimes, anti-Semitism, Sayers and Wimsey, plus two timelines. *282 pages.*

The Complete, Annotated Mysterious Affair at Styles
Agatha Christie

Mystery's most auspicious debut, Christie was only 25 when she introduced Hercule Poirot! With essays on Poirot, Christie, strychnine, women during the war, plus chronology and book lists. *352 pages.*

The Complete, Annotated Deluxe Secret Adversary
Agatha Christie

Christie's conspiracy thriller in which Tommy and Tuppence —based on herself and her husband?—fight socialists plotting to ruin England! With art from the newspaper edition and essays on thrillers and her 11-day disappearance and more! *478 pages.*

Don't miss future Peschel Press books: Visit Peschelpress.com or PlanetPeschel.com and sign up for our newsletter.

The 223B Casebook Series

Classic and newly discovered fanfiction written during Arthur Conan Doyle's life, with original art plus extensive historical notes.

The Early Punch Parodies of Sherlock Holmes
Parodies, book reviews, & cartoons. Includes parodies by R.C. Lehmann and P.G. Wodehouse. *281 pages.*

Victorian Parodies & Pastiches: 1888-1899
With stories by Conan Doyle, Robert Barr, Jack Butler Yeats, and James M. Barrie. *279 pages.*

Edwardian Parodies & Pastiches I: 1900-1904
With stories by Mark Twain, Finley Peter Dunn, John Kendrick Bangs, and P.G. Wodehouse. *390 pages.*

Edwardian Parodies & Pastiches II: 1905-1909
With stories by 'Banjo' Paterson, Max Beerbohm, Carolyn Wells, and Lincoln Steffens. *401 pages.*

Great War Parodies and Pastiches I: 1910-1914
With stories by O. Henry, Maurice Baring, and Stephen Leacock. *362 pages.*

Great War Parodies and Pastiches II: 1915-1919
With stories by Ring Lardner, Carolyn Wells, and a young George Orwell. *390 pages.*

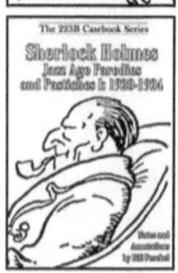

Jazz Age Parodies and Pastiches I: 1920-1924
With stories by Dashiell Hammett, James Thurber, and Arthur Conan Doyle. *353 pages.*

Jazz Age Parodies and Pastiches II: 1925-1930
With stories by August Derleth, Frederic Dorr Steele, and Edgar Wallace. *373 pages.*

ALSO: The Best of the 223B Casebook, featuring the best stories from 1888 to 1930.

The Rugeley Poisoner Series

A 3-book series from Peschel Press reprinting seminal works about Victorian poisoner Dr. William Palmer

The Illustrated Life and Career of William Palmer 1856	The Times Report of the Trial of William Palmer 1856	The Life and Career of William Palmer of Rugeley 1925
• A "quickie biography" written to cash in on the trial. • Gossip about Palmer's family, betting scams, and the stews of London. • More than 50 restored woodcuts. • Essays on medical training and racing. • Excerpts from Palmer's love letters. *225 pages*	• A trial transcript created by the Times newspaper, edited, corrected, and annotated. • More than 50 original woodcuts restored to better-than-new condition. • Essays on the trial judges and barristers, glossary of medical terms, and index to witnesses. *426 pages*	• Written by a doctor who interviewed witnesses and jurors. • Rare photos and art not seen since 1925. • Annotations define medical and legal terms and clarify obscure points. • Essays on Palmer's impact on modern culture, strychnine, and Rugeley today. *227 pages*

www.ingramcontent.com/pod-product-compliance
Lightning Source LLC
Chambersburg PA
CBHW030049100526
44591CB00008B/71